LNER 4-6-0 LOCOMOTIVES

LNER 4-6-0 LOCOMOTIVES

Their Design, Operation and Performance

DAVID MAIDMENT

First published in Great Britain in 2021 by
Pen and Sword Transport
An imprint of
Pen & Sword Books Ltd
Yorkshire - Philadelphia

ISBN 978 1 52677 254 1

A CIP catalogue record for this book is available from the British Library.

Typeset in Palatino by SJmagic DESIGN SERVICES, India.
Printed and bound in India by Replika Press Pvt. Ltd.

Pen & Sword Books Ltd incorporates the Imprints of Pen & Sword Books Archaeology, Atlas, Aviation, Battleground, Discovery, Family History, History, Maritime, Military, Naval, Politics, Railways, Select, Transport, True Crime, Fiction, Frontline Books, Leo Cooper, Praetorian Press, Seaforth Publishing, Wharncliffe and White Owl.

For a complete list of Pen & Sword titles please contact

PEN & SWORD BOOKS LIMITED
47 Church Street, Barnsley, South Yorkshire, S70 2AS, England
E-mail: enquiries@pen-and-sword.co.uk
Website: www.pen-and-sword.co.uk

or

PEN AND SWORD BOOKS
1950 Lawrence Rd, Havertown, PA 19083, USA
E-mail: Uspen-and-sword@casematepublishers.com
Website: www.penandswordbooks.com

All David Maidment's royalties from this book will be donated to the Railway Children charity [reg. no. 1058991] [www.railwaychildren.org.uk]

Other books by David Maidment:

Novels (Religious historical fiction)
The Child Madonna, Melrose Books, 2009
The Missing Madonna, PublishNation, 2012
The Madonna and her Sons, PublishNation, 2015

Novels (Railway fiction)
Lives on the Line, Max Books, 2013

Non-fiction (Railways)
The Toss of a Coin, PublishNation, 2014
A Privileged Journey, Pen & Sword, 2015
An Indian Summer of Steam, Pen & Sword, 2015
Great Western Eight-Coupled Heavy Freight Locomotives, Pen & Sword, 2015
Great Western Moguls and Prairies, Pen & Sword, 2016
Southern Urie and Maunsell 2-cylinder 4-6-0s, Pen & Sword, 2016
Great Western Small-Wheeled Double-Framed 4-4-0s, Pen & Sword, 2017
The Development of the German Pacific Locomotive, Pen & Sword 2017
Great Western Large-Wheeled Double-Framed 4-4-0s, Pen & Sword 2017
Great Western Counties, 4-4-0s, 4-4-2Ts & 4-6-0s, Pen & Sword 2018
Southern Maunsell Moguls and Tank Engines, Pen & Sword 2018
Southern Maunsell 4-4-0s, Pen & Sword, 2019
Great Western Granges, Pen & Sword, 2019
Cambrian Railways Gallery, Pen & Sword, 2019
Great Western Panniers, Pen & Sword, 2019
Great Western Kings, Pen & Sword, 2020
Great Western & Absorbed Railway 0-6-2 Tank Locomotives, Pen & Sword, 2020
Drummond's L&SWR Passenger & Mixed Traffic Locomotives, Pen & Sword 2020
Southern 0-6-0 Tender Locomotives, Pen & Sword, 2021

Non-fiction (Street Children)
The Other Railway Children, PublishNation, 2012
Nobody ever listened to me, PublishNation, 2012

Front cover photo:
B16/3 61444 at Doncaster ex-works, 29 October 1961. N.Fields/MLS Collection

Back cover photos:
B12/3 61572 at Norwich depot, 1961. Roy Hobbs/Transort OnLine Archive

B17/6 61657 *Doncaster Rovers*, 1958. MLS Collection

CONTENTS

PREFACE & ACKNOWLEDGEMENTS

I have been asked many times why I have only written about Great Western and Southern 'Locomotive Profiles' for the Pen & Sword series. My answer until now has been that I lived on the Southern and worked on the Great Western (or rather, its successor, BR's Western Region) and preferred to write about engines with which I'd been acquainted and therefore able to include some of my own experiences. My railway career later included the London Midland Region, but long after steam had retired (apart from the three ex GWR narrow gauge 2-6-2Ts of the Vale of Rheidol).

I did however have more than a passing acquaintance with the former LNER 4-6-0s, having a cousin who lived in Chelmsford with whom I spent a couple of weeks in the early 1950s, and I stayed with my best friend and his relatives near Doncaster in 1950 and seem to remember that the pair of us spent more time trainspotting on the cattle-dock at the station there than on visiting his various relations, the intended purpose of our three week vacation. My overriding remembrance of both occasions was the preponderance of Thompson's B1s, with which I confess we had little patience. However, I remember seeing the occasional North Eastern B16 in Yorkshire and both B12s and B17s in Essex. I regret I never even saw a Great Central 4-6-0, although 'Director' 4-4-0s appeared at Doncaster from Sheffield and I spied one solitary GC Atlantic (2909) from the top deck of a bus en route to a day's spotting in Sheffield. I wish we'd taken the train behind *Gerard Powys Dewhurst* or *Jutland* but I regret we couldn't afford the train fare. At the end of the 1950s, I found myself a couple of late afternoons a week, after college lectures and before evening commitments, free to indulge in a few trips out from Liverpool Street to Broxbourne, Bishop's Stortford or Shenfield behind B17s (*Sandringhams* or *Footballers*) or the occasional Thompson B2 rebuild, and on a couple occasions, the treat of a B12. I even tolerated the odd B1! I therefore consider myself presumptuous enough to tackle the history of the LNER 4-6-0s covering their design, construction, operation and performance.

I rely as ever on the comprehensive RCTS volumes on the LNER locomotives for technical descriptions as I'm no engineer and augment my own knowledge and experience of their operation and performance by decades of subscription to *Trains Illustrated* and its successors, and access to the complete set of *Railway Magazines* in my school library and more recently in the library of the Manchester Locomotive Society on Stockport station. As a member of the Rail Performance Society, I am able to research their archives of locomotive performance logs and for photographs

I acknowledge with thanks the magnificent and comprehensive archive held by the Manchester Locomotive Society and the help given by photo archivist Paul Shackcloth in accessing many of the photographs of former club members. Their collection of ex LNER 4-6-0 photographs is so large that I have had little need to look beyond their collections except for some additional colour slides by Roy Hobbs held in Peter Waller's Transport OnLine Trust archives. I have endeavoured to trace copyright owners of the photographs where ownership has been indicated, but if I have missed anyone, please contact the publisher.

I thank as ever my colleagues at Pen & Sword, John Scott-Morgan, Transport Commissioning Editor, Janet Brookes, Production Manager of the transport (and other) book themes, the design and marketing teams and my editor, Carol Trow.

As with my previous books, all royalties from the sales will be donated to the Railway Children charity (www.railwaychildren.org.uk) which I founded in 1995 and which flourishes from its base in Sandbach in Cheshire supporting projects for street children in India and East Africa, and partners the British Transport Police in the UK counselling runaway children picked up on our railway stations here. The charity has grown to be the largest international charity working exclusively for street children and finds a substantial part of its income from the generosity of people in the UK railway industry and from railway enthusiasts and societies throughout the country.

David Maidment
February 2020
www.davidmaidment.com

INTRODUCTION

The first really successful 4-6-0 express engines in the United Kingdom were Churchward's 2-cylinder 'Saints' and 4-cylinder 'Stars' for the Great Western, although several other companies felt the need to construct 4-6-0s around the same time to cope with the increasing train loads in the first decade of the twentieth century. However, neither the LSWR Drummond 4-6-0s nor the LNWR's 'Experiments' ever achieved the heights of the GWR engines or even consistently the performance levels of the companies' 4-4-0s. The East Coast Main Line via the Great Northern, North Eastern and North British relied on Atlantic 4-4-2s for their main express services and the Great Central had Atlantics and 4-4-0s, while 4-4-0s sufficed for the Midland. The Caledonian Railway and Glasgow & South Western both used 4-4-0s predominantly for their express work.

The first successful express passenger 4-6-0 locomotive, Churchward's 2-cylinder 6ft 8in 'Saint' class, No.98, the second of the class and still unnamed, at Swindon, March 1903. It was named *Vanguard* in March 1907 and renamed *Ernest Cunard* in December and renumbered 2998. The first, 100 *William Dean*, was built in February 1902. Locomotive Publishing Co/MLS Collection

The first London & North Western Railway express 4-6-0 was the 'Experiment' class, built in 1905. This example is 507 *Sarmation* and is seen at Camden. They were eclipsed by the 4-4-0 'George V' class for West Coast main line express haulage. F. Moore/ MLS Collection

Caledonian Railway No.912 of the '908' class. *Cardean* was a famous member of this class that worked Glasgow-Carlisle expresses regularly, but they were few in number and most Caledonian expresses were hauled by the successful McIntosh 'Dunalastair' 4-4-0s. F. Moore/MLS Collection

Drummond's attempt to improve his first 4-6-0 design, the F13, with E14 No.335 in 1907. This was even worse than the sluggish F13s and was not only guilty of poor steaming but was very heavy on coal. His T9, L12 and D15 4-4-0s were much more successful. A.R. Kingdom/John Scott-Morgan's Collection

The Great Northern Railway relied entirely on Ivatt's C1 Atlantics for its express traffic in the first decade of the twentieth century and continued to do so until the first Gresley pacifics were built in 1922. Here is 1427 in the immediate months after the Grouping, 1923. N. Fields/MLS Collection

The most successful use of the 4-6-0 wheel arrangement by these companies (that is, other than the Great Western) in the early years was for mixed traffic rather than top-link express passenger train working, and it was not until after the First World War that the 4-6-0 wheel arrangement was widely and successfully developed for express working – the LMS 'Royal Scots', the Southern 'King Arthurs' and 'Lord Nelsons' – and of course the ultimate development of Churchward's engines for the Great Western, the 'Castles' and 'Kings'. The North Eastern Railway had its 4-6-0s classified by the LNER as classes B13-B16, basically mixed traffic engines with its expresses in the hands of the 'R' 4-4-0s and 'V' Atlantics. The Great Northern relied entirely in the Ivatt Atlantics, using 4-4-0s and 2-6-0 moguls for mixed traffic work. The Great Central built its first 4-6-0s (identified later as B5s) in 1902 for its important fish traffic and fast freight work and although it built a series of 4-6-0 classes between 1903 and 1921, those intended for express passenger work gave way fairly quickly to the more successful 'Director' 4-4-0s and 'Jersey Lily' Atlantics. The one exception to this trend in the companies that formed the LNER, was the Great Eastern. Their development of the 'Claud Hamilton' 4-4-0 to the '1500' class (later B12) of 1911 was the one major 4-6-0 express engine success in the Eastern half of the country.

The very first British 4-6-0, the small-wheeled Highland Railway No.103, built primarily for freight work. It is here in the St Rollox Carriage Shop after withdrawal, preservation and restoration to Highland Railway livery, 16 August 1937. MLS Collection

The LN&WR George Whale 19in Goods 4-6-0 built for fast freight and mixed traffic duties from 1906. This example is No.285. F. Moore/MLS Collection

Churchward's master plan of 1901 included a 5ft 8in 4-6-0 version of his 'Saint' for freight and secondary passenger activity. A drawing was made in 1905, but in the event Churchward built a mogul, the 43XX, for this purpose. Collett then used parts of withdrawn 43XX to build eighty 'Granges' in 1936-7 which were virtually the 1905 design apart from the Collett side-window cab. They were among the most popular of GW engines to their crews and supervisors and lasted to the end of steam on BR's Western Region in 1965. F. Moore/MLS Collection

The 4-6-0s of the LNER, the subjects of this book, were, apart from the B12s, primarily intended for mixed traffic or secondary passenger train work, or were soon relegated to that work. The LNER inherited the 4-6-0s of the Great Central, Great Eastern and North Eastern Railways and for a couple of years after the Grouping in 1923, tried out the Great Central 'Sir Sam Fay' (B2) and 'Lord Faringdon' (B3) classes on the Pullman services of the East Coast Main Line but within a short time these became the preserve of the Ivatt Atlantics until sufficient Pacifics were available to replace them. The only 4-6-0s designed and built by Nigel Gresley were his B17 'Sandringhams' for the Great Eastern Section and later his B17 'Footballers' for the Great Central Main Line, express passenger work but on shorter distance subsidiary routes to the East Coast line. The final 4-6-0 design for the LNER was the Thompson B1, intended specifically as a mixed traffic locomotive derived in concept from the Great Western 'Halls' and the LMS 'Black 5s'. As well as mixed traffic work on the East Coast, the B1 largely took over the express work on the Great Central and Great Eastern Sections from the B17s, although the latter were improved by Thompson by reboilering them with the B1 boiler and some were rebuilt as 2-cylinder B2s (in hindsight, not necessarily an improvement).

This book will describe the design, construction, operation and performance of all these 315 4-6-0s inherited and 483 built by the LNER, most of which survived to ownership of British Railways' Eastern Region. I will tackle each class of the pre-Grouping companies in date order of their introduction, followed by chapters on engines built in the LNER regime, with a concluding chapter on engines rebuilt by Thompson from earlier 4-6-0 classes. Where possible, I will relate some of my own experiences with these engines, namely the rebuilt Great Eastern B12s, the North Eastern B16s, the Gresley B17s and the Thompson B1 and B2s. It is to my regret that I never was able to experience anything of the handsome Great Central 4-6-0s that failed to survive beyond the early years of my own burgeoning interest and ability to travel away from home under my own steam.

Chapter 1

THE ENGINEERS

John G. Robinson

John George Robinson was born at Newcastle-upon-Tyne on 30 July 1856, the second son of Matthew and Jane Robinson. He came from a railway family – his father was District Locomotive Superintendent of the Great Western Railway at Bristol in 1876 and his older brother worked for the GWR too. John was educated at Chester Grammar School and in 1872 started an engineering apprenticeship at Swindon Works as a pupil of Joseph Armstrong. In 1878, he became an assistant to his father at Bristol before joining the Irish Waterford & Limerick Railway as Assistant Locomotive, Carriage & Wagon Superintendent in 1884. He took on the Chief's post the following year and in 1896 the small railway became the Waterford, Limerick & Western Railway Company.

He appears to have been headhunted by the Great Central Railway directors after Johnson of the Midland had visited Ireland and mentioned to Robinson the impending retirement of Harry Pollitt, encouraging him to apply. He was the only applicant interviewed and was appointed as Locomotive and Marine Superintendent in 1900 and Chief Mechanical Engineer in 1902. He designed and built the successful 8K (LNER O4) 2-8-0 in 1911 which became the standard engine for the Railway Operating Division in France in the First World War and in 1920 was awarded the CBE. At the 1923 railway amalgamation, he declined the offer of the LNER to become its Chief Mechanical Engineer as he was already 66 years of age, leaving the post clear for Nigel Gresley, a younger man.

He was a member of the Railway War Manufacturing Sub-committee, and Member of the Institutes of Civil Engineers and Mechanical & Electrical Engineers. After retirement in 1923, he acted as a consultant to the LNER for a year. During his GCR days he had married and had three children, two girls and a boy, Matthew. He had a nephew who became Locomotive Superintendent at Neasden during the Second World War. He died in December 1943 aged 87 at Bournemouth.

Stephen D. Holden

Stephen Dewar Holden was born on 23 August 1870 in Saltney, Cheshire, the son of James Holden, a Quaker and Superintendent of the Great Western workshops at Chester, later Chief Assistant to William Dean at Swindon. His father then moved to Stratford as Locomotive Superintendent of the Great Eastern Railway in 1885 and Stephen was privately educated, then attended University College School, London, but left aged 16 to join Stratford Works and study under his father for four years.

He then worked in the Drawing Office for eighteen months and subsequently as a train running inspector. In 1892, he was appointed Suburban District Locomotive Superintendent and in 1894 a similar position at Ipswich. In 1897 he came Divisional Locomotive Superintendent followed by a number of other senior appointments, succeeding his father as Locomotive Superintendent of the Great Eastern Railway in 1908.

He was elected a Member of the Institute of Mechanical Engineers in 1910 and in 1911, designed his masterpiece, the 1500 class 4-6-0, one of the subjects of this book, in essence a development of his father's 'Claud Hamilton' 4-4-0s. He resigned in 1912 and died at Rochester on 7 February 1918, aged just 48, some seven years before the death of his father.

Wilson Worsdell

Wilson Worsdell was from a Quaker family, the tenth child, fourth son, of Nathanial and

Mary Worsdell and younger brother of William Worsdell, who would precede him as Locomotive Superintendent of the North Eastern Railway. He was born on 7 September 1850 at Monks Coppenhall in Crewe and was a pupil at the Friends' School at Ackworth in 1860. He left in 1867 and spent the first six months of that year in the Crewe Works Drawing Office. In July, he went to America and became an engineering pupil working for Edward Williams, Superintendent of Motive Power and Machinery at the Pennsylvania Railroad's Altoona Works. He returned to Crewe in 1871 in the Works under Francis Webb. He got experience in both the erecting shop and drawing office and was appointed assistant foreman at Stafford locomotive shed in 1874. He moved to Bushbury as foreman in 1876 and was in charge of the Chester depot in 1877.

He married Mary Elizabeth Bradford in 1882 and his son, Geoffrey, was born the following year, who broke the Quaker tradition by being educated at Charterhouse public school. He left Chester in March 1883 with a glowing testimonial from his depot staff and went as Assistant Mechanical Engineer of the North Eastern Railway at Gateshead. The Chief, Alexander McDonnell, was a controversial character and resigned at short notice in 1884 and his brother William became Locomotive Superintendent. Wilson was re-designated Assistant Locomotive Superintendent of the Northern Division in 1885 and his salary was increased by £100 to £600 a year. William retired on health grounds in 1890 and Wilson took over on 1 October at a salary of £1,100. He remained in charge until May 1910. He bought a home, 'Greenesfield House', adjacent to the Works, working closely with an outstanding General Manager, George Gibbs. Wilson's assistant was Vincent Raven and Walter Smith was his Chief Draughtsman.

He designed the M1 4-4-0 in 1895, an engine involved in the 1895 East/West Coast 'Race to Aberdeen' and went on a study tour to the USA in 1901. Influenced by what he saw, he designed larger twenty ton wagons and the outstanding Q6 0-8-0s and J27 0-6-0s which remained as last survivors of steam in the North East. He designed the enlarged 4-4-0 of class R (LNER D20) in 1899 and his S 4-6-0s were the first passenger 4-6-0s in the country.

He retired in May 1910 as Chief Mechanical Engineer, his duties including the design and maintenance of locomotives, carriage and wagons, tugboats and hydraulic machinery, having been responsible for the management of 18,500 staff, 2,142 locomotives, 4,000 passenger coaches and 98,000 goods wagons. He was involved in the electrification of North Tyneside in 1904 and the goods branch to Newcastle Docks and electric locomotive 26500, now preserved. He was well liked by his staff, ran a boys' club and became a JP in 1907. He was a keen fisherman, possessing a second house in Voss in Norway, and was President of the Association of Railway Engineers and Carriage & Wagon Superintendents of Great Britain and Ireland. He was much appreciated and remained as a consultant to the North Eastern Railway to the end of 1910. He moved home to South Ascot and died in 1920 aged 69 and was buried at All Souls, Ascot. He was honoured by the naming of a new Peppercorn A1 pacific 60127 *Wilson Worsdell* on 30 October 1950.

Sir Vincent Raven

Vincent Litchfield Raven was born on 3 December 1859, the son of the Rev Vincent Raven, at Great Fransham in Norfolk and was educated at Aldenham School in Hertfordshire. He joined the North Eastern Railway in 1877 as a pupil of the railway's Chief Mechanical Engineer, Edward Fletcher, and was appointed as Assistant Divisional Locomotive Superintendent at Gateshead in 1888, ascending to the senior post in 1893. He developed a simple form of cab signalling in 1895 and this was tried on the Newcastle-Alnmouth section of the North Eastern's main line, installed by 1899. It was eventually extended to cover the East Coast main line between Shaftholme Junction and Berwick although it was removed by the LNER.

He was appointed as Assistant to the Chief Mechanical Engineer, Wilson Worsdell in 1903. When Worsdell retired in 1910, he followed as Chief Mechanical Engineer and held the post until the Grouping at the end of 1922. He advocated the development of 3-cylinder engines, though with three separate sets of motion rather than Gresley's conjugated valve gear. For passenger work, he developed the successful Z class Atlantics which dominated the York-Edinburgh main line expresses until the Gresley pacifics grew in number, although Raven had built a small class of pacifics himself – the A2 'City' class, which never really surpassed the work of the Atlantics.

He was also a visionary regarding the scope for electrification and undertook the conversion of the North Tyneside service, and prepared plans for electrification of the York-Newcastle section at 1,500 volts D.C., though because of the war and impending Grouping it was never carried through and was abandoned by the LNER management. In 1915, he was appointed as Superintendent of the Royal Woolwich Arsenal and was knighted in 1917 for his wartime work there.

Although he retired in 1922, he was appointed as adviser to Nigel Gresley for a year, resigning in 1924 and became President of the Institute of Mechanical Engineers in 1925. He was subsequently appointed to the Royal Commission on the Australian New South Wales Government Railways.

He died on 14 February 1934.

Sir Nigel Gresley

Nigel Gresley was born in Edinburgh on 19 June 1876 where his mother had gone for medical treatment due to ante-natal complications, although his father was the Reverend Nigel Gresley, rector of Netherseal. He was their fifth child, the family originally coming from Gresley in Derbyshire. He attended a preparatory school in Sussex and then Marlborough College.

After leaving school he began an apprenticeship under F.W. Webb at Crewe Works, then spent a year undertaking practical work as an 'improver' in the fitting and erecting shops at Crewe. He moved in 1898 to the Design and Drawing Office of the Lancashire and Yorkshire Railway at Horwich under the guidance of John Aspinall. He had a short spell as foreman at Blackpool running shed and ran the materials test room at Horwich. In 1901, he was appointed as the Outdoor Assistant in the Company's Carriage & Wagon Department and the following year, Assistant Works Manager at the Newton Heath depot, promoted to be Works Manager in 1903. Further rapid promotion followed in 1904, when he became Assistant Superintendent of the L&Y Railway's Carriage & Wagon Department.

In 1905, he moved to the Great Northern Railway as Assistant Carriage & Wagon Superintendent at Doncaster and in 1906 assumed its leadership. He succeeded H.A. Ivatt as the GN's Chief Mechanical Engineer in 1911 and in 1920 was awarded the CBE for his wartime work at Doncaster. In 1923, J.G. Robinson was offered the senior post of CME of the new LNER Company but declined as he was near retirement and commended Nigel Gresley, who was duly appointed in 1923. He had designed and built the first engines of his 'Big Engine' policy in 1920 (the K3 mogul) and 1922 (the A1 pacific) but delegated many of the lesser designs to be developed by his Drawing Office staff or contractors under his direction and supervision, including that of the B17 described in this book.

During the 1930s he lived at Salisbury Hall, near St Albans, and had land where he developed his interest in breeding wild birds and ducks (the inspiration for the names of his A4 pacifics?). In 1936, he designed the 1,500v D.C. electric locomotives for the Woodhead electrification scheme although its implementation was delayed until after the Second World War. He was knighted in the 1936 New Year Honours after the triumph of the 'Silver Jubilee' high speed express and the exploits of his pacifics.

He died suddenly in office on 5 April 1941 and was buried at his father's church of St Peter's, Netherseal, Derbyshire.

Edward Thompson

Edward Thompson's father was Assistant Master and a Governor of Marlborough School, and a Greek scholar. Edward had three sisters and in 1889 was sent to a preparatory school in Reigate, moving to Marlborough in 1894. Gresley was also a pupil there, two or three years his senior. Edward left in 1899 and took a mechanical science degree at Pembroke College Cambridge, graduating in 1902.

He began at Beyer, Peacock as a pupil in the Drawing Office and in 1904 joined the Midland Railway at Derby Locomotive Works, becoming an 'Improver' at Derby shed, then in 1905 moving to Woolwich Arsenal. In 1906, he joined the North Eastern Railway as Assistant to the District Locomotive Superintendent at Hull Dairycoates. In 1909, he moved on to a similar position at Gateshead and went with Vincent Raven on a study tour to the USA in 1910. After Nigel Gresley's promotion as Locomotive Superintendent of the GNR in 1911, Thompson became Carriage & Wagon Supt. at Doncaster Works.

He married Vincent Raven's younger daughter, Guendolen,

in 1913 and in 1914 transferred to Peterborough as Assistant District Locomotive Superintendent. Raven was appointed as Superintendent of the Royal Ordnance Factory at Woolwich in 1915 and Thompson joined him in 1916 in the Movements branch of the Directorate of Transportation in France, where he was awarded the rank of Lt. Colonel and subsequently the OBE.

After the war, he became Superintendent of the GNR Carriage & Wagon Works and introduced the concept of conveyor belt construction after the Henry Ford example. Gresley moved him to Stratford in 1923 as Assistant Mechanical Engineer, and he occupied a flat in Baker Street. He visited Paddington on many occasions and was impressed with the sharp exhaust of the GW 4-6-0s. He learned of that company's long valve travel arrangements and economies (missing the Doncaster learning from the 1925 exchange with the GW's *Pendennis Castle* ?) and was influential in obtaining authority for the rebuilding of the GE B12s in 1933. However, his staff management was poor and his relationship with Gresley was not good. Gresley had criticised him on occasions in front of colleagues and staff and he resented this bitterly.

In 1933, Thompson was appointed as Mechanical Engineer for the North East Division at Darlington and was there five years, his wife dying during this period. In March 1938, he moved to Doncaster as Mechanical Engineer there and in April 1941 Gresley died suddenly. Although it seems that the LNER management was grooming J.F. Harrison as Gresley's successor, it was felt that he was still too young and Thompson, already sixty years of age, was appointed instead.

For years, Thompson had felt neglected and left outside of Gresley's core team and seized this opportunity he had been given with just five years left before retirement. The fact that this coincided with the Second World War was for him both a problem and opportunity, for the LNER needed engines that were simple and robust to stand up to intensive use and lack of maintenance. Thompson had been critical of Gresley's 3-cylinder conjugation valve gear arrangement and lack of standardisation in the way both the GWR and subsequently the LMS under Stanier had developed for their respective systems. Thompson drew up a similar list of requirements for the LNER with ten standard types although only the B1, K1 2-6-0 and L1 2-6-4T were completely new designs, and persuaded the LNER Board to authorise this, highlighting the failures of the Gresley 3-cylinder engines in traffic, especially during the first years of the war. The B1 4-6-0 concept was a more conventional replacement for Gresley's V4 2-6-2 of which only two had been built. That and the K1 were successful and the rebuilding of some of the Robinson O4 2-8-0s with the 100A boiler as O1s also was useful. However, the other standard requirements on his list were basically achieved by rebuilding some of Gresley's three cylinder engines, the A1/1 *Great Northern,* the P2 2-8-2s as A2/2s, the other A2 variants, the B17/B2 conversion, the two-cylinder D49, the K3/K5. The L1 design was really unnecessary as the Company already had the large V1/V3 2-6-2T class.

Gresley's former loyal staff were unhappy in this regime and his difficult manner had become unpredictable varying from charming, especially with women, to being autocratic and ruthless. He was a good chooser of assistants however and was efficient and cut costs at a time when this was a priority for the Company and the war effort. However, he harboured his continued resentment of Gresley and the way he felt he had been neglected and even undermined, and many of his staff believed that his locomotive policy was biased to a great extent by his desire to highlight the weaknesses in some of Gresley's designs. He retired in 1946 and the Drawing Office staff and others directly involved with the management of the LNER's Mechanical Engineering Department welcomed the more congenial Peppercorn to the helm.

Chapter 2

THE GREAT CENTRAL 4-6-9s, BEFORE LNER

The GCR class 8 (LNER B5) – 1902

Design and construction

Robinson had received his early training at Swindon and must have kept in touch and been aware of Churcward's standard design plans of 1901 which included a mixed traffic 4-6-0 with 5ft 8in coupled wheels though this concept was not developed until Collett's Hall and Grange classes. The Great Central had important perishable freight traffic – fish from the North Sea required to get quickly to Billingsgate Market in London. Robinson therefore designed the Company's first 4-6-0 locomotives specifically to handle this traffic and although they catered for other traffic, they were known from the first as 'fish engines'. Six locomotives numbered 1067-1072 were built in Glasgow by Neilson & Co. in 1902 at a cost of £3,700 each and a further eight (180-187) followed, constructed by Beyer, Peacock & Co. in 1904, costing £4,055 per locomotive.

The key dimensions were:

Cylinders (2 outside)	19in x 26in (B5/3: 21in x 26in)
Coupled wheel diameter	6ft 1in
Bogie wheel diameter	3ft 6in
Stephenson's valve gear	slide valves
Boiler pressure	180psi
Heating surface	1,795sqft (superheated: 1,568sqft)
Grate area	23.5sqft
Axleload	18 tons
Weight – Engine	65 tons 2 cwt (superheated: 64 tons 3 cwt)
– Tender	44 tons 3 cwt, (4,000 gallon: 48 tons 6 cwt)
– Total	109 tons 5 cwt (4000 gallon: 113 tons 8 cwt)
Water capacity	Initially 3,250 gallons, 4,000 from 1905/6
Coal capacity	6 tons
Tractive effort	19,672lbs

The Great Central Railway classified them as 'class 8' and the LNER identified them in their standard system as class 'B5'. Their cylinders and other parts were identical to that of the GC 0-8-0s (LNER Q4) and the boiler was similar though with a shallower grate to fit over the larger coupled wheels. It was initially unsuperheated. They remained unmodified until the Grouping, apart from 1072 which was experimentally fitted with a Schleyder ash consumer in the smokebox, passing the ash and any unburnt coal back to the firebox to ensure complete combustion. This cannot have been successful as no other engines were so modified and the equipment was later removed from 1072.

Shortly after the Grouping in 1923, one of the second batch, 184, was fitted with a larger superheated O4 boiler and a side-window cab. Between 1926 and 1936, the remaining engines of the class were superheated though with the original size Q4 boilers and 184 (by then renumbered 5184) received the smaller but superheated boiler and standard Robinson cab in 1927. The superheated boilers were, however, slightly higher pitched than the initial design, requiring the handsome Robinson chimney and dome to be cut down in size to meet the loading gauge, which rather marred their looks. The LNER classified the superheated engines as B5/3 and 5184 was B5/2 until it resumed the standard format. The unsuperheated engines were B5/1 until converted. Seven engines (5180, 5183, 5184, 5185, 5187, 6067 and 6072) received 21in diameter cylinders at the same time as superheating. By 1937 the class subdivisions were abandoned and they were just known as B5s.

Beyer Peacock 181, built in 1904, in lined Great Central livery at Leicester Central, 13 May 1910. W. Bradshaw/MLS Collection

Neilson & Co. 1067, built in 1902, with encased safety valves and tender with open coal rails at Woodford, 18 August 1923. W. Potter/MLS Collection

184 as rebuilt at Gorton with high pitched O4 type boiler, cut-down boiler mountings and side-window cab, classified by the LNER as the sole B5/2, July 1923. Bob Miller Collection/ MLS Collection

5180, B5/3, rebuilt with Q4 superheated boiler and 21in cylinders, at Woodford, 1931. It is fitted with a tender that retains the open coal rails. G.A. Coltas/ MLS Collection

5186, a B5 with the superheated Q4 boiler but retaining 19in diameter cylinders and with a tender with plated coal rails (and a very full load of coal), c1935.
W.A. Camwell/MLS Collection

Initially, they were equipped with 3,250 gallon tenders but the longer non-stop runs with the fast freight services taxed this and between 1905 and 1906 all were equipped with larger 4,000 gallon tenders. They received the GC lined green livery and at the Grouping they were repainted the freight livery – black with red lining – and renumbered 5180-5187 and 6067-6072. The lining was discontinued after 1928. However, they kept the brass beading over the splashers.

They performed their duties well enough and were largely unmodified, apart from superheating, during their long lives. Modifications to the blastpipe dimensions were made between 1936 and 1938 to further improve their steaming which seems to have been effective. However, although they performed the work for which they were designed, they clearly did not satisfy their designer or the GC Board for only fourteen were built whereas the 2 cylinder mixed traffic 4-6-0 became the widespread 'maid of all work' for the GW, LMS and after the Second World War, the LNER. Other attempts followed with a string of GC 4-6-0s, each class in small numbers.

One, 6070, was withdrawn in 1939, but the rest survived the Second World War and were withdrawn between 1947 and 1950. Seven (5182, 5183, 5185-7, 6069 and 6071) became British Railways engines in 1948 although none received their BR allocated numbers or livery. Two, 5186 and 5187, had received a revised LNER number, 1311 and 1312, in January 1946, but all (except 6070) were renumbered 1678-1690 later in 1946 to leave the 13XX numbers free for the new B1s. The last survivor was 1686 (ex 5182 and allocated 61686) condemned in June 1950. Despite their small numbers, most did last over forty-five years and only succumbed when replaced by the most successful LNER mixed traffic 4-6-0, Thompson's B1.

1689 (the former GC 186, LNER 5186) on shed in post-war condition, c1947. It was withdrawn in October 1949.
Lance Brown/MLS Collection

1681 (GC 1071, LNER 6071) on Lincoln shed alongside one of its sister engines, 8 June 1947. The tender is again well-stacked with coal.
W. Potter/MLS Collection

Brand new 1069, built by Neilson & Co. in 1902, with a train of four-wheel fish vans, c1903. Note the rerailing jack on the running plate above the cylinder and the original 3,250 gallon tender with open coal rails. Bob Miller Collection/MLS Collection

Operations

The locomotives were initially allocated between Neasden and Grimsby specifically for the fish trains from the port to London. At the same time, the GCR had built new 15 ton bogie fish vans for the traffic. Some of the second batch were allocated to Gorton, again for fast freight work. In addition to the perishable freight work, some of the Neasden engines were used on express passenger trains between Marylebone and Leicester. However, by the middle of the decade other GC 4-6-0s and 4-4-2s became available and by 1912, the B2 'Sam Fay' 4-6-0s and the first of the 'Director' 4-4-0s were in charge of the main passenger services. By the Grouping, the class was divided between Gorton, Immingham and Mexborough working fast freight and fish traffic to the Great Western via Banbury as well as to London and Manchester. The allocation at the Grouping was:

Mexborough:	5180, 5181, 5186, 6067-6072
Immingham:	5182-5184
Gorton:	5185

After a short stay by some of the class at Ardsley, they and the Mexborough engines moved to Doncaster in 1924. By 1928 the allocation had changed to:

Lincoln:	5181-5183, 5185, 6067, 6069
Doncaster:	5180, 6068, 6072
Woodford:	5184, 5186
Mexborough:	6070
Immingham:	6071

Four engines – 5180, 5186, 6068 and 6071 – were allocated to Woodford in 1929 and in addition to the fish

traffic to the GWR, worked other freight and stopping passenger trains. Between 1925 and 1931, the rest were allocated to Lincoln and worked local passenger trains to Cleethorpes, New Holland and March and some local goods traffic. However, by 1936 several had been transferred to Sheffield and Immingham. The complete allocation by the end of 1936 was:

Immingham:	5184, 5187, 6070
Lincoln:	5181, 5185, 6072
Sheffield:	5182, 5183, 5186, 6067, 6068, 6069
Woodford:	5180, 6071

Immingham's 6070 had a ten-coach 263 ton load on the 10.30am Manchester Central-Liverpool on 30 May 1939 which it worked up to 62½mph at Trafford Park and 64 down the 1 in 135 to Glazebrook after surmounting the same gradient at Flixton at 52mph minimum. The attempt to recoup a 4 minute late departure was thwarted however by a p-way slack at Padgate and arrival at Warrington was 5 minutes late, taking 20½ minutes for the 16.9 miles.

The prototype Neilson 1067 in original condition with saturated Q4 steam boiler at Nottingham Victoria at the head of an excursion train in 1922. Note the wrap-around cover for the safety valves. T.G. Hepburn/ MLS Collection

B5/3 5183, Lincoln based and before reallocation to Sheffield, leaving York with that city's portion of the *North Country Continental* strengthened by four non-corridor ex GNR coaches at the front, c1935. F. Moore/ MLS Collection

Woodford's B5 6071 with superheated boiler but still with 19in cylinders, leaving York with a cross-country train for Bournemouth formed of Southern Railway rolling stock which it will work as far as its home base, c1936. Cecil Ord Collection/ MLS Collection

The first withdrawal, 6070 of Immingham, took place in 1939 and 6071 moved to Gorton. The other two Immingham engines went to Mexborough in 1940 and by 1943, the allocation was:

Mexborough:	5180, 5181, 5182, 5184, 5185, 5186, 5187, 6067, 6071, 6072
Sheffield:	5183, 6068, 6069

During the war years, they were employed on heavy passenger trains between Sheffield and Hull and the only log I have discovered of any engine of the class at that time was on this route on 25 November 1944. Mexborough's 5180 worked the 335 ton 10am from Sheffield, departing 14 minutes late, and was heavily delayed by signals around Tinsley, taking 13¾ minutes to the Rotherham stop. It took just over 13 minutes over the colliery slack affected six miles to Mexborough, including more signal delays at Kilnhurst and a further fifteen minutes for the five miles to Doncaster including a seventy-five second stop at Conisbrough. Arrival at Doncaster was 21 minutes late.

The influx of the new Thompson B1s in the immediate post-war period displaced them from the Sheffield – Doncaster area and three, by then numbered 1679, 1680 and 1686, moved to Trafford Park, Manchester, replacing D9 4-4-0s on the Cheshire Lines Committee (CLC) routes. Included in their duties were special and excursion trains, including Grand National Race trains. I have traced the log of one run by a B5 on the CLC, not particularly distinguished but probably typical of the period. The load, however, was quite substantial for the class and route. I give some outline timings and speeds which were logged by the recorder.

Liverpool Central-Manchester Central
4.15pm Liverpool-Hull
1680 (ex 6069)
10 chs, 318 tons
9 October 1946

Miles	Location	Times	Speeds	Schedule	Gradients
0	Liverpool Central	00.00		1 L	
1.5	Brunswick	04.38	34		1/348F
2.4	St Michael's	06.24	34		1/200 R
5.1	Mersey Road	08.24	44		1/750 F
5.8	Cressington	09.24	39	½ L	
8	Hunts Cross West Jn	11.54	33/32	1 L	1/195 R (2 miles)
11.5	Hough Green	17.51	52/33		1/185 F/1/185 R
13.1	Farnworth	21.06		T	
0		00.00		1 L	
1.9	Widnes East Jn	03.55	43	1L	1/230 F
3.8	Sankey	06.01	53½		1/200 F
5.4	Sankey Jn	07.35	pws 30*	½ L	
6.1	Warrington Central	10.43		¾ L	
0		00.00		1½ L	
1.9	Padgate	03.37	43	2¼ L	1/180 F
6.1	Glazebrook	09.17	38/43		1/240 R/ L7
7.4	Irlam	11.45	45/37	2¼ L	L/1/135 R
9.7	Flixton	14.46	50		1/135 F
13.5	Trafford Park Jn	19.06	47/40	1¾ L	L/1/180 R
14.5	Throstle Nest East Jn	20.10	46	1¾ L	1/230 F/1/132 R
16.9	Manchester Central	24.59		1½ L	

1686 (**GC** 183, LNER 5183) destined to be the last survivor in 1950, here piloting a B7 4-6-0, No.5475, on the 4.55pm relief Manchester London Road-Cleethorpes at Torside on the Woodhead route, 10 June 1946. J.D. Darby/MLS Collection

However, within a year they had moved again, and the 1947 allocation was:

Mexborough:	1679, 1680, 1686
Lincoln:	1681, 1683, 1684, 1685, 1689

Other engines were withdrawn in 1947 and all the remaining engines, by now in poor condition, concluded their careers at Mexborough on local freight and banking duties at Dunford Bridge. The last survivor was 1686, the only member of the class to reach 1950.

1680 (GC 1069, LNER 6069) on freight banking duties near Penistone, 13 September 1948. It was withdrawn two months later. MLS Collection

The GCR class 8C (LNER B1, later B18) – 1903

Design & construction

Before the GCR Atlantics and 4-6-0s for express work, the main passenger services were in the hands of Pollitt's and Robinson's 4-4-0s (the latter becoming LNER D9 class).

In 1903, Beyer, Peacock produced the design of an express passenger version of Robinson's class 8 – an identical 4-6-0 with 6ft 9in wheels – just before they constructed the second batch of the 'fish engines' in 1904. Only two were built by Beyer, Peacock, the first, numbered 195, having 19½in cylinders whilst 196 had the same 19in cylinders as the 6ft 1in engines. Clearly aware of Churchward's comparison between his 2 cylinder 4-6-0s and the experimental conversion of the type to Atlantic 4-4-2s, Robinson got Beyer, Peacock to build a couple of 8B Atlantic versions of the 8C at the same time and these were numbered 192 and 194. The key dimensions of the two 4-6-0s were:

Cylinders (2 outside)	19½in x 26in (196, 19in x 26in)
Coupled wheel diameter	6ft 9in
Bogie wheel diameter	3ft 6in
Stephenson's valve gear	slide valves
Boiler pressure	180psi
Heating surface	1,911sqft
Grate area	26.24sqft
Axleload	18 tons 10 cwt
Weight – Engine	71 tons
– Tender	48 tons 6 cwt
– Total	119 tons 6 cwt
Water capacity	4,000 gallons
Coal capacity	6 tons
Tractive effort	17,729lbs (196)

Robinson's 4-4-0 No.106 (later LNER D9) at Manchester, c1903. MLS Collection

In order the fit the boiler and Belpaire firebox over the 4-6-0 wheel arrangement, the grate was rather shallow and the ashpan was only 7in deep at the back and was without a rear damper risking the lack of air for efficient combustion. Although there is little evidence that this caused poor performance of the 4-6-0s, it was the Atlantics that were preferred and multiplied, the wheel arrangement allowing for deeper fireboxes and ashpans on the additional Atlantics constructed, suggesting that the flaws in the design of the 4-6-0s had been detected.

195 was rebuilt with a Robinson designed superheater in 1912, although it was subject to a boiler exchange during a Works visit in 1920 and received a saturated steam boiler (the boiler was interchangeable with the Robinson 8F (LNER B4) of which ten were built in 1906 with 6ft 7in coupled wheels). Its cylinders were also enlarged to 21 inches. After the Grouping, a superheated boiler similar to that of the O4 2-8-0s was provided for both engines, although with the shallower grate to accommodate the rear coupled large pair of wheels. 196 also got 21in cylinders when it was superheated at the Grouping. The revised post-Grouping changed dimensions were:

Cylinders (2 outside)	21in x 26in
Stephenson's valve gear	10in piston rings
Heating surface	1,724sqft (incl 242sqft superheating)
Engine weight	72 tons 18 cwt
Tractive effort	21,658lbs

The prototype Atlantic, 192, constructed by Beyer, Peacock as class 8B in comparison with the 8C 4-6-0 at Nottingham Victoria, c1903. MLS Collection

Postcard of the first 8C 4-6-0, No.195, in Works Grey livery for the company's official photograph, 1903.
MLS Collection

An excellent portrait of 196 in original condition as built, taken during the first decade of the twentieth century.
Bob Miller Collection/ MLS Collection

Another minor alteration but one which changed their appearance was the reduction in size of the boiler mountings to fit the LNER loading gauge (the GC London extension had more generous gauge allowances). The Robinson pattern chimney was reduced by 1¼ inches using a plain taper version common to other LNER engines. The proposed electrification of the Woodhead route in the 1930s was also a factor requiring the reduction in height of GC engine fittings to give safe clearance from the overhead lines. The four Ramsbottom safety valves were replaced by twin Ross pop valves encased in a rectangular covering. The GCR standard smokebox door with wheel and handle was replaced by twin handles on 5195, although 5196 retained its GCR variety until withdrawal.

Unlike the 'fish engines' which had received the GCR lined black freight livery, both the 6ft 9in classes received the Great Central lined green passenger livery, although curiously the 4-6-0 got lined LNER green after the Grouping and the more numerous and popular passenger Atlantics got lined black. The 4-6-0s were renumbered 5195 and 5196 adding the extra 5000 as on all ex GCR engines at the Grouping. The locomotives were now identified as LNER class B1, although this was changed on the building of Thompson's B1s in 1943, when the two GCR engines became class B18. During the Second World War both were repainted plain black and in 1946 they were renumbered again, being allotted 1470 and 1471 (which were never carried) before finally being repainted 1479 and 1480 in the autumn of 1946. Both were withdrawn in December 1947, just before nationalisation.

5195 in LNER lined apple green livery at Woodford, c1928. Note altered dome shape and 'flowerpot' chimney.
W.L. Good/MLS Collection

A classic shot of 5195 in the last days before the Second World War at Skelton Junction, York, 1939. The boiler mountings are different again with short but improved chimney shape and flatter dome. W. Potter/MLS Collection

It is difficult to recognise the same locomotive as that in the photograph at Skelton Junction. In fact, it is sister engine, ex 5196, renumbered 1480 in 1946 and seen here two months after withdrawal stored at Dukinfield, 1 February 1948. Another Robinson 4-6-0 is behind, possibly 1479, but it looks as though it might be one of the B5s with higher pitched boiler such as 1680 (ex 6069) which was condemned at the same time. N. Fields/ MLS Collection

Operations

Both engines were initially allocated to Gorton while comparisons with the 4-4-2s were carried out. Although there is no account indicating any failure of the 4-6-0s, the Atlantics were favoured for replication, unlike similar trials on the Great Western. Perhaps the need for extra adhesion on the South Devon banks influenced the argument there, although traffic levels on the GWR undoubtedly required heavier trains than the recently opened Great Central main line. The 4-6-0s for express passenger work on the Great Central remained isolated, the wheel arrangement being developed only for mixed traffic and freight work, until increasing loads at the end of the decade saw another Robinson 4-6-0 attempt for an express passenger locomotive in the shape of the B2 'Sir Sam Fay' engines of 1912. Although the 6ft 7in 8Fs (LNER B4s) were developed from the 8Cs, in fact they were intended for fast freight, fish and mixed traffic duties.

After this initial trial period, both engines were allocated to Neasden depot and worked express passenger trains from Marylebone to Leicester until more of the Atlantics became available when they moved to Sheffield and worked the Manchester-King's Cross through coaches between Sheffield and Grantham. A *Railway Magazine* article by Cecil J. Allen in April 1914 records the run of 196 on an unspecified date with the return working, the 11-coach 6.5pm from King's Cross which the 8C took over at Grantham.

196 as constructed, at Marylebone ready to depart with the 3.20pm Marylebone-Manchester which it will work to Leicester, c1922. Bob Miller Collection/MLS Collection

Grantham-Retford,
6.05pm King's Cross-Manchester
196
11 chs, 320 tons

Miles	Location	Times	Speeds	Schedule	Gradient
0	Grantham	00.00		T	
6 ¼	Hougham	08.35	75		1 in 300 F
14 ¾	Newark	15.45	73½		L
21 ¼	Carlton	21.10	67	(Now inside 'even time')	L
27	Tuxford	26.55			1 in 200 R
	Markham Box	-	48½		L/1 in 200 R
33 ¼	Retford	34.40		2¼ E	

195 moved back to Neasden in 1916 and was regularly rostered to the very heavy 10.5pm Marylebone-Manchester mail train. However, after the war both engines moved to Immingham and were used on secondary passenger services and continued there until 1926. They then moved to Woodford for the Sheffield-Banbury cross-country services and were both there for most of the 1930s. They were also used on the fish traffic to the GWR, but they were less popular for

196 shortly before the Grouping passing Abbey Lane Coal Sidings Box with a Sheffield-Swindon train, c1922. W.A. Brown/ MLS Collection

195 on a similar duty with a Sheffield-Swindon train formed mainly of GWR coaches, shortly after the Grouping but before repainting in LNER livery, c1923. W.A. Brown/MLS Collection

this type of work with their large driving wheels. They were occasionally loaned to Leicester when that depot was short of power.

I have turned up one run in the Rail Performance Society's archives timed by John Wrottesley, the father of a friend I meet occasionally. His son, Michael, will not mind me saying that his father's notebooks are incredibly difficult to decipher, but as far as I can see, after a day spent at the races near Gatwick and a night in a London Hotel, he caught the 8.45am Marylebone back to his home in Brackley. The times quoted are below and I have estimated speeds from the average times.

Marylebone-Brackley
8.45am Marylebone-Woodford
5196
5 chs, 173/183 tons
21 September 1938

Miles	Location	Times	Est.Speed	Schedule	Gradients
0	Marylebone	00.00		T	
	Kilburn	06.50			1 in 100 R
5.2	Neasden	09.30		½ L	1 in 90 F
	Wembley Park	11.00			1 in 91 R
9.2	Harrow-on-the-Hill	14.50		¾ L	
0		00.00		¾ L	
1.4	North Harrow	02.45			1 in 176 F
2.3	Pinner	03.50	60		L
4.6	Northwood	06.45		½ L	
0		00.00		1 L	
1.4	Moor Park	02.35			1 in 176 F
2.4	Watford South Junction	03.35	60	1¾ L	
3.5	Rickmansworth	04.55	40*	1 L	1 in 243 R
5.7	Chorley Wood	08.35	36		1 in 100/106 R
7.9	Chalfont	11.55	40	1L	1 in 105 R
10	Amersham	15.00	40		1 in 105 R
15.1	Great Missenden	20.10	70	1 ¼ L	1 in 160 F
	Dutchlands Box	-	50		1 in 125/163 R
19.6	Wendover	25.10	60		1 in 117 F
21.9	Stoke Mandeville	27.25	63		1 in 117 F
24.1	Aylesbury	30.05		¼ L	
0		00.00		½ L	
	Waddesdon Manor	06.45			L
6	Quainton Road	08.05			1 in 160 R
6.3	Quainton Rd Junction	08.35		1¼ L	L
9	Grendon Underwood Jn	11.05	65	¾ L	1 in 176 F
11	Calvert	12.55	60		1 in 176 R
16.5	Finmere	18.45		¼ L	
0		00.00		T	1 in 176 F/ 1 in 176 R
4.8	Brackley	06.45		¾ L	

In March 1940, both were allocated to Colwick to act as station pilot and standby engine at Nottingham Victoria and run local services to Grantham. 5196 soon moved, however, to Leicester for similar duties at Leicester Central. There are records of substitutions on main line services following locomotive failures such as 5195 reaching Manchester on the morning Hull-Liverpool express which presumably it took over at Nottingham. In 1946 both were moved to Neasden but only for nine months when they returned to Colwick before finally languishing at Annesley from whence they were both withdrawn in December 1947.

5195 piloted by C1 exGN Atlantic 4454 on a heavy postwar passenger train on the Woodhead line, c1946. W. Potter/MLS Collection

The GCR 8F (LNER B4) – 1906

Design and construction

The ten engines of the 8F class were built by Beyer, Peacock & Co. in 1906 and were straight developments of the earlier 8C class with the coupled driving wheels less by three inches at 6ft 6in, the only significant difference. Later, they were equipped with thicker tyres so that at the Grouping the LNER drawings showed wheel diameter of 6ft 7in. Although a 4-6-0 with such wheel dimensions would have been considered suitable for express passenger work on other railways, in fact they were designed specifically to handle the fast developing fish and perishable traffic from Lincolnshire and the North Sea ports for the London markets, and augmenting the class 8 (B5) engines built for this traffic in 1902. They were numbered 1095-1104 and were painted in the GCR lined green livery initially although later, black. They were provided with the standard 4,000 gallon tenders with plated coal fenders although there were exchanges with other engines throughout their lives and some received the earlier style tenders with coal rails. The key dimensions were:

Cylinders (2 outside)	19 in x 26in (six rebuilt as B4/2 with 21in x 26in)
Coupled wheel diameter	6ft 6in (later 6ft 7in)
Bogie wheel diameter	3ft 6in
Stephenson's valve gear	slide valves
Boiler pressure	180psi
Heating surface	1,951sqft
Grate area	26.24sqft
Axleload	18 tons 8 cwt
Weight – Engine	70 tons 14 cwt
– Tender	48 tons 6 cwt
– Total	119 tons
Water capacity	4,000 gallons
Coal capacity	6 tons
Tractive effort	18,178lbs

1097 was involved in the ceremony to mark the commencement of building a new dock at Immingham in July 1906 and received the name *Immingham* in honour of the occasion, the first GCR 4-6-0 to be named and the only one in this class – it kept its name to the end of its long career.

At the Grouping the engines were renumbered 6095-6104, identified as class B4 and were painted in the LNER apple green livery until the onset of the Second World War when they reverted like many other engines to plain black livery. All received superheaters between 1926 and 1928 and six of the ten (6095, 6098, 6100, 6101, 6103 & 6104) had their 19in cylinders widened to 21in with 10in piston valves, increasing their tractive effort to 22,206lbs. The superheated engines had 1,975sqft of heating surface and the B4s with enlarged cylinders weighed an extra ton. The locomotives with saturated steam boilers were then classified B4/1 and the superheated engines B4/2. Once they were all superheated the 19in cylinder engines became B4/1 and the 21in engines B4/2. Like the earlier 4-6-0s, the boiler mountings were reduced in height to meet the LNER standard loading gauge.

An official photograph of 1097, still unnamed, in Works Grey on a postcard, 1906.
MLS Collection

1097 after naming *Immingham*, c1907. Real Photographs/MLS Collection

1100 and crew posing at Leicester, 4 May 1910. W. Bradshaw/MLS Collection

6097 ***Immingham*** in resplendent LNER lined apple green livery at Liverpool (Brunswick) shed, July 1937. MLS Collection

Lincoln's B4/2, 6104, thought to be at Nottingham Victoria, c1938. W.L. Good/ MLS Collection

6095 was withdrawn in July 1939, but reprieved because of the looming hostilities and lasted until 1944, when it was condemned after a collision at Woodhead. The rest were withdrawn between 1947 and 1950, all except 6095 being renumbered 1481-1489 in 1946. Four survived nationalisation but none were repainted with their BR number. 1482 *Immingham* was repainted LNER green in 1946 and became something of a celebrity in its remaining years being the last withdrawn in November 1950.

6104 in post-war condition with an unidentified V2 at Sheffield Darnall depot, 14 October 1945. J.D. Darby/MLS Collection

B4/2 1488, formerly GC 1103, LNER 6103, at Gorton a month before it was withdrawn, 26 September 48. N. Fields/MLS Collection

***Immingham*, renumbered** 1482 but repainted in LNER lined green, still in good condition, at Leeds Ardsley depot, 22 May 1949. H.D. Bowtell/ MLS Collection

1482 *Immingham*, now the sole survivor of the class, just four months before its withdrawal and still looking in reasonable condition, Ardsley, 16 July 1950. MLS Collection

Operations

As intended, the 8Fs were spread between Neasden, Gorton and Grimsby to work fish and fast freight services to London, the GW via Woodford and Banbury and across the Pennines to Manchester and Liverpool. They operated passenger expresses also though more on the Nottingham-Sheffield-Manchester route than on the Leicester and London services. During the First World War, 1095, 1097-1099 and 1104 were reallocated to Mexborough and were involved in troop train movement, especially to Banbury and the SR and GWR ports. The *Railway Magazine* of 1914 published a run when an 8F worked the 2.15pm Manchester-Marylebone between Sheffield and Leicester, the highlights shown alongside:

Sheffield-Leicester
2.15pm Manchester-Marylebone
1102 – Gorton
180 tons to Nottingham
250 tons to Leicester
c1913

Miles	Location	Times	Speeds	Schedule	Gradients
0	Sheffield Victoria	00.00		T	
1.6	Darnall	04.20	pws 15*		1/144/155 R
4.9	Woodhouse	09.35			1/ 137 F
12	Staveley	17.50	51½		1/176 R
17.9	Heath	26.20	42		1/100R
26.5	Kirkby Bentinck	36.35	60		1/132 F/ 1/132 R/L
32.4	Hucknall	43.00	65/sigs 20*		1/130 F
38.2	Nottingham	50.25	(48 net)	1½ L	
0		00.00		1½ L	
4.4	Ruddington	06.25	pws		L
9	East Leake	12.25	46		1/176 R
13.6	Loughborough	17.20	66		1/176 F
18.4	Rothley	22.35	55		1/264 R
23.4	Leicester Central	28.20	(27 net)	3¾ L	

An early shot of the final B4, 1104, on a lightweight up Bradford – Marylebone express near Neasden, c1912.
MLS Collection

At the Grouping they became involved in the ex GNR East Coast main line services being based at Sheffield, and also travelling to York, Hull, Manchester and Leicester. The LNER motive power management were involved in some early testing and trials with the pre-grouping engines they'd inherited. The B4s' main line work from Sheffield was short-lived and four (1100-2 and 1104, not yet wearing their newly allocated numbers) were sent to March for freight work on the former Great Eastern, but their activity was limited because their height exceeded much of the GE's loading gauge. This was therefore short-lived also and they returned to Sheffield and Mexborough. When the latter's fish train diagrams were transferred to Doncaster, the B4s followed them. By the end of 1924, they were on their travels again and 6100 went to Ardsley. New England had four for goods train work to Ferme Park but by 1925 they had moved to Ardsley also. By the end of the year all ten B4s were allocated to Ardsley and Copley Hill and found regular work on the Leeds portions of King's Cross expresses from Doncaster as the Gresley Pacifics were too heavy until bridge renewals took place in 1933. They shared this work with Gresley's K2 and K3 moguls, but although the latter were more powerful, the B4s were better riders and seemed more popular with the crews. They also worked excursion traffic from the Leeds area to London, Aintree and the East Coast seaside resorts. On one excursion 6104 took 427 tons from Doncaster-Retford (17.4 miles) in just over 20 minutes reaching 70mph near Ranskill. It then ran the 33.1 miles on to Grantham in 39 ½ minutes. There is a log of one run from Doncaster to Wakefield on the 10.10am King's Cross which Pacific 2560 *Pretty Polly* had worked to Doncaster.

Doncaster-Wakefield
10.10am King's Cross-Leeds & Bradford
6100 – Ardsley
13 chs, 390 tons
16 March 1931

Miles	Location	Times	Speeds	Schedule	Gradients
0	Doncaster	00.00		¾ L	
2.8	Castle Hills	05.20			L
4	Carcroft	06.40	54		
6.5	Hampole	09.10	60		1/440 R
8.6	South Elmsall	11.40	50		1/220 R/ 1/350 F
11.8	Hemsworth	15.25	48/53		1/150 R
14.4	Nostell	18.35	49		
15.9	Hare Park	21.20	pws 40*		1/150 F
18.2	Sandal	23.50	55		
19.8	Wakefield Westgate	26.10	(25 net)	T	

John Wrottesley timed 6101 on the 5.45pm King's Cross from Doncaster to Leeds on 16 October 1931. Pacific 2743 *Felstead* brought the heavy train down from London and 6101 had eight coaches including two heavy dining cars. It left Doncaster 3¾ minutes late and took 24 minutes 25 seconds to Wakefield (3 late) and averaged 46.5mph from Carcroft to Sandal including over three miles of 1 in 150 up to Fitzwilliam followed by four miles of descent at the same gradient, arriving Wakefield 3 minutes late and departing 4¼ late. It then climbed the 1 in 100/122 to Ardsley summit in 8 minutes 50 seconds for the 4½ miles uphill from the start, clearing the summit at an excellent 43mph but was delayed on the approaches to Leeds arriving 5 minutes late.

They also worked out of Sheffield on the Woodhead route to Manchester and I have details of a number of runs in the summer of 1938 between Penistone and Guide Bridge, comparing the efforts of two B17 'Footballers', A1 pacific *Tracery* and B4 6104. The B4 was working a relief train consisting of five bogie coaches, the other three were on a train leaving Penistone at 6.55pm, all with six coaches. The most interesting part of the log is the time between Hazlehead and Dunford Bridge, the last 2¼ miles of 1 in 130/124/135 continuously from the Penistone stop to Woodhead Tunnel. 6104 and B17 2864 *Liverpool* averaged 43mph over this section, the A1 41mph and *Hull City* 38mph. The A1 was 5 seconds faster to the summit from the Penistone start, but the B4 beat the B17s by 30 and 45 seconds. 6104 and 2864 were

6100 at Doncaster with a stopping train for Wakefield and Leeds, 26 May 1931.
MLS Collection

6098 near Hadley Wood with a Leeds-London excursion train, c1935.
Photomatic/MLS Collection

content with 60mph on the descent through Crowden and Torside, the other B17 and the A1 just touching 70. All were set for meeting the 32 minute schedule with ease until signal checks from Godley Junction onwards. 6104 completed the journey to Guide Bridge in 30¾ minutes net.

When the Gresley Pacifics were allowed to work through to Leeds, three of the redundant B4s (6095, 6103 & 6104) were reallocated to March once more and this time worked passenger turns with surprisingly the same route availability as the B17s. This included the former M&GN line through to Cromer, also Norwich and Cambridge, though most of their work was towards Lincoln which became their home in 1935. This included the York – Lincoln stage of the Harwich boat train in both directions and stopping services to Grantham. In 1939, 6096 and 6097 moved to Lincoln also though 6103 went to Retford. The allocation just before the Second World War in the summer of 1939 stabilised as:

Leeds Copley Hill	6098, 6099, 6100, 6101, 6102
Lincoln	6095, 6096, 6097, 6104
Retford	6103

During the Second World War, changes were minor – 6103 returned to Lincoln and the Copley Hill engines stayed in the area but were based at Ardsley. Although the Harwich Boat Train had been withdrawn, there was still a Colchester-York daily service which was heavily used and sometimes loaded to fifteen or sixteen vehicles which were entrusted to the B4s. The Ardsley engines were primarily involved in freight movement which became the priority during the war years. They returned to the Leeds expresses on the Leeds-Bradford as well as the Leeds-Doncaster sections. A number of logs recorded during the wartime years are of interest. 6097 was in charge of the 3.15pm York-Selby-Hull with a load of 392 tons on 12 July 1941and ran the 13.8 miles start-to-stop in 20 minutes 10 seconds, gaining 2¾ minutes on the schedule. On 12 July 1941, 6101 had just four bogies on the 5.23pm Doncaster-Leeds and ran the 19¾ miles in 23 minutes exactly four minutes less than the scheduled time. It sustained 50mph to the top of the two miles at 1 in 150 to Hemsworth and averaged 68mph from Nostell to Sandal down the long 1 in 150, touching a maximum of 75mph. Of greater interest is the run on 11 July 1942 in the other direction when 6101 had a load of 14 coaches.

Wakefield-Doncaster
1.25pm Leeds
6101 – Copley Hill
14 chs, 480 tons
11 July 1942

Miles	Location	Times	Speeds	Schedule	Gradients
0	Wakefield Westgate	00.00		3 L	
1.25	Sandal	03.35			1 in 100/150 F
3.75	Hare Park	06.50	46		1 in 150 R
5.25	Nostell	09.30	34		1 in 150 R
8	Hemsworth	12.53	50		1 in 150 F
11	South Elmsall	16.00	58/60		1 in 150 R (1 mile)/ 1 in 150 F
13.25	Hampole	18.20	58		1 in 200 F
15.7	Cardroft	21.00	57		1 in 440 F
18.1	Bentley Halt	23.35	pws		L
19.75	Doncaster	26.45	(26 net)	¼ E	

Train loads at this time were very heavy and the best run I've come across on this section was with a K3 mogul which ran from Wakefield to Doncaster in 25½ minutes net with a 16 coach 550 ton load. A1s *Prince Palatine* and *Sceptre* matched the B4's time but with an extra coach. After the war, their work changed little at first and the allocation in January 1947 was (using the 1946 allocated numbers):

Ardsley	1484, 1485, 1486, 1487 (ex 6099-6102)
Copley Hill	1483, 1488 (ex 6098, 6103)
Lincoln	1481, 1482, 1489 (ex 6096, 6097, 6104)

The Ardsley engines worked summer excursions to Scarborough, Skegness and Filey and were joined by the green painted 1482 *Immingham* which was the last survivor, the rest succumbing quickly to the large number of Thompson B1s flooding the system.

The GCR class 8G (LNER B9) – 1906

Design and construction

1906 saw the introduction of another variation of the class 8 series, this time with 5ft 4 in coupled wheels and clearly intended for the faster freight work, the heavy slow coal trains being in the hands of the O4 2-8-0s. These were also constructed by Beyer, Peacock immediately after the last 8F had been delivered. They received numbers following on, the ten being identified as 1105-1114. They had similar boilers to the 8C and 8F designs apart from a shorter firebox. They were equipped with the standard GC 4,000 gallon tender. Key dimensions of this design were:

Cylinders (2 outside)	19in x 26in
Coupled wheel diameter	5ft 4in
Bogie wheel diameter	3ft 6in
Stephenson's valve gear	slide valves
Boiler pressure	180psi
Heating surface	1,951sqft (1,568sqft incl 230sqft superheating from 1924)
Grate area	23.75sqft
Axleload	18 tons
Weight – Engine	67 tons 6 cwt
– Tender	48 tons 6 cwt
– Total	115 tons 12cwt
Water capacity	4,000 gallons
Coal capacity	6 tons
Tractive effort	22,438lbs

B9, 1113, constructed in October 1906 in the condition and livery as built, c1912. MLS Collection

They wore the standard Great Central lined green livery. No significant changes were made before the Grouping when the ten engines were renumbered 6105-6114, but they then received the LNER goods plain black livery. Between 1924 and 1929 all were superheated and as each was rebuilt it became class B9/2, with all being known again as B9s after the last (6114) was superheated in April 1929. Just one example (6109) received similar treatment to the earlier 4-6-0s, being fitted with 21in diameter cylinders and piston valves at the same time as getting the superheater in November 1924, increasing its tractive effort to 27,410lbs. Performance was considerably improved and it is surprising the others of the class were not modified in similar fashion, but presumably the cost could not be justified. The weight of the superheated engines reduced slightly to 50 tons 14 cwt and the axleload to 17½ tons. The GC original design was just within the LNER loading gauge, but the higher pitched superheated boiler required the cutting back of the boiler mountings, some of the engines acquiring small 'flowerpot' chimneys. These were replaced in the 1930s by a plain chimney of the same height.

6111 was withdrawn in July 1939 but reinstated because of the impending war scenario. In 1946 all were still in existence and were initially allocated numbers 1342-1351, but then changed to 1469-1478 to avoid clashing with the new B1s. Four engines – 1469, 1470, 1475 and 1476 – were received into BR ownership and two, 61469 (ex 1105) and 61475 (ex 6111) received their BR numbers. 61475 was the last to be withdrawn in May 1949, having been the first as 6111 in July 1939, before its reprieve.

6106, superheated with higher pitched boiler and cut-down boiler mountings and in LNER plain black goods livery at Trafford Park Sidings, July 1939. W. Potter/ MLS Collection

1475 (ex GC 1111) standing on the turntable siding at Manchester Central station, 24 April 1947. This locomotive did receive its BR number and was the last survivor withdrawn in May 1949. H.C. Casserley/MLS Collection

61469, one of the two B9s that survived long enough to acquire their BR numbers, at Heaton Mersey a couple of months before its withdrawal, 19 February 1949. MLS Collection

Operations

The ten engines were initially split between Gorton and Lincoln depots, the Gorton engines working freight services from Manchester to London, Hull and Grimsby. The Lincoln engines worked freight mainly over the Woodhead route to Manchester. For a short time 1114 was based at Bradford and worked a freight nightly to Marylebone. The allocation at the Grouping in 1923 was:

Gorton	6106, 6109, 6110, 6113, 6114
Lincoln	6105, 6107, 6108, 6111, 6112

The Lincoln engines were transferred to Gorton in 1925, the whole class then being based there, but in 1927 Nos. 6105, 6106, 6110 and 6111 moved to Trafford Park and four, though not necessarily the same ones, were there throughout the 1930s with the remainder at Gorton. They worked freight during the week and excursions to Liverpool and Southport and to race meetings at Aintree and Haydock Park. Two regular turns for the

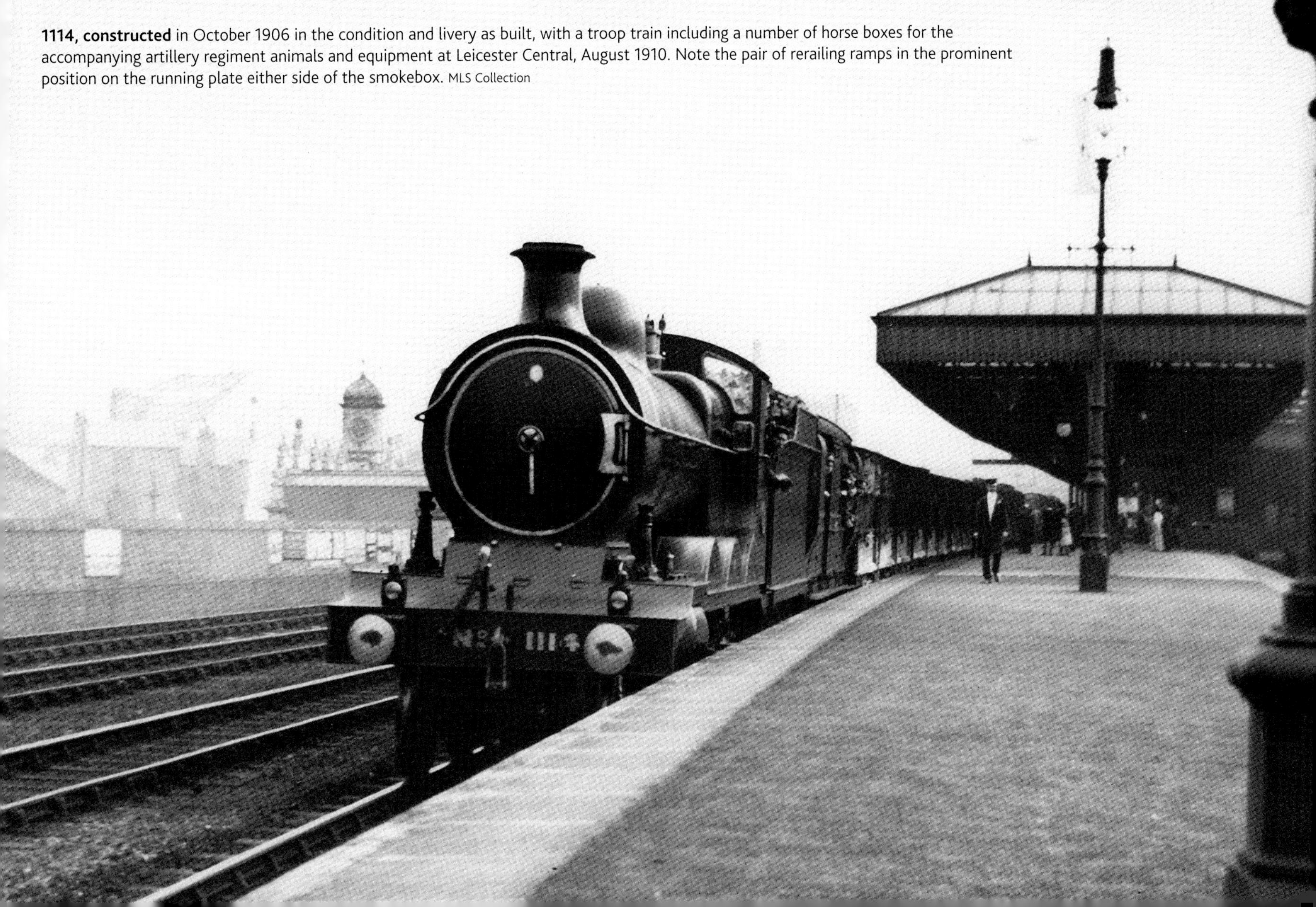

1114, constructed in October 1906 in the condition and livery as built, with a troop train including a number of horse boxes for the accompanying artillery regiment animals and equipment at Leicester Central, August 1910. Note the pair of rerailing ramps in the prominent position on the running plate either side of the smokebox. MLS Collection

Gorton engines were the 7.15pm Ardsley-Lincoln and the 7.50pm Ardsley-Marylebone part-fitted freights. They also worked local stopping passenger trains in the Manchester area. At peak holiday times they could work as far as Scarborough or the Lincolnshire coast. Trafford Park's 6105 was recorded unusually on an express to Liverpool in 1937, and 6106 in the war years, details below:

Manchester Central-Liverpool Central

		2.45pm Manchester Central			**10.30am Manchester Central**			
		6105			**6106**			
		8 chs, 192/205 tons			**7 chs, 205 tons**			
		15 May 1937			**15 March 1943**			
Miles	**Location**	**Times**	**Speeds**	**Sch**	**Times**	**Speeds**	**Sch**	**Gradients**
0	Manchester Central	00.00		4¼ L	00.00		2¼ L	
1.6	Throstle Nest East Jn	03.31	50	4¾ L	03.57	35	3 L	1/100, 1/132 F
2.5	Trafford Park Jn	04.24		4¾ L	05.01	39		1/230 R
3.3	Trafford Park	05.38	47		06.35	35		
6.3	Flixton	09.09	56		10.43	45½		1/135 R
8.4	Irlam	11.42	50/57		13.58	32/46		1/135 F
9.4	Glazebrook East Jn	12.38	58	6 L	15.04	46	3¼ L	L/ 1/240 F
14	Padgate	17.48	60/56	7 L	21.31		3¾ L	
					00.00		3¾ L	L
15.7	Warrington Central	19.50		6¼ L	04.49		5½ L	1/234 R
		00.00		6½ L	00.00		5 L	
1	Sankey Junction	02.46		6¼ L	02.50	pws/42	2¾ L	1/180 F
2.5	Sankey	04.40	47		05.12	pws 26*		L
4.3	Widnes East Jn	07.18	41/35	7¾ L	08.42	32 ½	4¾ L	1/158 R
6.2	Farnworth	09.52		8¼ L	12.29		5½ L	
		00.00		8¾ L	00.00		5¾ L	
1.6	Hough Green	03.09	60		03.32	47		1/185 F
3.7	Halewood	05.31	52	8¼ L	06.17	33	6 L	1/185 R
5.2	Hunts Cross	07.14	44		08.38	32 ½		1/185 R
6.7	Garston	08.59	51		10.56	47		1/195 F
7.4	Cressington	09.44	58	9½ L	11.49	48	7½ L	1/400 F
9.9	St Michaels	13.12			14.41	sigs		
13.1	Liverpool Central	16.14		9 L	22.42		11¼ L	

It was unusual to roster a B9 to a 45 minute express in 1937 and the small-wheeled 4-6-0 dropped nearly five minutes on the tight schedule. The timing was eased to 56 minutes during the war years and 6106 would just about have kept the schedule apart from the two engineering slacks and signal checks from St Michaels in.

After 6111's reinstatement in 1939 it went to Stockport (Heaton Mersey) working the Liverpool coaches off the London mail train from Godley Junction returning on a freight to Dewsnap Yard. In 1941 6111 was replaced by 6105 and 6107.

From the summer of 1945 all were stationed on the CLC lines at Stockport, Trafford Park and Liverpool Brunswick. They worked both freight and passenger trains with the exception of the Manchester-Liverpool expresses. Six were withdrawn in 1947, 1470 (6106) and 1476 (6112) in 1948 and the BR renumbered 61469 and 61475 in April and May 1949 respectively.

6107, with new superheated boiler received in January 1929, at Manchester London Road with a stopping train to Macclesfield, 1 June 1936. MLS Collection

6105 with a Hartford-Dunford freight in black LNER wartime livery, 7 August 1944. R.D. Pollard/ MLS Collection

6105 on the Cheshire Lines Committee route with a local stopping train near Cheadle, August 1945. N. Fields/ MLS Collection

1475 (ex 1111) on an unfitted freight train at Wilbraham Road, 20 May 1948. J.D. Darby/ MLS Collection

1475 again, active with a heavy unfitted class 'H' freight at Levenshulme, 19 August 1948. R.E. Gee/ MLS Collection

The last survivor, now numbered 61475 but the LNER still prominent on its tender, at Levenshulme on the 8.50 Liverpool Brunswick-Dewsnap freight, just two months before its withdrawal, 18 March 1949. R.E. Gee/ MLS Collection

The GCR class 1 (LNER B2, later B19) – 1912

Design and construction.

The next 4-6-0 design of Robinson's was strikingly different from the earlier Robinson/Beyer, Peacock machines. It looked different as well as being innovative in its technical design. For a start it had two inside cylinders – at 21½ inch diameter, this was unusually large for an inside cylinder locomotive. The boiler was large, 5ft 6in diameter with a generous heating surface and was the first of the GC 4-6-0s to be constructed with a superheater. Six locomotives were built, No.423 named after the Company's General Manager *Sir Sam Fay* in December 1912. 424-427 followed in the winter of 1913 and after a gap, 428 named *City of Liverpool* in December 1913. The most significant dimensions were:

Cylinders (2 inside)	21½ in x 26in
Coupled wheel diameter	6ft 9in
Bogie wheel diameter	3ft 6in
Stephenson's valve gear	10in piston valves
Boiler pressure	180psi
Heating surface	2,817sqft (incl superheater 440sqft)
Grate area	26sqft
Axleload	19 tons 10 cwt
Weight – Engine	75 tons 4 cwt
– Tender	48 tons 6 cwt
– Total	123 tons 10 cwt
Water capacity	4,000 gallons
Coal capacity	6 tons
Tractive effort	22,700lbs

423 had a raised running plate over the driving wheels and a continuous straight splasher and was presented in the GC lined green livery and, for a while, a copper-capped chimney (as it was intended at the time to exhibit the engine at an international display in Belgium).

424-427 appeared unnamed at first, 425 in green livery like 423, though inexplicably for its new express engines, 424, 426 and 427 were painted in the Company's freight livery of black with red lining. 428 then appeared in green and all had acquired the passenger livery by the Grouping.

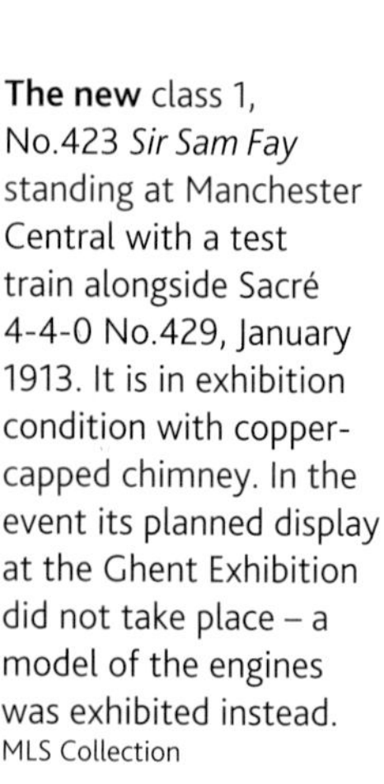
The new class 1, No.423 *Sir Sam Fay* standing at Manchester Central with a test train alongside Sacré 4-4-0 No.429, January 1913. It is in exhibition condition with copper-capped chimney. In the event its planned display at the Ghent Exhibition did not take place – a model of the engines was exhibited instead. MLS Collection

The unnamed engines were then also named after cities served by the Great Central, the six therefore being:

423 *Sir Sam Fay*
424 *City of Lincoln*
425 *City of Manchester*
426 *City of Chester*
427 *City of London*
428 *City of Liverpool*

The choice of names is a little strange in that three of the main cities it served were omitted – Sheffield, Nottingham and Leicester. Perhaps more of the class had been foreseen. However, some concerning defects of the class soon became apparent and instead of more express 4-6-0s, Robinson produced his 'Director' 4-4-0s (LNER D10s) the following year and these outclassed the 4-6-0s and with the Atlantics covered all the main express work, relegating the new 'Sam Fays' to secondary passenger activity in the northern regions of the railway.

The weaknesses soon revealed themselves. The steam passages were restricted, the grate area for such a large engine was small and too shallow (to give clearance over the rear coupled wheel), the ashpan was inadequate and the boiler design proved unsatisfactory. Axlebox design was also found wanting and frequent overheated bearings were a consequence. These flaws were obviously quickly apparent to the designer and corrected in the design of the new 4-4-0s. As a result some modifications were made to the 4-6-0s, initially with boiler design, the first attempt reducing the number of tubes and superheater elements, and a more successful second which reduced still the number of tubes but increased the flues. This became the standard boiler then for all six locomotives having a heating surface of 2,387sqft including superheater provision of 343sqft.

The other major change occurred just before the Grouping when 427 had its cylinder diameter reduced to 20in followed by 424 in May 1922 and 423 in October. The others retained their 21½ in cylinders until 5426 (ex 426 – all had

4-4-0 'Director' 437 *Charles Stuart-Wortley* shortly after construction and with the lessons from the experience of 423 and its sisters, c1913. MLS Collection

5,000 added to their numbers at the Grouping) which was converted in August 1938, although perversely 5423 got a new set of 21½in cylinders to replace its 20in in the previous year. The smaller cylinders reduced the tractive effort to 19,644lbs. The engines with the cylinder size as built became class B2/1 and the 20in engines B2/2.

During the coal strike of 1921, all except 425 were fitted with the Unolco oil burning system, retaining it for less than six months. A recurrence of industrial strife in the coal and related industries in 1926 caused four of the engines to be refitted (minus 5425 and 5427 this time). It lasted from the summer of 1926 to March 1927.

They were painted in the standard LNER passenger lined apple green livery after the Grouping until replaced by wartime plain black and were allocated numbers 1472-1477 in a 1943 renumbering scheme. However, these were not carried and 5426 was withdrawn in December 1944 and 5424 in November 1945, so at the 1946 LNER renumbering scheme, the remaining members of the class became 1490-1493. None received a BR number as all were withdrawn in 1947, the last being 1492 (ex 5427)

5423 *Sir Sam Fay* in LNER days and livery, standing under the coal stage at Gorton depot, c1930. G.A. Coltas/ MLS Collection

5428 *City* *of Liverpool* in LNER livery, awaiting its next duty at Sheffield Victoria, 3 September 1932. MLS Collection

5425 *City* *of Manchester* waits impatiently at Sheffield Victoria at the head of an express, 12 May 1935. G.A. Barlow/ MLS Collection

which had lost its name (*City of London*) when B17 2870 received that name for the *East Anglian* new service in 1937.

One of the nameplates and workplates of 425 *City of Manchester* now have pride of place in the clubrooms of the Manchester Locomotive Society on Stockport station, whose archive has been the source of most of the photographs in this book (see photos in Colour Section).

5427 ***City*** *of London* departing from Manchester Central with an express, July 1937. W. Potter/MLS Collection

5424 ***City*** *of Lincoln* at the city after which it was named, 1 May 1938. J. Suter/MLS Collection

The end – the withdrawn 1491 (ex 425 *City of Manchester*) renumbered in 1946, at Gorton, awaiting cutting up, 6 July 1947. N. Fields/MLS Collection

Operations

The six locomotives were allocated when new to Gorton depot and were put to work on the company's main expresses between Manchester and Marylebone. However, they were supplanted by the 'Director' 4-4-0s the following year and 424, 426 and 427 (three of the four black ones) were sent to Immingham for the Hull-Manchester services whilst those remaining at Gorton were relegated to fast freight work towards London. This remained the pattern until the Grouping, when all the engines were returned to Gorton. The *Railway Magazine* published a run of *Sir Sam Fay* in 1913, shortly after its construction and I give the outline on the next page.

3.20pm Marylebone-Sheffield
423 *Sir Sam Fay* – Gorton
185 tons
1913

Miles	**Location**	**Times**	**Speeds**	**Schedule**	**Gradients**
0	Marylebone	00.00		T	
9.2	Harrow-on-the-Hill	13.35		½ L	
17.2	Rickmansworth	22.25	slack	½ L	
	Chalfont	-	39		1/105 R
23.6	Amersham	32.30	40		1/105 R
28.8	Great Missenden	-	75		1/160 F
37.9	Aylesbury	45.50		¾ L	
44.1	Quainton Road Jn	51.50	45*	¼ E	
54.5	Finmere	-	56½		1/176 R
59.3	Brackley	67.12	60		1/176 F: 1/176 R
69.1	Woodford	76.40		¾ L	
	Braunston	-	79		1/176 F
83.2	Rugby	89.33			
90	Lutterworth	-	56½		1/176 R
103.1	Leicester Central	108.25		½ E	
0		00.00		T	
5	Rothley	06.33	76½		1/176 F
10	Loughborough	10.33	58½		1/176 R
14.5	East Leake	14.48	75		1/176 F
22.5	Arkwright Street	22.05			
23.7	Nottingham	23.43		¼ E	
0		00.00		T	
5.5	Hucknall	08.17			
11.5	Kirkby	15.47	44		1/132 R
20	Heath	25.22			
37.8	Sheffield	46.15	(45½ net)	1½ E	

Cecil J. Allen quoted that the run was made 'with the utmost of ease'.

In a *Railway Magazine* of October 1924 another B2 run is quoted in the up direction in comparison with a 'Director' 4-4-0. Although no dates are given, I suspect it was a run also around 1913/14, rather than post-war. The 'Director' was 501 *Mons* with the same load and I show its comparative speeds in the last column.

Leicester-Marylebone
427 *City of London*
265 tons

Miles	**Location**	**Times**	**Speeds**	**'501' speeds**	**Gradients**
0	Leicester Central	00.00			
4.7	Whetstone	06.53			
9.2	Ashby	12.27	46½	50	1/176 R (7 miles)
13.1	Lutterworth	17.04	75½	80½	1/176 F

Leicester-Marylebone
427 *City of London*
265 tons

Miles	Location	Times	Speeds	'501' speeds	Gradients
19.9	Rugby	23.07	64	70½	
24.6	Braunston	27.18	70	76	L
31.6	Charwelton	35.26	45½	50	1/176 R (6 miles)
34	Woodford	38.00			
37	Culworth	40.44		sigs and eased thereafter	
40.6	Helmdon	44.04			
43.8	Brackley	47.06	78½	75	1/176 F
48.6	Finmere	50.57	66	64½	1/176 R
54.3	Calvert	55.33	79½	79	1/176 F
56.3	Grendon U'wood Jn	57.17			
58.7	Quainton Road Jn	59.32	slack		
65.1	Aylesbury	65.55	65	64½	
69.8	Wendover	71.47	40		1/117 R (6 miles)
74.3	Great Missenden	77.23	74		1/125 F
79.5	Amersham	82.19	53		1/160 R
	Chorley Wood	-	65½		
85.9	Rickmansworth	88.56	slack		
89.4	Northwood	93.24	65		
93.9	Harrow-on-the-Hill	98.27	slack		
98.3	Neasden	102.42	65½		
103.1	Marylebone	109.17	(108 net)		

Arrival was just over a minute late and Cecil J. Allen compared the run unfavourably with that of the 4-4-0 which had only eased after the signal check at Culworth to avoid more checks from the train in front.

426 *City of Chester* at Guide Bridge, c1920.
MLS Collection

Oil burning 424 *City of Lincoln* at Willesden Green with a Marylebone-Manchester express during the coal strike of 1921. MLS Collection

Oil burning 423 *Sir Sam Fay* hauling an excursion train formed of 'Barnum' coaches near Alexandra Palace on the GN main line, 1921. MLS Collection

5425 which had retained 21½ in cylinders was given a trial on the GN Pullman services on the East Coast main line, but clearly did not measure up to requirements as it soon returned back to the northern end of the former Great Central system. They all remained Gorton based until 1929, when two (5423 and 5426) moved to Sheffield which then had two on its books - though the individual engines changed - until 1939. The Sheffield locomotives worked passenger trains to Manchester, York, Cleethorpes and Hull. They also worked the Bradford - Marylebone service as far as Leicester on occasions.

The B2s' work to London on the main expresses was short-lived and they spent more time on services over the Woodhead route. O.S. Nock unearthed a short but first class example of their work there, which occurred four years after the grouping and is as good as anything seen there by an LNER 4-6-0.

Guide Bridge-Penistone
5423 *Sir Sam Fay*
268/285 tons
7 June 1927

Miles	Location	Times	Speeds	Gradients
0	Guide Bridge	00.00		
2.32	Newton	05.35	33½	1/97 R: 1/185 R
3.27	Godley Junction	07.15	36	1/143 R
4.32	Mottram	09.35	45	1/462 R
6.75	Dinting	12.30	45	1/122 R
7.65	Hadfield	13.40	40	1/100 R
10.30	Torside Box	18.05	33½	1/100 R: 1/117 R (6 miles)
12.29	Crowden	21.30	36	1/117 R

5423 then caught up another train which was still threading the Woodhead Tunnel where the gradient eased to 1 in 200 and followed it being checked by signals all the way to Penistone, 23.33 miles reached in 41 minutes 45 seconds. Mr Nock calculated that 5423 was producing 911 dhp on the climb before checked at Crowden. A log found in the Rail Performance Society archives found 5428 *City of Liverpool* four years later taking over the 11pm Marylebone mail train at Sheffield working it through to Godley junction where it was relieved by a 4-4-0.

Sheffield Victoria-Godley Junction
11pm Marylebone-Manchester (dep Sheffield 2.51 am)
5428 *City of Liverpool*
7 chs, 200 tons
6 September 1931

Miles	Location	Times	Speeds	Gradients
0	Sheffield Victoria	00.00		
2.9	Wadsley Bridge	09.45	slow/ floods	1/132 R
4.8	Oughty Bridge	14.05	30* floods	1/132 R
8.8	Wortley	21.35	32	1/120 R
13	Penistone	28.25	37	1/131 R: 1/100 R
16.75	Hazlehead	35.25	32	1/128 R
19	Dunford Bridge	39.00	38	1/135 R
22.2	Woodhead	43.25	43	1/200 F (Woodhead Tunnel)
24.2	Crowden	45.25	60	1/117 F
28.6	Hadfield	50.15	55 easy	1/117 F
29.5	Dinting	51.30		1/100 F
33	Godley Junction	56.55		

425 *City* *of Manchester* working a GN line Pullman express during the short period when they were tested on these services, at Finsbury Park, 1923. MLS Collection

5425 *City* *of Manchester* darkens the landscape as it climbs to Woodhead summit with a return Scarborough-Manchester five shilling excursion, c1926. MLS Collection

5428 ***City*** *of Liverpool* drifts down from Woodhead summit east of Dunford Bridge with a Manchester-Marylebone express, c1928. F. Moore/ MLS Collection

In January 1933, 5423 was involved in a collision with a goods train at Loughborough and the braking system seems to have been suspect as 5427 was subsequently involved in brake trials with a GN Atlantic. During the tests, 5427 was recorded at 84mph, the fastest known speed achieved by any engine of the class. One was utilised on the Lincoln-York section of the Harwich Boat Train in 1936 (appropriately 5424 *City of Lincoln)* and was joined at Lincoln by 5427 in 1939. 5424 was timed in 1935 with 235 tons on a Marylebone-Leicester express, taking 107½ minutes for the 103.1 miles, significantly better than the 1913 log, covering the 6.4 uphill miles from Rickmansworth to Amersham in 9 minutes 22 seconds (average 41mph) and averaging 75mph from Wendover to Aylesbury which suggests a maximum over 80 as speed would have moderated through Aylesbury.

Other records of the B2s in the late 1930s indicate their use on stopping and semi-fast trains between Manchester and Sheffield, 5425 with 8 coaches taking the 13 downhill miles from Penistone to Sheffield in 21 minutes with stops at Wortley and Oughty Bridge and a run on the 6.32pm Hull to Doncaster with 5426 and 283 tons on 4 July 1936. The 23.7 miles to Goole took 35½ minutes, a loss of 3½ minutes part caused by signal checks approaching Goole. Speeds were only in the low 50s. A minute was regained on to Doncaster despite a check at Thorne Junction but again speeds were modest. 5424 on the Harwich boat train on 28 January 1939 had a 13 coach load of 425 tons gross southbound from York and took exactly 20 minutes for the 13.8 miles to Selby dropping a minute. The *Railway Magazine* of June 1939 describes three runs from Manchester Central to Liverpool, comparing 5427 *City of Liverpool* with two runs by B17 2816 *Fallodon* all with loads in the 195-215 ton range. 5427 with 205 tons ran the 15.7 miles to Warrington in 16¾ minutes appreciably faster than both 2816's times though one was delayed by signals approaching Warrington, its net time being identical to that of the B2. 5427 reached 62mph at Trafford Park, fell to 55½ at Flixton and reached a maximum of 72 after Glazebrook, midway between the speeds of the two B17 runs at this point. It was the fastest on the 6.1 mile hop to Farnworth - 8 minutes 21 seconds compared with 2816's 8.36 and 8.45, top speed 59mph. The 12.2 miles on to Liverpool was plagued with signal checks throughout after an initial 67 before Hunts Cross and 59/64 at Garston. The net running time for the 34 miles with two stops was 40 minutes for 5427, and 39½ and 43 minutes for 2816.

Although the boat train was withdrawn during the war the Colchester-York service remained and was often very heavily loaded – up to sixteen bogies on occasions. These engines were powerful enough and good at acceleration from rest though at the expense of heavy coal and water consumption and reliability. Then 5423 was sent to Immingham followed by the remaining Sheffield engines so that during the war all were based in Lincolnshire. Their wartime work included troop trains via Woodford, freight traffic and some heavy through services from East Lincolnshire to London King's Cross.

Sheffield regained 5423 and 5428 in 1942 and these were replaced at Immingham by 5424 and 5427 from Lincoln. The Sheffield engines worked Hull-Liverpool trains between Sheffield and Manchester. Then in 1945 all those remaining were moved to Immingham where they stayed until withdrawn from service – the last four in 1947. The last to go was 1492 (ex 427) in November.

5424 *City* *of Lincoln* leaving Retford with the 2.20pm Cleethorpes-Manchester semi-fast train, 25 July 1936.
MLS Collection

The GCR class 1A (LNER B8) – 1913

Design and construction

The 1A was a straight freight engine version of the 'Sam Fay' class – an inside two-cylinder 4-6-0 with 5ft 7in coupled wheels. The first, No.4 *Glenalmond,* named after the home of the Company's Chairman, was built at Gorton in June 1913 and was very similar in appearance to 423-428, apart from the straight running plate rather than raised area over the coupled wheels. Key dimensions:

Cylinders (2 inside)	21½ in x 26in
Coupled wheel diameter	5ft 7in
Bogie wheel diameter	3ft 6in
Stephenson's valve gear	10in piston valves
Boiler pressure	180psi
Heating surface	2,387sqft (incl 343sqft superheating)
Grate area	26sqft
Axleload	19 tons 10 cwt
Weight – Engine	74 tons 7 cwt
– Tender	48 tons 6 cwt
– Total	122 tons 13cwt
Water capacity	4,000 gallons
Coal capacity	6 tons
Tractive effort	27,445lbs

Despite suffering from the same design faults as the class 1, ten more were built a year later between July 1914 and January 1915. They were numbered 439-446 and 279, 280 in that order and three of these were also named:

439 *Sutton Nelthorpe*
446 *Earl Roberts of Kandahar*
279 *Earl Kitchener of Khartoum*

The naming of freight engines was unusual. 439 was named after a Director left off the list of names given to the D10 4-4-0s and the two military names were clearly deemed appropriate in the patriotic first months of the First World War. They were given the GC freight livery of black with red lining. Three engines, 279, 443 and 445, were equipped with Unolco oil-burning systems in 1921 and

Mixed traffic
4-6-0 class 1A, LNER B8, No.446 *Lord Roberts of Kandahar* at Gorton, c1920. Bob Miller Collection/ MLS Collection

Oil burner No.279 *Earl Kitchener of Khartoum* at Gorton, 1921.
MLS Collection

445 retained it until 1923, burning experimentally finely ground coal with the oil.

Despite their substandard performance, no significant changes were made by GC management and it was June 1927 before the 21½ in cylinders were lined up to 20in for 5004 and 5443. After the Grouping, all were also fitted with the final modified boiler of the B1 (B19) including 28 element superheater, completed by 1934. The 20in cylinder engines were identified as B8/2s, although only 5004 retained this size. Tractive effort was reduced to 23,750lbs for this pair. Although varying chimneys and dome shapes appeared, the height of the cab was not reduced so their route availability was restricted and they stayed mainly on the former GC routes.

They were renumbered with an extra 5,000 by the LNER as all other GC engines and in 1946 were allocated 1349-1359. Although five survived nationalisation, none took their allocated BR numbers and all were withdrawn before their new numbers clashed with the Thompson B1s being constructed.

The first B8, 5004 *Glenalmond* after having its inside cylinders lined up to 20in and being reclassified B8/2, at Neasden, 10 May 1933.
W.L. Good/MLS Collection

B8/1 5439 *Sutton* *Nelthorpe*, named after one of the GC directors whose name was not used for the 4-4-0 'Director' class, c1935.
W.L. Good/MLS Collection

Operations

No.4 *Glenalmond* was allocated to Gorton in the first year while it was the lone example and the engines constructed in 1914 were distributed between Gorton, Neasden and Immingham. They shared in the working of the fast freight and fish trains joining the class 8s (B5s) and 8Fs (B4s) in this activity. All three classes undertook this work until the advent of the 9Q (B7) mixed traffic engines in 1920. Some then went to Leicester for its freight turns to Banbury and Manchester, others went to Annesley. Like the other mixed traffic locomotives, they also worked excursions and summer relief trains to the East Coast resorts and London.

In 1923 at the Grouping, the allocation of the eleven engines was:

Gorton	5280, 5439, 5442, 5443, 5444, 5445
Annesley	5004, 5279, 5440, 5441, 5446

As more B7s were built, four (5441, 5443, 5444, 5446) went to the GE section at March working freight to Lincoln and Doncaster via the GN & GE Joint Line, but their height restricted their operation south of March and they soon returned to the former GC railway. However, a year later the authorities tried again, this time with 5280, 5440, 5442, 5444 and 5445. Their area of operation was similarly restricted and once more they returned to their original haunts,

439 *Sutton* *Nelthorpe* on a heavy freight at Guide Bridge, c1922. MLS Collection

Nottingham receiving several at Colwick to join those already operating out of Annesley.

In 1928 the allocation was:

Colwick	5004, 5279, 5280, 5439, 5440, 5441, 5443, 5445
Annesley	5442, 5444, 5446

They worked overnight goods trains to Manchester and Hull and from 1933, the accelerated coal trains between Annesley and Woodford. 5279 and 5440 were transferred from Colwick to Annesley to join the three there for these new diagrams. In the 1930s their involvement in excursion traffic was considerable, but unfortunately there are no records or logs of any of their runs that I can find.

Their war service from 1939, like that of the other ex-GC mixed traffic engines, covered troop trains as well as increased wartime freight traffic, both of which were especially busy via the Woodford-Banbury link. In June 1943, the whole class was based at Annesley and remained there for the rest of the war. Two, 5280 and 5441, were withdrawn in the spring of 1947, but the rest of the class were transferred as a block to Sheffield Darnall in April 1947 and remained there until their withdrawal. Four of them were withdrawn there before much used and the remaining five worked the slower goods trains over the Woodhead route and on the CLC to Northwich. They could also be found occasionally on stopping passenger trains to York, Doncaster or Leeds. The last survivor was 1357 (the GC 446) *Earl Roberts of Kandahar*, although the photograph of this engine in April 1948 appears just to show a bare back plate where the nameplate should have been.

5280 waits in the sidings at Skegness with a return excursion train to Bulwell Common made up of Gresley steel bodied rolling stock painted in blue and duck-egg green, 3 June 1934. MLS Collection

5446 ***Earl*** *Roberts of Kandahar* pilots a C4 Atlantic on a semi-fast train composed of ex-Great Central short underframed six wheel coaches near Bagthorpe, c1946. MLS Collection

1355 (formerly GC 444) with a train of refrigerated containers, c1947. N. Harrop/ MLS Collection

1358 (formerly GC 279) *Earl Kitchener of Khartoum* on a down goods train at Cheadle, 20 March 1948. N. Fields/ MLS Collection

1357 (ex GC 446) *Earl Roberts of Kandahar* on an unfitted freight at Ashley, 26 April 1948. Note the blank back plate where the nameplate had been fixed. MLS Collection

The GCR 9P (LNER B3) – 1917

Construction and design

The first of Robinson's largest passenger engines appeared from Gorton Works towards the end of 1917 and although it bore a strong external likeness to his class 1s of 1912, it was a four cylinder engine with Stephenson link motion, the inside cylinders driving the front coupled axle and the outside cylinders driving the middle axle. It was numbered 1169 and named *Lord Faringdon* after the Company's Chairman. Its key dimensions were:

Cylinders (4)	16 in x 26in
Coupled wheel diameter	6ft 9in
Bogie wheel diameter	3ft 6in
Stephenson's valve gear	8in piston valves
Boiler pressure	180psi
Heating surface	2,387sqft (incl 343sqft superheater)
Grate area	26sqft
Axleload	20 tons
Weight – Engine	79 tons 2 cwt
– Tender	48 tons 6 cwt
– Total	127 tons 8 cwt
Water capacity	4,000 gallons
Coal capacity	6 tons
Tractive effort	25,145lbs

The 1917 prototype, 1169 *Lord Faringdon* in Works Grey for official photographic purposes, 1917. MLS Collection

The use of four cylinders rather than the huge inside cylinders of the class 1s (B2s) and the revised motion layout enabled increased size bearings and eliminated one of the major weaknesses of the 'Sam Fay' class, namely the problems of hot boxes. However, although the engine was free-running and fast, it was very heavy on coal. Despite this, after a gap of three years five more were built between June and October 1920 and named:

1164 *Earl Beatty*
1165 *Valour* (the Great Central's 'Remembrance' engine)
1166 *Earl Haig*
1167 *Lloyd George* (removed in 1923 when politically inappropriate)
1168 *Lord Stuart of Wortley* (replacing the name *Charles Stuart Wortley* of 'Director' 4-4-0 437 which was then named *Prince George*)

The six locomotives received the GC lined green livery, standard 4,000 gallon tenders and were similar in outline to the large boilered inside cylinder class 1 4-6-0s apart from the raised running plate over the outside cylinders. At the Grouping they were renumbered 6164-6169 and repainted in the LNER lined apple green livery.

In 1921 three of the class – 1165, 1167 and 1169 - were fitted with the

1165 ***Valour*** at Manchester London Road on Armistice Day 11 November 1920.
MLS Collection

1165 *Valour* on the turntable at King's Cross station, 1923. It is still in Great Central livery and clearly shows the detail of the nameplate which was to commemorate the lives of Great Central employees who died in the 'Great War'. Bob Miller Collection/MLS Collection

6168 *Lord* *Stuart of Wortley* also on the King's Cross station turntable, but now in LNER lined apple green livery and renumbered, c1925. MLS Collection

Unolco oil burning system, with large rectangular tanks mounted in the tender. The engines only retained the system for two months and unlike some other GC classes, the class did not feature in the oil burning conversions during the 1926 coal emergency.

Because of their high coal consumption and the increasing cost of coal after the strikes of 1921, 1926 and the economic problems of the Depression, the LNER management sought to improve their efficiency and reduce their running costs and in 1929 Gresley rebuilt 6166 and 6168 with Caprotti valve gear. This improved their coal consumption, though not entirely, as the small 26sqft grate area continued to be a weakness in the design. The class 9Ps had been redesignated class B3 in the LNER classification system, and the Caprotti valve engines became B3/2s, the Stephenson Link motion engines becoming B3/1. Then, somewhat belatedly, another two, 6164 and 6167 were converted in 1939 and 1938 respectively, leaving the original 6169 and 6165 unaltered to the end.

The B3s were on Edward Thompson's list for rebuilding as two cylinder machines along with other multi-cylinder classes, and in 1943 6166 was rebuilt in the style of his new B1s but retaining its 6ft 9 in wheels. However, this was not a success and the B3/1s and B3/2s were left in those forms until withdrawal, which commenced with B3/2 6168 in September 1946 and all the rest, apart from the rebuilt 6166 in 1947. The remaining B3s were renumbered 1494-1498 in the LNER 1946 renumbering scheme. The final rebuilding and operation of 6166 as a B3/3 is recounted in chapter 7 (Thompson's Rebuilds').

6168 *Lord Stuart of Wortley*, after rebuilding with Caprotti valve gear and being redesignated class B3/2, at Gorton in September 1929.
MLS Collection

6164 *Earl* *Beatty*, which remained as a B3/1 until June 1939 when it was also rebuilt as a B3/2, but seen here earlier around 1935. It also has the GC open style rather than side-window cab. MLS Collection

B3/1 1494 *Lord* *Faringdon* (ex 6169) in poor post-war condition, in plain black and renumbered 1494, at Langwith shed, 24 August 1947, just four months before withdrawal. MLS Collection

B3/2 1495 (ex 6164) *Earl Beatty,* after withdrawal in September 1947, with other stored locomotives including a B7/2 mixed traffic engine behind (probably 1394, ex 5481, the first to be withdrawn in April 1948), at Gorton, 12 October 1947. MLS Collection

Operations

1169 was allocated to Gorton at first, but moved to Immingham with the new 1164 and 1168 when they were built in 1920. 1165-1167 went from the Works to Gorton shed. The Gorton engines ran express trains to London but not the fastest which remained in the hands of the 'Director' 4-4-0s and Atlantics. The 9Ps were used on the heavier slower trains with more stops where their power and acceleration were useful. The Immingham engines had even less top-link work and ran the Hull-Manchester services. However, Cecil J. Allen in the May 1922 and September 1924 editions of the *Railway Magazine,* published the logs of three early runs with these engines on Marylebone-Manchester expresses.

		Marylebone-Sheffield, 1921 **1166 *Earl Haig*** **221/230 tons**			**1169 *Lord Faringdon*** **219/230 tons**			
Miles	**Location**	**Times**	**Speeds**	**Schedule**	**Times**	**Speeds**	**Schedule**	**Gradients**
0	Marylebone	00.00		T	00.00		T	
5.1	Neasden	09.05	64½		08.40	70½		1/90 F
9.2	Harrow	13.20		¼ L	12.30		½ E	
11.4	Pinner	15.55	52		14.40	61		
17.2	Rick'sworth	22.15		¼ L	20.15		1 ¾ E	
19.4	Chorley Wood	25.30	41		23.30	39		1/105 R
23.6	Amersham	31.45			30.15			1/105 R
28.8	Gt Missenden	36.45		1 ¾ L	35.15	74	¼ L	1/160 F/ 1/125 R
33.3	Wendover	41.15	66		39.40	75		1/117 F
38	Aylesbury	45.35		½ L	43.30	55*	1½ E	
44.4	Quainton Rd	52.10		¼ L	50.40		1¼ E	
46.8	Grendon U Jn	54.55	59		53.20	54		
48.8	Calvert	56.50	66		55.20	64½		
54.5	Finmere	62.30	60/53		61.20	57/48½		1/176 R
59.3	Brackley	67.30	56½		66.30	51		1/176 R
62.5	Helmdon	70.55			70.10			
66.1	Culworth	74.20	75		73.45	72½		1/176 F
69.1	Woodford	76.50		¾ L	76.25		½ L	
71.5	Charwelton	79.10			78.40		L	
78.5	Braunston	85.25	76½		84.55	76½		1/176 F
83.2	Rugby	89.40			89.20			
90	Lutterworth	96.20	61		97.00	61		
93.9	Ashby	100.10			100.55			1/176 F
98.4	Whetstone	103.55	75		104.35	77 ½		1/176 F
103.1	Leicester	108.55		T	109.00		T	
0		00.00			00.00			
2.3	Belgrave	04.10			04.15			1/176 R
5	Rothley	07.05			07.20			1/176 F
9.8	Loughboro'	11.30	71 ½		11.35	76		
12.6	Barnston Box	14.30	55		14.20	57½		1/176 R
19	Ruddington	20.10	71 ½		19.50	76½		
22.5	Arkwright St	23.30			22.50			
23.4	Nottingham	25.55		1 L	24.50		¼ E	
0		00.00			00.00			
1.6	Basford	04.00			04.15			
5.8	Hucknall	09.30			09.25	55		1/130 R
10.8	Kirkby Jn	16.40	39½		16.20	43		1/132 R
17.9	Pilsley	25.10			24.00	65/52		1/132 F: 1/132 R

		Marylebone-Sheffield, 1921						
		1166 *Earl Haig*			1169 *Lord Faringdon*			
		221/230 tons			219/230 tons			
Miles	**Location**	**Times**	**Speeds**	**Schedule**	**Times**	**Speeds**	**Schedule**	**Gradients**
26.2	Staveley	34.10	67		31.40	76½		1/100 F
30	Killamarsh	37.40			35.15			
33.2	Woodhouse	41.05			38.40	sigs		
36.2	Darnall	45.05			43.10			
38.2	Sheffield	47.50		¾ L	46.15	(45½ net)	¾ E	

Although these runs were competent enough and broadly kept time, Cecil J Allen commented that they were inferior to the logs he'd received recording the performance of the 'Director' 4-4-0s. The log below is of a run recorded with 1164 before it was transferred to the ex-GN main line in 1924, with one extra coach.

Marylebone-Leicester, c1923
1164 *Earl Beatty*
8 chs 258/275 tons

Miles	Location	Times	Speeds	Schedule
0	Marylebone	00.00		T
5.1	Neasden	09.20	65	¾ L
9.2	Harrow	13.50	44½/61¾ L	
	Northwood	16.15	70½	
17.2	Rickmansworth	22.10		¼ L
19.4	Chorley Wood	25.00	33	
23.6	Amersham	32.05		
28.8	Gt Missenden	37.30	71½	2½ L
33.3	Wendover	42.05	77½	
37.9	Aylesbury	45.55		1 L
44.1	Quainton Road Jn	52.00		
46.8	Grendon Underwood	54.25		
48.8	Calvert	56.15	67	
54.5	Finmere	61.55	68/52½	
59.3	Brackley	67.00	72	
62.5	Helmdon	70.40		
66.1	Culworth	74.10	58	
69.1	Woodford	76.45		¾ L
71.5	Charwelton	79.10		
78.5	Braunston	85.15	83½	
83.2	Rugby	89.00	64	
86.8	Shawell	-	70½	
90	Lutterworth	95.55	53	
98.4	Whetstone	103.45	74	
103.1	Leicester	108.25		½ E

The prototype, 1169 *Lord Faringdon,* at Guide Bridge with a GC London express, c1920. MLS Collection

Three 9Ps were fitted with oil burning apparatus during the 1921 coal strike. The equipment was only in place for two months and this rather poor quality photo of 1165 *Valour* leaving Manchester London Road is included as a rare image of that event, 1921. H. Parrish/ MLS Collection

At the Grouping, the former Locomotive Running Superintendent of the Great Central was appointed to a similar position for the southern section of the LNER and he brought over the three Immingham B3s (6164, 6168 and 6169) to King's Cross shed to work the new Pullman service introduced between Leeds and London via the GN main line. This made an interesting comparison with the Ivatt Atlantics which had dominated the Pullman expresses with their very free-steaming boiler and exceptionally large firebox and grate area. The B3, on the other hand, had large cylinders and boiler but restricted size firebox and grate areas that needed expert firing to produce the necessary steam. Their performance on the Leeds Pullman service was erratic with some crews mastering them, but others preferring the easier task of firing the Atlantics. The regular King's Cross crew of 6168 did some good work and 6165 (which came to King's Cross from Gorton with 6166 and 6167 in August 1923) featured in a log published in Cecil J. Allen's regular article in the *Railway Magazine* in 1924.

Wakefield-King's Cross (*The West Riding Pullman*), 1923
6165 *Valour*
8 Pullmans, 291/300 tons

Miles	Location	Times	Speeds		Gradient
00	Wakefield	00.00	30(pass)	T	
1.7	Sandal	02.35	49		1/100 F
4	Hare Park	05.45			
5.5	Nostell	08.00	40		1/150 R
8	Hemsworth	11.00			
13.3	Hampole	15.45	74		1/150 F
17.1	Castle Hills	19.00			
19.9	Doncaster	22.30	30*	½ E	
24.6	Rossington	28.10	55 1/2/ 50		L/ 1/198 R
28.2	Bawtry	32.10	67/ sigs 10*		1/198 F
32	Ranskill	36.20			
37.3	Retford	43.00		2 L	
42.2	Markham Box	48.55			1/200 R
44.6	Dukeries Junction	51.30			
49.5	Carlton	55.35	77½		1/200 F
55.8	Newark	61.00	68	1 L	L
60.5	Claypole	65.05	60		1/300 R
64.4	Hougham	69.15			
66.2	Barkston	71.15	49		1/200 R
70.4	Grantham	76.20	57½	¼ E	
73.9	Great Ponton	80.20			1/200 R
75.8	Stoke Box	82.35	53½		
78.8	Corby Glen	85.30			1/178 F
83.7	Little Bytham	89.20	85		1/200 F
87.3	Essendine	91.55			
91.1	Tallington	94.50			
96.4	Werrington Junction	99.05			
99.5	Peterborough	103.10		2¾ E	
103.3	Yaxley	108.25			
106.5	Holme	111.25	68		L

Wakefield-King's Cross (*The West Riding Pullman),* 1923
6165 *Valour*
8 Pullmans, 291/300 tons

Miles	Location	Times	Speeds		Gradient
112.4	Abbots Ripton	117.20	48		1/200 R
113.9	Leys Box	119.15			
117	Huntingdon	122.15	66/sigs	2¾ E	1/200 F
124.2	St Neots	130.10			
131.8	Sandy	137.55			l/ 1/264 R
138.9	Arlesey	145.30			
144	Hitchin	151.25		½ E	1/200 R
147.3	Stevenage	155.50	47		1/200 R
150.9	Knebworth	159.55			
153.9	Welwyn	163.15			
158.2	Hatfield	167.05	74	T	1/200 F
163.2	Potters Bar	172.10			
166.7	New Barnet	175.35			1/200 F
173.5	Finsbury Park	181.45			
175.9	King's Cross	186.00		1 E	(182½ net)

As well as the Pullman trains, they also worked a Hull train as far as Grantham and other lesser services including milk and parcels trains. However, the high coal consumption was unacceptable – there were even some instances of the locomotives running out of coal on the GN main line.

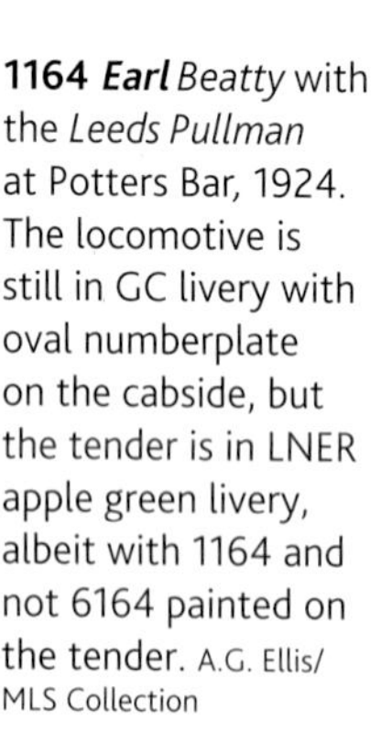

1164 *Earl* *Beatty* with the *Leeds Pullman* at Potters Bar, 1924. The locomotive is still in GC livery with oval numberplate on the cabside, but the tender is in LNER apple green livery, albeit with 1164 and not 6164 painted on the tender. A.G. Ellis/ MLS Collection

1167 ***Lloyd*** *George* waits at Belle Isle to back down to King's Cross to pick up an East Coast Pullman train while GN Atlantic C1 1460 heads north with another, as GN J52 tanks shunt the Yard. 1167's name was removed shortly after this at the order of the LNER Board when Lloyd George was involved in political scandal. H. Gordon Tidey/MLS Collection

6165 *Valour,* in full LNER livery, on a heavy East Coast express thought to be the 5.37pm King's Cross-Hull, c1927. MLS Collection

Their work on the East Coast main line was not consistently successful and as the number of Gresley pacifics increased they were deemed redundant there and were transferred back to the former GC lines in 1927, initially all six to Gorton, then 6166 and 6169 moved to Neasden. The Gorton engines had turns to London including the return fast 3.20pm Marylebone with its 109 minute booking to Leicester (103.1 miles). However, by the 1930s they replaced the B2s in the Sheffield No.2 link. The Neasden engines worked the Manchester/Liverpool night mail to and from Leicester and the 2.32am newspaper train to Sheffield as far as Nottingham. Both were reasonably heavy trains but had fast schedules because of the urgent nature of the mails and newspaper traffic. The GC main line with its long steady gradients on 1 in 176, up and down, produced uphill speeds of mid 50s and downhill speeds of mid 80s on these services with the B3s. Apparently such work called for strenuous and continuous labour on behalf of the regular firemen. In 1927 6164 took 300 tons but dropped 1½ minutes on the schedule exerting a maximum drawbar pull of 936hp on the climb to Amersham, speed held between 36 and 38mph. Maximum speed was 76½mph at Braunston. 6164 was active again on the route a couple of years later.

Marylebone-Leicester, c1929
6164 *Earl Beatty*
5chs 175/185 tons

Miles	Location	Times	Speeds	Schedule	Gradients
0	Marylebone	00.00		T	
5.1	Neasden	07.35	68	1 E	
9.2	Harrow	11.45	60	1¼ E	
	Northwood	16.15			
17.2	Rickmansworth	20.30	20*	1½ E	
19.4	Chorley Wood	23.30	49½		
23.6	Amersham	28.35	50		
28.8	Gt Missenden	33.15			
33.3	Wendover	37.50	easy		
37.9	Aylesbury	41.45		3¼ E	
44.1	Quainton Road Jn	47.30			
46.8	Grendon Underwood	50.40			
48.8	Calvert	52.30	66		
54.5	Finmere	58.25	58/55		
59.3	Brackley	63.40			
66.1	Culworth	71.05	70/62		
69.1	Woodford	73.55		2 E	
71.5	Charwelton	76.25	58		
78.5	Braunston	82.35	78		
83.2	Rugby	86.40			
86.8	Shawell	90.20	pws		
90	Lutterworth	94.05			
98.4	Whetstone	101.45	70		
103.1	Leicester	106.25	(105 ¼ net)	2½ E	

With this light load, 6164 made a fast start and good climb to Amersham, but then eased to avoid running too far ahead of time. However 'Director' 5510 *Princess Mary* took six coaches to Leicester in 103¾ minutes net, and later B17 2840 *Somerleyton Hall* on two separate occasions matched 6164's time with 7 coaches, 250 tons gross. This was one of three B17s that replaced the B3s on these turns in 1934 but only for a year or so, as their smaller ex-Great Eastern style tenders held insufficient water and coal for their reliable operation. The same B3, 6164, had 9 coaches of 306 tons tare on a Sheffield-Manchester train in April 1927 and sustained 34-36mph in the 1 in 120 through Deepcar, increasing to 40mph on the 1 in 131 before Penistone. The load reduced there to six coaches (228 tons) and 6164 accelerated to 40mph on the 1 in 124 through Hazlehead Bridge and 43 on the final 1 in 135 to Woodhead Tunnel, drifting at a maximum of 64mph on the descent before passing Hadfield in 21¼ minutes for the 15.7 miles from Penistone. B3/1 6167 (unnamed) took 108 minutes (106¼ net) in 1931 on the 4.55pm Marylebone-Leicester/Manchester with a fast start and good climb to Amersham (45mph) but lapsed between Aylesbury and Woodford (short of steam?) then recovered touching 82mph at Braunston and 79 at Whetstone. However, the return of the B3s on top-link turns only lasted a further year as the new B17/4s (the 'Footballers') had larger LNER standard tenders.

By 1936 the Neasden had the Caprotti engines 6166 and 6168 in its allocation which performed very reliably. Then when 6167 was rebuilt in 1938 it replaced unrebuilt 6165 there. The Immingham engines from 1928 had worked a daily Cleethorpes-Leicester service and in the summer, Immingham-King's Cross boat trains.

In the March edition of the 1931 *Railway Magazine*, Cecil J. Allen reported on the run of a B3 with a very heavy load on the East Coast main line. B3/1 6169 *Lord Faringdon* was heading a Grimsby-King's Cross excursion with 13 coaches, 425 tons, a full 460 gross, which it worked up to 65mph by Holme (7 miles in 9 minutes 25 seconds from the Peterborough start. 49 minimum at Leys summit, 71 at Huntingdon, 70 at Offord, 68½ at Sandy and Hitchin was passed in 46¼ minutes for the 44½ miles start to pass at 50mph. 6169 may have been winded by this effort as speed fell back to 43 at Knebworth and then the rest of the journey was spoiled by prolonged signal checks all the way to King's Cross, eventually taking 89¾ minutes (80 net). This was comparable with Gresley pacific average runs with similar loads.

B3/1 6165 *Valour* and B2 5424 *City of Lincoln* doublehead a Grand National special train at Glazebrook in March 1939. W. Potter/ MLS Collection

B3/2 6166 *Earl Haig* at Sheffield Victoria, at the head of an express for Leicester and London, 12 May 1935. G.A. Barlow/ MLS Collection

On 17 June 1933, a Caprotti B3/2, 6168 *Lord Stuart of Wortley* headed the 5.11pm from Guide Bridge to Penistone, a Manchester-Cleethorpes train, with an 8-coach 265 ton train. It left Guide Bridge 8½ minutes late and regained two of them running to Penistone in 35 minutes (34½ net). It took 12¾ minutes to climb the 7.6 miles of gradients varying from 1 in 77 to 1 in 462 and averaged 37mph over the 1½ miles at 1 in 100 and 3 miles at 1 in 117 between Hadfield and Crowden, but was then checked by signals before entering the Woodhead Tunnel. 6168 demonstrated its ability to run fast on a 240 ton Leicester-Nottingham 23.4 mile start-to-stop even time performance:

Leicester-Nottingham, c1936
6168 *Lord Stuart of Wortley* (with Caprotti gear)
228/240 tons

Miles	Location	Times	Speeds	Gradients	Schedule
0	Leicester	00.00			T
2.3	Belgrave	04.18			
5	Rothley	07.06		1/176 F	
9.9	Loughborough	11.01	82½		
12.9	Barnston	13.29	65½	1/176 R	
14.4	East Leake	14.47			
19	Ruddington	18.16	84		
22.5	Arkwright Street	21.01			
23.5	Nottingham	23.12			¾ E

In January, 1938 six months before its conversion to B3/2, 6167 worked a fish train from Cleethorpes to Leicester, timed between Worksop and Nottingham Victoria, augment by three bogie passenger carrying vehicles. I am showing it below as it is a rare example of the log of a fish train that so many of the Robinson 4-6-0s were designed to work.

Worksop-Nottingham Victoria
12.39pm Cleethorpes-Leicester
6167
3 coaches + 24 fish trucks, 395 tons gross
27 January 1938

Miles	Location	Times	Speeds	Schedule	Gradients
0	Worksop	00.00		T	
2.1	Shireoaks	04.58	31/38		1/150 R
5.2	Kiveton Park	10.42	28		1/140 R
6.4	Kiveton Bridge	12.52	37/33		L: 1/179 R
8	Waleswood	15.07	45/30*	¼ L	1/115 F
9.8	Killamarsh Junction	18.35	30*	½ L	1/115 F
12.2	Eckington	22.46	46		
14.3	Staveley Town	25.32	44	½ E	1/176 R
16.5	Duckmanton N Jn	29.36	24		1/100 R
20.1	Heath	37.21	33	¼ L	1/100: 1/264 R
23.9	Tibshelf Town	43.21	50		1/132 F
26.7	New Hucknall	46.48	46		
28.7	Kirkby Bentinck	49.30	46		L
29.6	Kirkby S Junction	50.42		¼ E	
31.9	Annesley S Junction	53.26	55		1/132 F
34.6	Hucknall	57.20	pws 31*/35		1/130 F
37.1	Bulwell Common	61.28	38	2½ L	1/130 F: 1/330 R
38.3	Bagthorpe Junction	63.26	37	2½ L	1/130 F
40.4	Nottingham Victoria	68.53	sigs	2¾ L	

I conclude this section by looking at the performance of the Caprotti B3/2s in their final year of express working just before the outbreak of the Second World War. First, 6167 was at the head of the 10am Marylebone-Bradford as far as Leicester routed via the GW joint line as far as Ashendon Junction.

Marylebone-Leicester via High Wycombe
6167, B3/2
6 chs, 207/215 tons
11 February 1939

Miles	Location	Times	Speeds	Schedule	Gradients
0	Marylebone	00.00		T	
5.1	Neasden South Jn	08.36	59/41*	¼ L	
8.8	Sudbury Hill	13.08	52		1/264 R
11.6	Northolt Junction	16.43	pws 30*/20*	¾ L	Subsidence & bridge repair
13.4	Ruislip	20.25	45	2½ L	
16.1	Denham	23.21	61		
18.7	Gerrards Cross	26.02	59		1/175 R
	Seer Green	-	58 ½		1/254 R
23	Beaconsfield	30.20	67/73½		1/225 F
27.9	High Wycombe	35.36		1½ L	
0		00.00			
2.2	West Wycombe	04.18	46		
4.9	Saunderton	07.34	51		1/164 R
8.1	Princes Risborough	10.52	73	¼ L	1/100: 1/88 F
13.5	Haddenham	15.08	79		1/176 F
17.5	Ashendon Junction	18.28	73/67*	T	L
23.4	Grendon Underwood Jn	23.42	70/65	¾ E	
25.4	Calvert	25.28	56/64		
31.1	Finmere	30.44	70/54		1/176 R
35.9	Brackley	35.30	69/61		1/176 F: 1/176 R
39.1	Helmdon	38.52	56/ pws 27*		1/176 R
43.9	Culworth Junction	45.10	58	¾ L	
45.7	Woodford	47.53		¼ L	
(Woodford – Rugby – several slacks/checks)					
0	Rugby	00.00		2 L	
3.6	Shawell	04.46	61/58		1/176 F: 1/176 R
6.8	Lutterworth	08.03	70/62		1/176 F: 1/176 R
10.7	Ashby	11.22	76		1/176 F
16.2	Whetstone	14.58	73/76		1/176 F
19.9	Leicester	19.58		1 L	

Note – inside 'even time' start – pass High Wycombe-Finmere and Rugby-Whetstone.

6166 on the 5pm Bradford Exchange with six coaches ran the 47.7 miles from Woodford to High Wycombe in 45 minutes 43 seconds on 1 December 1937, and was timed by Mr N. Harvey on a Sunday in July 1939 up from Rugby via the Aylesbury route with a heavy load of 360 tons. Mr Harvey had gone down to Rugby on the Sunday 9.50am Marylebone-Nottingham with Caprotti 6167 and 360 tons which had dropped over six minutes on the easy 100 minute schedule with just two p-way slacks at Northwood and Braunston to excuse it. 6167 could manage no more than 25mph on the climb to Amersham, 72 below Wendover and averaged only 48mph over the undulating but predominantly uphill stretch from Finmere to Helmdon. However, 6166 on the 7.47pm off Rugby in the evening put up a much better performance. It ran the 45.3 miles from Rugby to Aylesbury in 45 minutes 49 seconds, gaining over three minutes on schedule, with a maximum of 80mph at Calvert on the long 1 in 176 descent from Finmere. The 28.7 miles on to Harrow took 39½ minutes start to stop, dropping just half a minute despite a signal check at Pinner. It accelerated out of Aylesbury on the 1 in 117 climb to 38mph and held 36-38 to the summit between Wendover and Great Missenden. In a final dash to the terminus it beat the 15 minute schedule for the 9.2 miles by a minute and a half with 70mph past Neasden.

The allocation at the beginning of 1939 was:

Neasden	6166, 6167, 6168
Immingham	6164, 6165, 6169

Then 6164 was rebuilt with Caprotti gear and the three Immingham engines moved to Woodford to work West of England trains from Banbury to Sheffield and later in 1939 the GC main line received some Gresley pacifics. Train loads in the war years grew considerably and if a pacific was not available a B3 was a better substitute than a 4-4-0 or 4-4-2. In 1942 two B3s (6164 and 6165) returned to the GN main line at Copley Hill to tackle some of the enormous loads (up to nineteen coaches) on the King's Cross expresses between Doncaster and Leeds. 6164 which was a high mileage engine was soon replaced by 6169 and the two B3/1s did sterling work. 6169 on one occasion replaced a failed V2 on a 540 ton train which it worked successfully as far as the Grantham engine exchange point. Then at the end of 1942 the Gresley pacifics working on the former GC lies were recalled to the East Coast line to handle the very heavy trains there (and the diminishing pacific availability due to lack of maintenance capacity) and both B3s returned to Gorton with 6164, now repaired, from Woodford.

At the end of the war, the Gresley pacifics and V2s returned, and the Gorton engines finished at Immingham working expresses and semi-fast services between Cleethorpes and Sheffield and Grimsby and Peterborough. Then in 1947, two B3/1s now numbered 1494 and 1496 (ex 6169 and 6165) went to Lincoln and the Neasden B3/2s, 1495 (6164), 1498 (6167) and B3/3 1497 (6166) were transferred to Immingham. All except 6166 were withdrawn before nationalisation in January 1948. The judgement on the Robinson 4-6-0s, particularly the ones designed for express passenger work, is that the weaknesses in firebox and ashpan design, coupled with the LNER engineering management's belated recognition of the value of long-travel valves as designed by the GWR for their passenger 4-6-0s as early as 1902 meant that they never fulfilled their promise in traffic. They may have looked magnificent but must have been a great disappointment to their designer, whose reputation rests on his 4-4-0s, 4-4-2s and the sturdy 2-8-0s.

The GCR 8N (LNER B6) – 1918

416 was built at Gorton in 1918, a 5ft 8in coupled wheel version of the company's 8M 2-8-0s. The presumption is that they were intended as an improved version of the 1913 1A 5ft 7in inside cylinder engines (LNER B8), having their two 21in cylinders outside to improve the bearings and avoid the common overheating of the previous class. Two more, numbered 52 and 53, were built in 1921, but were then superseded by the 4-cylinder 9Q class (LNER B7) which were constructed also from 1921. 416 was built with the old style GC open cab, but the latter two had the side-window cab. The dimensions of the three engines were:

Cylinders (2 outside)	21 in x 26in
Coupled wheel diameter	5ft 8in
Bogie wheel diameter	3ft 6in
Stephenson's valve gear	slide valves
Boiler pressure	180psi
Heating surface	2,123sqft (incl 308sqft superheating)
Grate area	26.24sqft
Axleload	18 tons 4 cwt
Weight – Engine	72 tons 18 cwt
– Tender	48 tons 6 cwt
– Total	121 tons 4 cwt
Water capacity	4,000 gallons
Coal capacity	6 tons
Tractive effort	25,798lbs

Despite only being a small class and overlooked in favour of the B7s, they had a good reputation and were a true mixed traffic locomotive. They were renumbered 5052/3 and 5416 at the Grouping and 1346-1348 in the LNER 1946 renumbering scheme, being withdrawn in 1947 before the new B1s required a further renumbering.

Two photos of Great Central Railway 8N, No.53, built at Gorton in 1921 and photographed when new. A. Brown/ MLS Collection

The left hand side of the 8N, here the other 1921 engine, No.52, seen at Gorton shed, 1922. MLS Collection

The prototype 8N built in 1918 and seen here at Gorton, 24 February 1923. It is still in Great Central livery and retains the GC oval numberplate on the cabside but the tender is lettered L&NER, a short lived lettering. By 1924 the engine would be renumbered 5416 and the tender inscription would just be simply LNER. Bob Miller Collection/ MLS Collection

Operations

416 was initially allocated to Gorton but was transferred to Neasden in 1919. The 1921 pair were allocated to Woodford and were joined by 416. Their work was the Banbury-Sheffield inter-railway traffic until many of the B7s were able to replace them. By the Grouping, all three had returned to Gorton. From there they worked overnight freights between Manchester and Hull over the Woodhead route. They then moved to Sheffield between 1925 and 1927, before moving to Ardsley in the West Riding and finally in 1929/30 to Bradford from where they were engaged in excursion work and specials to Manchester, Liverpool, Banbury and the Lincolnshire and Yorkshire coastal resorts.

This period of activity ceased in 1934, when they moved back to Sheffield, working freight and passenger trains in all directions radiating from that city. This acted as their base throughout the war years until 1946 when all three finished their last year art Ardsley on local goods work, 1346 (5416) being withdrawn in November 1947 and the other two in December.

B6 5416 in plain black LNER livery waits at York to take over a southbound train, probably a cross-country train to Leicester, Woodford and the GWR, 1929. Bob Miller Collection/MLS Collection

B6 5053 at Glazebrook with a Grand National special train for Liverpool Aintree, March 1939. W. Potter/MLS Collection

A war-stained 5053 stands with a passenger train at Mexborough, 14 October 1945. N. Fields/MLS Collection

The GCR 9Q (LNER B7) – 1921

The 9Q was a Robinson 4-cylinder 9P (B3) with 5ft 8 in diameter coupled wheels instead of 6ft 9in. They were built at the same time as the last two locomotives of the 8N class and Robinson very quickly decided to increase the numbers of the 9Q rather than the 2-cylinder mixed traffic engine. A total of thirty-eight were built, twenty-eight by the Great Central Railway in 1921/2 and the last ten by the LNER as class B7. The GCR engines were numbered 31-38, 72, 73 & 78 and 458 – 474, and the post-Grouping engines, 475-482 and 5483, 5484. All except the last two above had 5000 added to their numbers after 1923. The main dimensions were:

Cylinders (4)	16 in x 26in
Coupled wheel diameter	5ft 8in
Bogie wheel diameter	3ft 6in
Stephenson's valve gear	8in piston valves
Boiler pressure	180psi
Heating surface	2,387sqft (incl 343sqft superheating)
Grate area	26sqft
Axleload	19 tons 10 cwt
Weight – Engine	79 tons 10 cwt
– Tender	48 tons 6 cwt
– Total	127 tons 16cwt
Water capacity	4,000 gallons
Coal capacity	6 tons
Tractive effort	29,952lbs

Of all the various attempts that Robinson made to produce a successful mixed traffic 4-6-0, this was probably the best and certainly the class most multiplied. However, like the 9P passenger engines, they were heavy on coal and were nicknamed 'Colliers' Friends' and other such epithets implying a rather too healthy appetite for coal. The main disadvantage that they seemed to have compared with the

No.32 built at Gorton in July 1922, at Leicester in the same year. Bob Miller Collection/MLS Collection

GW 4-6-0s and Maunsell's mixed traffic engines was the continued use of short-travel valve gear, an insight that did not impact on the LNER motive power team until the 1925 GW 'Castle'/LNER 'A1' exchange. They were sufficiently successful in carrying out their duties for no significant rebuilding to have taken place, though Thompson did intend to provide them with the 100A (B1) boiler and two instead of four cylinders. The plan, which was never executed is explored more fully in Chapter 7 which covers the Thompson rebuilds.

The post-Grouping engines, LNER numbering 5475-5484, were built to the LNER loading gauge rather than the more generous Great Central one, with 4in reduced chimney height, low domes, cut down cabs and shortened safety valves. These were identified in LNER records as class B7/2. 5480, 5482, 5483 and 5484 also appeared with modified cylinders and larger steam chests, recognisable by vertical instead of sloping cylinder covers and square longer valve chest casting. When the cylinders of earlier engines required renewal, theses improved cylinders were usually used and thirteen were fitted between 1936 and 1947 in addition to the original four – the engines so equipped are identified in the Appendix. As the locomotives were being built during the 1921 coal strike when some examples of different classes were fitted with oil burning equipment, one 9Q, 72, was built as an oil burner with the standard GC Unolco system, although not until June 1922 and it was removed two months later.

32 a year later at Neasden, 28 April 1923. Bob Miller Collection/MLS Collection

No.72 built in June 1922 was oil burning from its construction but was converted back to coal in August. It was the only9Q/ B7 that was fitted with oil burning equipment after the 1921 coal strike and shortage and none were converted during the 1926 General Strike. 72 is seen here in photographic Works Grey, June 1922. MLS Collection

458 built in October 1921 seen here at Nottingham Victoria, 1924. It was renumbered 5458 in November 1924, but it has already had 'LNER' stencilled on the tender, but retaining the GC number. Bob Miller Collection/MLS Collection

B7/1 5035, built in August 1922, at Gorton in LNER Goods lined black livery, April 1936. MLS Collection

5468 built in March 1922 in LNER plain black livery, 1939. W.L. Good/ MLS Collection

All had the standard 4,000 gallon GC tender and were painted lined black initially and in LNER days, just black. They were allocated the numbers 1360-1397in 1946 and all bore this number, with two gaining the BR version of this number, 61391 (ex 5478) and 61396 (ex 5483). Then, as the increasing number of Thompson B1s claimed these numbers, the remaining twelve in 1949 were renumbered in the 61702-61713 series. The first withdrawal in April 1948 was 1394, the B7/2 former 5481, but withdrawals then came thick and fast and only four survived to 1950, 61711 (alias 5478, 1391 and 61391) outliving the others by five months being condemned in July.

1367 (ex 5459) in LNER wartime black livery, at Trafford Park shed on the Cheshire Lines Committee, 14 June 1948. W. Potter/MLS Collection

A filthy B7/1 1376 (ex 5468) at Gorton, 26 September 48. It was supplied with the modified cylinders and steam chest in March 1936. It was condemned three months after this photo was taken.
MLS Collection

A B17/1, 1386 (ex 5034) that was overhauled and provided with strengthened new front end to the frames after frame distortion was discovered in the 1940s. It is recognisable by the curved extension in front of the smokebox. Behind is ex-works J11 64366, both at Gorton, 28 May 1949. The B7 was withdrawn a month later.
J.D. Darby/MLS Collection

A B7/2 with cut-down cab, small chimney and shallow dome, also renewed front end frame, and as initially painted after nationalisation as E1391, at Gorton, 13 March 1948. This engine was renumbered 61391 in January 1949, 61711 in April 1949 and was the last survivor of the class, withdrawn in July 1950. J. Davenport/ MLS Collection

A B7/1 in final guise – 61707, formerly 5474 and 1382, withdrawn in June 1949, seen here at Gorton just a few days earlier on May 28th. It has a renewed front end and it would appear that the tender has not been repainted but still bears the LNER lettering. J.D. Darby/MLS Collection

Operations

The twenty-eight 9Qs redesignated B7s at the Grouping took over much of the mixed traffic work of the earlier B4, B5 and B9s and almost immediately were joined by the ten built just after the Grouping. The pre-Grouping engines were allocated as follows:

Gorton 10
Neasden 6
Woodford 4
Immingham 3
Leicester 3
Sheffield 2

The final ten went to Gorton (seven) and Neasden (three) though two of the Gorton engines moved on soon to Immingham. The two at Leicester (5032 and 5033) moved on in 1924 and two were allocated to Annesley, but thereafter the allocation remained similar until the Second World War, although individual engines moved around between these depots.

The Gorton engines were rostered primarily to fast freight work, vacuum brake fitted trains to London, Grimsby, Lincoln, Leeds, York and Liverpool. This included perishable meat traffic in refrigerated vans from Liverpool Docks. The crews that operated these services had wide route knowledge and also operated many of the pre-war excursion trains to coastal resorts, London and race meetings. Their predominance on fast freight

B7/1 5459 near Rickmansworth with a Great Central line express in the late 1920s. F. Moore/ MLS Collection

work lasted until the mid-1930s when Gresley's 3-cylinder K3 moguls came on the scene and in 1935 four were allocated to Gorton for this type of work, and by 1939 had displaced the B7s largely on this activity. 5031 spent some time in the late 1930s at Liverpool and the B7s retained their work at Neasden until 1941.

A B7 was allocated to a mid-week excursion from Liverpool to York, possible a special for York races, and the main points of interest are tabled below:

Liverpool Central-York
11.20am Liverpool excursion
5073 – Gorton
9 chs, 297/320 tons
18 September 1929

Miles	Location	Times	Speeds	Gradients
0	Liverpool Central	00.00		¾ E
6.25	Hunts Cross West Jn	10.20	45	1/195 R
10.5	Hough Green	15.05	60/53	1/185 F: 1/185 R
15.8	Sankey	20.35	65	1/158 F
19.5	Padgate Junction	26.45		
24.5	Glazebrook	31.50	58/55	
27.5	Flixton	35.15	60	
31.5	Trafford Park Junction	40.15	sigs 15*	
32	Throstle Nest S junction	43.05/50.30	sigs stand	
37.2	Levenshulme	61.25		1/100 R
39	Hyde Road	65.10	29	1/100 R
41.4	Guide Bridge	69.15		
0		00.00		
3.25	Godley Junction	07.10	38	1/77 R: 1/143 R
6.8	Dinting	12.30	40	1/122 R
8.6	Valehouse	16.00	32	1/100 R
	Torside Box	19.25	25/ sigs 5*	1/117 R
12.2	Crowden	24.40	22½	1/117 R
14.1	Woodhead	-	sigs stand (1 ½ min)	
17.3	Dunford Bridge	38.40		
20	Hazlehead	41.30	60	1/124 F
23.3	Penistone	46.45		
0		00.00		
7.4	Barnsley Exhange	14.45		Colliery subsidence slacks
16.6	Mexborough	30.20	sigs 5*	
23.75	Doncaster	41.15		
0		00.00		
4.2	Shaftholme Junction	07.25		
7	Moss	10.30	58	
10	Balne	13.35	60	
11.25	Heck	15.00	56½	
13.8	Templehurst	17.35	60	
18.4	Selby	22.45	slack	
22.5	Riccall	28.55		

Liverpool Central-York
11.20am Liverpool excursion
5073 – Gorton
9 chs, 297/320 tons
18 September 1929

Miles	Location	Times	Speeds	Gradients
25.2	Escrick	31.55	57	
30.25	Chaloners Whin Junction	37.35		
32.2	York	41.40	(arr at 2.53pm)	

Return Excursion
9.10pm York-Liverpool
5073
9 chs, 297/320 tons
18 September 1929

Miles	Location	Times	Speeds	Gradients
0	York	00.00		2½ L
13.8	Selby	21.45	sigs	
25.2	Moss	36.05	59	
			Sig stop (2½ mins)	
32.2	Doncaster	50.05		
0		00.00		
7.1	Mexborough	13.00		Colliery subsidence slacks
16.5	Barnsley Exchange	31.20		
23.75	Penistone	49.40	sig stop (35 secs)	
27.5	Hazlehead	60.05	31½	1/124 R
29.75	Dunford Bridge	64.20	32	1/135 R
33	Woodhead	68.40		
39.4	Hadfield	75.05	60	1/117 F
43.8	Godley Junction	80.20	sigs	
47.1	Guide Bridge	88.05		
0		00.00		
4.3	Levenshulme	06.55	50	1/100 F
9.3	Throstle Nest S Junction	14.20	20*	
10	Trafford Park Junction	16.05		
12.7	Urmston	19.30	45/50	
17	Glazebrook East Junction	26.00		
21.9	Padgate Junction	31.40		
25.5	Sankey	35.50	58	
29.2	Farnworth	40.25	48	1/158 R
34.4	Hunts Cross	46.20	60/50	1/185 F: 1/185 R
36	Garston	48.50		
0		00.00		
5.4	Liverpool Central	10.00	(arr 12.42am)	

This run is typical of B7 performance on passenger excursion traffic – slogging uphill and 60mph maximum on the level or downhill, with much running in the 50s.

A speedier effort but with a lightweight train only is the following log with the prototype 1921 built B7 found in the July 1931 edition of the *Railway Magazine*:

Sheffield-Manchester London Road
4.55pm Marylebone-Manchester
5072 – Gorton
5 chs, 175/180 tons
c1930

Miles	Location	Times	Speeds	Schedule	Gradients
0	Sheffield	00.00		T	
4.9	Oughty Bridge	08.15	44		1/132 R
8.8	Wortley	13.35	47		1/120 R
12.9	Penistone	18.50	43½		1/100 R
16.7	Hazelhead	24.05	43½		1/124 R
18.9	Dunford Bridge	27.10	43	1¾ E	1/135 R
22.1	Woodhead	30.45		2¼ E	
24.1	Crowden	32.25	71½		1/117 F
26	Torside Box	34.05	68		1/117 F
29.4	Dinting	37.30	pws		1/100 F
31.5	Mottram	40.55			
33	Godley Junction	43.40	pws		
36.3	Guide Bridge	47.40			
38.6	Gorton	50.50			
40.5	Ardwick	53.15			
41.3	Manchester London Rd	55.20	(52 net)	¼ L	

The B7s worked the Woodhead route regularly often on the last leg of expresses, mainly for their hill-climbing ability. They also worked stopping trains over the route and I have a log of 5469 with 263 tons on the 7.41pm from Penistone to Sheffield which touched a maximum of 63mph on the descent through Wortley before a p-way slack at Deepcar caused the train to exceed its 17-minute schedule for the 13 miles by 45 seconds (net 15¾ mins).

Woodford's allocation worked passenger trains to the Great Western via Banbury and more were added to their allocation in the late 1920s for the fitted goods and fish trains over the same route and right through to and from Grimsby. By 1941, the Woodford allocation had grown to seventeen engines of the class, adding stopping passenger and coal trains from Woodford to Marylebone to their regular duties. In 1933 the schedules and diagrams for the Annesley-Woodford coal trains were improved and Annesley received 5032, 5471 and 5472 to work these trains.

The Immingham engines, including 5036-5038, 5467 and 5478, worked via Sheffield to Manchester via the Woodhead route, from Cleethorpes to Leicester on passenger services, boat train work and excursion traffic to London. Sheffield's two had been augmented in the 1930s and by 1938 consisted of 5033, 5462, 5471, 5480, 5481 and 5483.

Their work changed significantly in the Second World War. Their fast freight work had been largely taken over by the K3s by then and they were used on military traffic, especially troop train movements, including the transport of American forces landing at Liverpool and

An unidentified B7/2 with the revised cylinders works a Grand National race special for Aintree on the Cheshire Lines Committee route in the late 1930s. MLS Collection

A B7/1 in the 546X series enters Manchester London Road with the 3.10pm from Sheffield, 7 August 1933. It appears to have another Robinson 4-6-0 at the rear of the train although this may be an illusion with the engine passing on the adjacent track.
MLS Collection

B7/2 5477 arrives at Manchester London Road with the 8.45am from Marylebone which it has worked over the Woodhead route from Sheffield, 7 August 1933.
MLS Collection

Woodford's B7/2 5484 with modified cylinders and steam chest with a train of GW coaches on a cross-country express at Staverton Road, near Rugby, June 1939.
MLS Collection

B7/1 5037 on a down goods train at Godley Junction, 1 June 1939.
C.A. Appleton/MLS Collection

B7/1 with a fast freight including empty cattle trucks for returning to Fishguard Harbour at Staverton Road near Rugby, June 1939.
G.A. Coltas/MLS Collection

being taken to bases in Lincolnshire and East Anglia. Gorton was the base for much of their wartime activity and in 1943, all thirty-eight B7s were allocated there. Some would be lent to subsheds on the CLC-Trafford Park, Stockport and Liverpool Brunswick when those depots were short of power.

I have found, unusually, a wartime log (6 June 1943) of a B7 on the Sunday 4.45pm Nottingham-Marylebone train via the GW joint line. 5472 had a load of just six coaches, and stopped at all the main stations as far as Woodford and Brackley. It ran the 35.8 miles from Brackley to High Wycombe in 48 minutes 3 seconds with speed in the upper 50s most of the way, maximum 59 at Finmere, minimum of 52 at Saunderton summit. It arrived in High Wycombe five minutes early. The 27.8 miles to Marylebone took 43 minute 4 seconds, a minute less than schedule with a maximum speed of 59mph at Ruislip (passed 3 minutes early). I'm unsure whether the speed was governed at this time by a maximum of 60mph, or whether the ease of the wartime schedule demanded no more.

At the end of the war, many were moved from Gorton to Sheffield – nine in 1945 and a further nine in 1946, though four returned to Gorton in 1947. By this time they were operating slow and local goods trains, stopping passenger trains and an occasional relief or excursion. Their end was foreseen by the large scale construction of the Thompson B1s, although they outlasted most of the other GC 4-6-0s, the class being still intact at nationalisation although twenty were withdrawn during that year (1948) and most of the rest in 1949, leaving just four in 1950, with 61711 (ex 5478, 1391) being finally withdrawn in July. They were engines that could be worked hard (and were) and were impressive to watch, although their fuel consumption was heavy (some 60-65lbs per mile on average). Because of their power they received the BR classification 6MT, putting them surprisingly in the same freight power group as the V2s although the latter were granted '7' for passenger work.

B7/1 5474 on a return excursion to Sheffield and beyond with a set of LMS coaches, on the climb to Woodhead Tunnel near Valehouse, 17 August 1946. J.D. Darby/ MLS Collection

1385 (ex 5033) at Godley Junction with a hopper train from Spink Hill to Liverpool Huskisson Dock, c1947. 1385 has received modified cylinders and steam chest. Note the revised smokebox door handles. MLS Collection

B7/2 1397 (ex 5484) at Ashley with a stopping passenger train, 9 August 1947. 1397 has the modified cylinder layout and smokebox door handles. MLS Collection

B7/1 1370 (ex 5462) with modified cylinders and new frame front end on the 10.40am Manchester-Hull near Torside Box on the climb to Woodhead Tunnel, 12 April 1947. It has recently visited Gorton Works for a light overhaul, evidenced by the repainted smokebox. J.D.Darby/MLS Collection

B7/1382 (5474) at Wilbraham Road with an unfitted up goods train, 13 May 1948. J.D. Darby/ MLS Collection

B7/1 1367 (5459) with an up goods train at Penistone, 14 April 1949. N. Fields/MLS Collection

B7/2 61710 (ex 1388, 5475) at Skelton Junction, York, with an unfitted goods train, 23 July 1949. N.H. Spilsbury/MLS Collection

Chapter 3

THE NORTH EASTERN 4-6-0s

The NER class S (LNER B13) – 1899

The North Eastern Railway had been party to the rail races to Scotland that climaxed in 1895 and had used 4-4-0s, a 4-2-2 and a 4-4-0 with large 7ft 7¼ in coupled wheels for their fastest trains in that decade. In 1899, the NER Locomotive Superintendent, Wilson Worsdell, produced a 4-4-0 with a larger boiler, the NER 'R' class, that became well-acclaimed and was reclassified D20 by the LNER and then, to cope with the increasing train loads, designed and constructed a 4-6-0 ordered from Gateshead Works in 1898. Ten numbered 2001-2010, were delivered in 1899 and 1900 and were identified as NER class 'S'. These were the first 4-6-0 engines built for express passenger work in the UK – the Highland 4-6-0s that preceded them were for freight work and known as the 'Jones Goods'. Their key dimensions were:

Cylinders (2 outside)	20in x 26in
Coupled wheel diameter	6ft 1¼in
Bogie wheel diameter	3ft 7¼in
Stephenson's valve gear	8¾in piston valves (2001-3 built with slide valves)
Boiler pressure	200psi (2001-3; remainder reduced to 175psi)
Heating surface	1,769sqft
Grate area	23sqft
Axleload	19 tons 7 cwt
Weight – Engine	62 tons 8 cwt (2001-3) 62 tons 19 cwt (remainder)
– Tender	38 tons 12 cwt (2001-3) 41 tons 2 cwt (remainder)
– Total	101 tons (2001-3) 104 tons 1 cwt (remainder)
Water capacity	3,701 gallons (2001-3) 3,940 gallons (remainder)
Coal capacity	5 tons
Tractive effort	2001-3: 24,136lbs; remainder 21,119lbs

One of the first ten of the class as constructed, 2008, built in 1900.
MLS Collection

Initial experience of these three engines was one of disappointment in that they did not seem as free running as the 'R' 4-4-0s. Their slide valves were replaced by piston valves in line with the 'Rs' and the later 'S' class locomotives were all built with piston valves. The first three engines also had short cabs and tenders as the 4-6-0s did not fit easily onto the turntables in use at the beginning of the century. The ten S's express work was short-lived, partly because of the superiority of the Rs and partly because five S1s with 6ft 8½in coupled wheels were built in 1901 and 1902.

However, the usefulness of the 6ft 1in engines on fast freight and secondary or heavy passenger services was sufficient for the NER Board to authorise a further thirty to be built between 1906 and 1909. In the custom of most of the pre-grouping railways at that time, they were numbered in somewhat haphazard fashion filling in gaps between existing engine numbers. The additional thirty S class were numbered as follows:

1906 build: 726, 740, 757, 760, 761, 763, 766, 768, 775 & 1077
1908 build: 738, 739, 741, 743-749
1909 build: 750-756, 758, 759, 762

760, constructed in 1906, still in pristine condition, c1907. Loco Publishing Co/ MLS Collection

New piston valves and cylinders were fitted to the 2001-2010 series over a period stretching from January 1901 (2001) to July 1924 (2002), most being rebuilt between 1916 and 1918. The first to be superheated was 751 in November 1913, and all bar 2002, 739, 759 and 761 had been superheated by the Grouping. The last to be superheated was 739 in February 1925. The superheated engines had 1,773.6sqft of heating surface including 378sqft of superheating. However, boiler pressure was reduced to 160psi, engine weight increased to 65 tons 2 cwt and tractive effort reduced to 19,309lbs. The short smokeboxes were replaced when superheated with a longer version. The first thirty were dual fitted with Westinghouse and vacuum brakes. The last ten had air brakes only until the Grouping.

The locomotives were painted when built in the NER lined green livery, but this had been replaced by black by the beginning of the First World War. 2009 and 2010 received gold lining when working the royal train in 1900. 2006 won a gold medal at the 1900 Paris Exhibition a replica being displayed on the centre splashers. 2006 was painted in LNER lined apple green livery for its inclusion in the 1925 Darlington centenary procession (see Colour Section painting). The S class was designated B13 in the LNER classification and apart from 2006, all received the LNER goods livery of black with red lining, although the lining was dispensed with after 1928.

They became redundant when traffic levels fell at the time of the Depression and the first withdrawals took place in 1928 (2004, 2005 and 2007). Most had gone by 1938, 748, 753 and 759 being withdrawn in October of that year leaving just 761. However, that locomotive was taken into Departmental stock in September 1934 and was used as a counter-pressure engine for testing purposes of other locomotives, being renumbered 1699 in 1946 and withdrawn finally in May 1951.

743 built in 1908 with Westinghouse and vacuum brake systems and with the slightly enlarged smokebox after being superheated in 1917, seen here c1920. MLS Collection

738 built in 1908 in LNER black livery with brass edges to the splashers, c1935. F. Moore/ MLS Collection

The sole survivor, 1699 (ex 761) used as a counter-pressure test engine, outside the Darlington Works Paint Shop where it was based between 1934 and 1951, 4 July 1948. N. Fields/ MLS Collection

Operations

The intention was to use the ten Gateshead based S locomotives of the first series on main line expresses between Newcastle and Edinburgh to avoid the hitherto common practice of double-heading. However, not only were the R 4-4-0s found superior for express passenger work, but they were also replaced by the S1 4-6-0s and in 1903 by the successful V Atlantics (LNER C6). Therefore, the first series found themselves allocated to fast freight work and excursion traffic which they accomplished with competence, and the 1906-1909 constructed locomotives were introduced to this type of work immediately. Later, they were supplanted on this traffic by the S3 (LNER B16) series. The allocation at the Grouping was:

Tweedmouth:	738, 739, 741, 745, 747, 754, 2001, 2007 (8)
Newcastle Heaton:	752, 759, 757, 761, 1077, 2002, 2003, 2005 (8)
Leeds Neville Hill:	743, 750, 753, 762, 2006, 2008 (6)
Blaydon:	756, 766, 775 (3)
Hull Dairycoates	726, 740, 744, 746, 748, 749, 751, 755, 758, 760, 763, 768, 2004, 2009, 2010 (15)

By the mid-1920s, both B16s and Gresley K3s had replaced the Heaton allocation, and a few passed to the Southern Area Motive Power

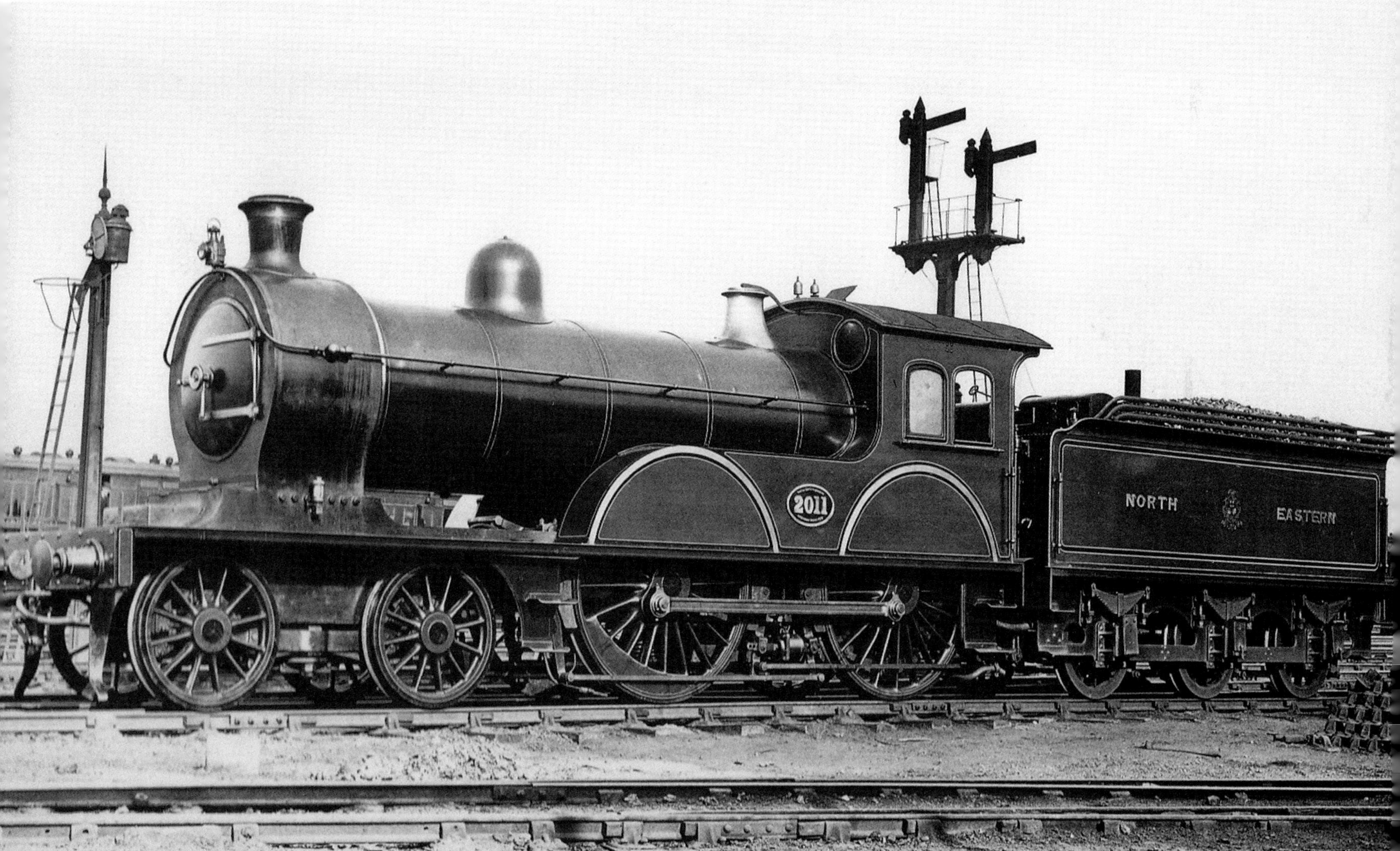

The first of the 1899 built R 4-4-0s, 2011, as constructed c1900. The Rs were capable of working the NER express traffic and quickly displaced the S 4-6-0s from their intended work. F. Moore/ MLS Collection

Division to sheds like Doncaster and Colwick. York and Ardsley also acquired a few in their declining years. The types of work remained parcels and fitted goods trains, passenger stopping trains and the occasional excursion to race meetings or seaside resorts. They covered stopping passenger trains over the Border from Berwick to Edinburgh and could be found working empty stock and local services in the Edinburgh area between turns.

As stated earlier, withdrawals commenced in 1928, although those remaining could still be found occasionally on important services between Leeds and Harrogate or Leeds and Newcastle. 2006 was still the prestige engine of this fleet and was used on passenger services such as the Sunday Pullman between Leeds and Harrogate.

In 1934 the nine remaining survivors were based at:

Hull Dairycoates:	726, 738, 748, 751
Leeds Neville Hill:	753, 759, 762
Tweedmouth:	754
York:	775

1906 built 766 with a down goods train near Darlington, June 1927. Photomatic/MLS Collection

One of the 1899 engines, 2002, pauses with a southbound freight at York, c1929. 2002 was the last of the class to be superheated in 1924.
W.L. Good/MLS Collection

752 at Croft Spa with a lightweight fast freight service, c1932.
Photomatic/MLS Collection

The Hull engines had regular fish train diagrams as far as Doncaster where a K3 or B17 (if for the GC Woodford and GWR) would take over. By 1938, the remaining four were in poor condition and were withdrawn. However, 761, withdrawn in September 1934, was transferred to Departmental stock to replace 756 which had been used as a counter-pressure test engine since March of that year. The superheater was removed and 761 was kept in the Darlington Paint Shop. After nationalisation in 1948, numbered 1699 since 1946, it was moved to BR's Rugby Testing Plant, but was scrapped in May 1951.

There are few records of the performance of the B13s in service and the only log I've discovered is of the 6.44pm Harrogate-Leeds in January 1936, when 759 piloted D49 No.297 *The Cottersmore* with a load of nine bogie vehicles weighing 316 tons. The 22.3 miles were completed in 36 minutes 15 seconds including the observance of two p-way slowings and signal checks approaching Leeds, net time of 32 minutes against the scheduled 34. The pair averaged 48mph on the 1 in 70/87 to Bardsey, falling to 30mph at the summit but the downhill stretches were hindered by the p-way slack after Scholes.

The NER class S1 (LNER B14) – 1900

Design & construction

Dissatisfied with his S 4-6-0s for fast East Coast passenger train work, Worsdell had five similar engines, but with 6ft 8¼in coupled wheels, constructed in 1900-1901. Their dimensions were:

Cylinders (2 outside)	20in x 26in
Coupled wheel diameter	6ft 8¼in
Bogie wheel diameter	3ft 7¼in
Stephenson's valve gear	8¾in piston valves
Boiler pressure	200psi
Heating surface	1,769sqft
Grate area	23sqft
Axleload	19 tons 10 cwt
Weight – Engine	67 tons 2 cwt
– Tender	41 tons 2 cwt
– Total	108 tons 4 cwt
Water capacity	3,940 gallons
Coal capacity	5 tons
Tractive effort	22,069lbs

The first of the five S1 class reclassified by the LNER as B14s, No.2111, in NER lined green livery shortly after construction, 1901. Loco Publishing Co/ MLS Collection

2113 as constructed at Gateshead Works in 1901. F. Moore/MLS Collection

These locomotives were equipped with Schmidt superheaters between 1913 and 1917, providing 1,857.8sqft heating surface including 390.1sqft superheating. The boiler pressure was reduced to 175psi and tractive effort because of this was just 19,310lbs. As with the S class, their smokeboxes were slightly lengthened when superheated improving their appearance and they were reclassified as B14s by the LNER. All had both Westinghouse and vacuum brakes. They were painted in the NER lined green livery although after 1912 they were black with lining of white, gold and red. During the First World War, they were black with red lining and the LNER restored their passenger lined apple green livery which they retained until withdrawal, which commenced with 2111 and 2115 in the summer of 1929. The last survivor was 2112 withdrawn from traffic in April 1931.

2115 which was superheated in April 1917 in LNER lined green livery, c1928 a year before withdrawal. MLS Collection

Operations

Initially the S1s replaced the Ss on the heaviest expresses between York and Edinburgh, but it was not long before they too were relegated to secondary services by the R 4-4-0s and the Atlantics. In 1906 a series of tests were carried out between York and Newcastle with the S and S1 4-6-0s, the V and Compound Atlantics and the R 4-4-0. The S1 performance with 365 tons failed to meet the schedule of the test service train, the 1.52pm York-Newcastle non-stop, with nothing over 71mph. Both the S and S1 suffered from shallow grates and a small grate area and could not maintain sufficient steam to service its large cylinders over sustained long periods requiring hard running. After 1907, they were mainly engaged in main line freight work, including perishables and fish traffic from Scotland.

2113 at Edinburgh Waverley with a Newcastle train, 7 August 1911. G.M. Shoults/MLS Collection

They were all allocated to Gateshead until the autumn of 1924 when four were transferred to Hull Botanic Gardens. They were clearly not entirely satisfactory for the Hull passenger work and were soon removed to the freight depot Hull Dairycoates. The fifth member, 2115, was moved to York. 2113 moved to Selby for summer traffic on the Bridlington line. Two were withdrawn in 1929, but the other three worked relief passenger trains to Bridlington and freight services in the Hull and Scarborough areas.

2111 at York on a southbound express, a few months after being superheated, 1914.
W.L. Good/MLS Collection

The B15 – 1911

Design and construction

The Worsdell 4-6-0s had not been successful as express passenger engines but they were very satisfactory for mixed traffic activity. Vincent Raven succeeded Wilson Worsdell in 1910 and developed the already successful Atlantics as the class Z for the express work, so Raven intended his 4-6-0s for mixed traffic work. It had been intended to order more of the S class, but Raven developed the design to incorporate a larger boiler as used on other engines, and twenty S2s were constructed, the first two, 782 and 786, being delivered in December 1911. The order was completed by the end of 1912 of nineteen conventional engines. The key dimensions were:

Cylinders (2 outside)	20in x 26in
Coupled wheel diameter	6ft 1¼in
Bogie wheel diameter	3ft 7¼in
Stephenson's valve gear	8¾in piston valves
Boiler pressure	180psi (175psi when superheated))
Heating surface	2,297sqft (later 2,366sqft incl 545sqft superheating)
Grate area	23sqft
Axleload	19 tons 4 cwt
Weight – Engine	68 tons 17 cwt (70 tons 14 cwt superheated)
– Tender	41 tons 2 cwt
– Total	109 tons 19 cwt (111 tons 16 cwt superheated)
Water capacity	3,940 gallons
Coal capacity	5 tons
Tractive effort	21,723lbs (later 21,555lbs when superheated)

The first seven were built without superheating, but they were built with superheaters from 797 in May 1912 onwards. The first seven were superheated later, between 1919 (788) and 1928 (786 and 795). The last engine of the twenty was 825 and this was experimentally fitted with Stumpf Uniflow cylinders which allowed the cooler used exhaust steam to flow onwards rather than return causing condensation in the cylinder. It ran trials against 797, a conventional S2, in 1913 between Newcastle and York which identified some value in the system – enough anyway for Raven to equip one of his Z Atlantics with a similar system. However, the advantages were not sufficient to offset the costs of the unique S2 and it was converted to the standard cylinder layout in 1924. The different dimension of this engines were as the above superheated locomotives except:

Walschaerts valve gear	Piston valves with Uniflow
Axleload	19 tons 9 cwt
Weight – Engine	71 tons 14 cwt
– Total	112 tons 16 cwt

782 - 795 were delivered in NER lined green, but the rest were black and the earlier engines were painted black at the first general overhaul. As with the other NER 4-6-0s, the smokebox was extended slightly on superheating. All were dual-brake fitted until the LNER standardised the vacuum brake in 1928, but the B15s retained their Westinghouse air brake until 1932. They all received the standard NER 5 ton, 3,940 gallon tender.

797 was built in May 1912 and was the first of the class to have included a superheater from initial construction. It is seen here on shed, c1920. MLS Collection

825 was the last of the batch, built in March 1913 experimentally with Stumpf Uniflow cylinders, a system unique to the UK, but found on the Continent. The system ensured the exhaust steam flowed on in the same direction and did not return and cause condensation in the cylinders. It was tested against 797 (see photo above) between Newcastle and York in 1913 and in 1919 the same system was incorporated in the design of the last Z Atlantic. However, the improvement over the conventional engines was insufficient to offset the cost and it was converted to normal cylinder arrangements in 1924. It is in Works Grey for the company photograph, March 1913. MLS Collection

825, still with the Stumpf Uniflow cylinders in 1923. It was rebuilt in conventional style the following year. MLS Collection

782 built in December 1911 and superheated in 1926, on shed shortly after the Second World War and before receiving its allotted revised number of 1313 which it did not carry as it was withdrawn in December 1946. W.A. Camwell/MLS Collection

Five of the first ten were withdrawn in the autumn of 1937, but the onset of the Second World War reprieved the rest which were withdrawn between 1944 and 1947. They were initially allocated the numbers 1313-1327 in 1946, but then, to avoid confusion with the new Thompson B1s, were reallocated 1691-1698, six having been withdrawn in 1946. However, only 1693 (ex 815), 1695 (ex 819), 1696 (ex 820) and 1697 (ex 821) carried the new number.

Operations

The first ten S2s were allocated to Heaton whilst the next nine were allocated to York (five), Hull Dairycoates (three) and Leeds Neville Hill (one). The experimental Stumpf Uniflow engine joined the first ten at Heaton. Although Raven had designed them for mixed traffic duties, they did have some express duties including the East Coast section of trans-Pennine trains

786, the second example of the class, built in December 1911, on a down Scotch express at Beningborough, 1914. The four-wheel flat wagon behind the tender is an oddity on an express. 786 is in NER lined green livery and was withdrawn in 1937. MLS Collection

for Manchester and Liverpool. However, Raven had designed a 3-cylinder Atlantic, the Z, which soon ousted them from any top-link work and they settled into the mixed traffic duties for which they were designed.

At the Grouping, their allocation and work remained unchanged until B16s were available in sufficient numbers for the Heaton allocation to be replaced and five more were sent to York. Doncaster and Darlington also had one or two and, as more B16s were built, the B15s were relegated to basic goods train work. Like the other NER mixed traffic 4-6-0s, they found their way onto summer relief and excursion trains when power shortage was most acute. They also worked trains from Hull to the former GC line at Sheffield and via the Woodhead line to Mottram Yard.

There are hardly any logs recorded of B15s at work, but I found one short snippet in the archives of the Rail Performance Society, but with only a lightweight 102 ton four-coach train. 824 was working the 4.52pm Leeds-Selby-Hull on 23 October 1936 and ran the 20.7 miles from Leeds to Selby in 25¾ minutes, some 2¼ minutes under schedule. 68½mph was achieved after Micklefield and speed was maintained in the mid-60s until Hambleton.

823 with a southbound stopping train at York, c1922. E.S. Cox/MLS Collection

825, the Stumpf Uniflow engine, working a heavy goods train at an unidentified location, c1920. Photomatic/MLS Collection

820 toils out of the Woodhead Tunnel with a heavy unfitted train of coal for Manchester, c1926. 820 was the last survivor of the class withdrawn in December 1947 just before nationalisation. J.A. Peden/MLS Collection

Some withdrawals took place pre-war and in 1939 Leeds Starbeck had a couple and Neville Hill five, but the largest number was at Hull Dairycoates (eight). These fifteen nearly survived the war although four were condemned in 1944. Post-war, the remaining engines were based at Hull, employed almost exclusively on goods train work. The last survivor was the former 820, renumbered 1696 in May 1946. It was withdrawn in December 1947.

The NER class S2 (LNER B16) – 1911

Design and construction

Vincent Raven took over from Wilson Worsdell in 1910 and after developing the latter's S series 4-6-0s in his two cylinder S2, turned to the design and construction of three cylinder engines, his Z Atlantics for main line work. There was still a need for mixed traffic locomotives, but the onset of the First World War meant that further development was put on hold until the end of the conflict. After designing a three cylinder heavy freight locomotive for the Durham and Northumberland coalfields, the T3 (LNER Q7) 0-8-0, he designed a 4-6-0 with 5ft 8in coupled wheels and three cylinders driving the leading coupled axle with independent Stephenson valve gear. Ten S3s, as they were identified, were ordered at the end of 1918 and Nos. 840-849 were built at the NER's Darlington Works and put into traffic in 1920 and 1921. Before delivery of these, a further twenty-five were authorised and were completed by June 1921. They were numbered (filling in the gaps) as 906, 908, 909, 911, 914, 915, 920-934, 936, 937, 942 and 943. Further engines of the class were ordered in March 1922 but only three of the twenty had been delivered before the Grouping in 1923, when the LNER classified them as B16s. The order was completed by the LNER, Nos. 2363-2382 being constructed in 1922 and 1923 and a final batch, numbered 1371-1385, ordered at the last minute in December 1922, was completed in January 1924. Their key dimensions were:

Cylinders (3)	18½in x 26in
Coupled wheel diameter	5ft 8in
Bogie wheel diameter	3ft 1in
Stephenson's valve gear	8¾in piston valves
Boiler pressure	180psi (175psi when superheated))
Heating surface	1,958sqft (incl 392sqft superheating)
Grate area	27sqft
Axleload	20 tons
Weight – Engine	77 tons 14 cwt
– Tender	46 tons 12 cwt
– Total	124 tons 6 cwt
Water capacity	4,125 gallons
Coal capacity	5 tons10 cwt
Tractive effort	30,031lbs

Their livery was black with a single red lining, the lining removed from 1928. They were dual fitted with Westinghouse air and vacuum brakes, the air brake

846 built in March 1920 and seen in Works Grey for photographic purposes. It was rebuilt by Gresley as a B16/2 in 1940, renumbered 1406 in December 1946, then 61475 in December 1949. It was withdrawn in April 1963. Real Photographs/MLS Collection

943 built in June 1921 in LNER plain black livery, c1927. It remained unrebuilt as a B16/1, was renumbered 61433 at nationalisation and was withdrawn in November 1959. It is still fitted with the Westinghouse air-brake system which would be removed five years later. MLS Collection

system being removed between 1932 and 1936. The tender was slightly larger than the NER standard tender with four plated coal rails, holding 4,125 gallons of water. A number of modifications were made from 1932 to correct problems identified on their fast freight work. New axleboxes, horn guides and steel horn stays were fitted and additional mechanical lubrication, suggesting that the engines suffered too frequently from hotboxes. The springing of the coupled wheels was also improved.

In 1937, Gresley rebuilt 2364, using Walschaerts valve gear for the outside cylinders and his design of derived motion for the inside cylinder, taking into account the learning about longer lap valves and increased travel. The bogie had to move forward to provide clearance for the motion and the frame was lengthened and a new cab design provided.

The rebuilt engine was then classified B16/2, the unrebuilt engines becoming B16/1s. Six further B16/1s were converted to B16/2s between 1937 and 1940 (846, 926, 2366, 2367, 1372 and 1374). The modified dimensions were:

Walchaerts/Gresley conjugated gear, 9in piston valves

Length	Extended by 1ft
Wheelbase	Extended by 9in
Axleload	20 tons 3 cwt
Weight – Engine	79 tons 4 cwt
– Total	125 tons 16 cwt

Edward Thompson also decided to rebuild a B16/1 but instead of a drastic rebuilding to two cylinders as in his other rebuilding programmes, he retained the three cylinders but instead of replicating the Gresley derived gear, he modified the engines with three independent sets of Walschaerts motion. The first to be rebuilt was 922 in April 1944 and was classified as B16/3. Sixteen further B16/1s were rebuilt between 1944 and 1949 – 843, 847, 921, 924, 1371, 1378 (61461), 1380 (1463), 1381, 1384, 1385 (1465), 2363 (61434), 2368, 2373, 2377, 2378, 2382 (1453). The numbers in brackets were their numbers at the time of their rebuilding. The B16/3 altered dimensions were:

As B16/2 except:

Walchaerts valve gear	3 independent sets
Axleload	20 tons
Weight – Engine	78 tons 19 cwt
– Total	125 tons 11 cwt

842, the third S3 to be built in December 1919, at York, c1932. Renumbered 1402 in 1946 and 61402 in 1948, it was renumbered again, 61471, to make way for the B1 of that number in 1949. N. Harrop/MLS Collection

2364, built in November 1922, the first B16 to be rebuilt by Gresley with Walschaerts valve gear and derived motion for the inside cylinder, as a B16/2in June 1937. It is in Works Grey for its official LNER photograph. It was renumbered 61435 in 1948 and was the last survivor of the B16s, withdrawn in July 1964.
F. Moore/MLS Collection

2364 in unlined black livery on Darlington shed, 16 April 1938.
MLS Collection

1449, formerly 2378 built in July 1923, rebuilt by Thompson in September 1944 with independent Walschaerts gear to all cylinders, at York, 6 July 1947. MLS Collection

925 was destroyed during the summer of 1942 through enemy action, but the rest remained active until the first withdrawals took place in 1958. The B16s were renumbered 1400-1468 in 1946 and 61400-61468 at nationalisation, but 61400-61409 were renumbered again in December 1949 to make way for the last ten Thompson B1s. They adopted the numbers 61469-61478. The B16/1s and the rebuilds received the BR mixed traffic lining of red, cream and grey from 1950 onwards. The B16/1s were extinct by the end of 1961. Two B16/3s, 61417 and 61439 were withdrawn in 1962, but the remaining B16/2s and B16/3s were withdrawn during 1963 and 1964. Eleven were withdrawn in June 1964 – four B16/2s and seven B16/3s – and the last survivor, B16/2 61435 ex 2364, the first to be rebuilt in 1937,was withdrawn in July 1964. The highest mileage was achieved by B16/2 61455 (ex 1372) of 1,159,799 miles.

61441, a B16/1 in BR guise, black with mixed traffic red, cream and grey lining, at York, 25 May 1952. The only visual change from its original state, apart from livery, is the replacement of the NER ring by two handles to release the smokebox door. J. Davenport/MLS Collection

B16/1 61427 (ex 932) showing off its BR mixed traffic livery after overhaul at Darlington in April 1956. It would be withdrawn in March 1960. T.K. Widd/MLS Collection

B16/2, 61435, the former 2364, ex-works after overhaul at Darlington and just repainted in the new BR mixed traffic livery, 14 September 1950. As stated earlier, this was the last B16 survivor in 1964. J.D. Darby/ MLS Collection

B16/3 61444 (ex 2373) at York, 25 May 1952. It was one of the eleven B16/2s and B16/3s withdrawn in June 1964. J. Davenport/MLS Collection

Operations

On completion of the construction of the seventy B16s in 1924, their initial allocation was:

York:	844, 845, 847-849, 908, 911, 915, 921, 923, 925, 927, 933, 936, 942, 1371, 1374, 1377, 2364, 2366, 2368, 2370, 2372-2374, 2376, 2378, 2380, 2382 (29)
Heaton:	840-843, 846, 906, 914, 922, 930, 932, 934, 937, 943, 1372, 1373, 1379, 1383, 1385 (18)
Gateshead:	920, 2363, 2365, 2367, 2369, 2371, 2375, 2377, 2379, 2381 (10)
Tweedmouth:	909, 924, 926, 928, 1375, 1376, 1378, 1384 (8)
Neville Hill:	929, 931, 1380
Darlington:	1381, 1382
Selby:	2368

Their work was mixed traffic, supplementing that of the earlier B13, B14 and B15s and the Gresley GN K3s. As the number of K3s multiplied, B16s from Heaton and Tweedmouth moved to Hull Dairycoates and as many as twenty-three were there by 1931. Their work included express passenger trains from Hull to Sheffield. Scarborough received 845 in 1930 working regular coal traffic and returning empties from Gascoigne Wood Yard and summer relief passenger work until 1943. They were frequent performers on the regular Hull-York, Hull-Sheffield and Hull-Scarborough passenger trains and in the summer they were invaluable for the Saturday relief trains to the Yorkshire coast and mid-week excursions. Many of these services loaded to ten or even twelve coaches and taxed the D49 and D20 4-4-0s which were the other regular engines for such services. It is said that on a summer Saturday in the 1930s as many as thirty different B16s could be seen at Scarborough in a day.

By the mid-1930s depot allocations had changed and the situation at the end of 1935 was:

Hull Dairycoates:	840-843, 846, 906, 909, 925, 928, 930, 933, 934, 936, 937, 942, 1371, 1374-1376, 1378, 1384, 1385, 2367, 2369, 2379, 2380 (26)
York:	844, 847, 908, 911, 921, 923, 926, 927, 1372, 1373, 1377, 2364, 2366, 2370-2374, 2376, 2378, 2382 (21)
Neville Hill:	848, 849, 914, 924, 929, 931, 1379, 1380, 1383 (9)
Gateshead:	2375, 2377
Darlington:	915, 1381, 1382
Tyne Dock:	922, 943
Blaydon:	932, 2365
Scarborough:	845

However, the Newcastle area engines moved on in 1937, with Hull getting another five, York three and Darlington, one. This removed the sighting of B16s in Scotland as the Newcastle and Tweedmouth engines had worked freights and stopping passenger trains northwards. The York and Hull engines worked predominantly freight trains to Normanton, Wakefield, Sheffield and Nottingham, although stopping passenger trains and excursions (seaside and race trains) were common fare. Gresley Pacifics were not allowed to travel to Hull and the Hull portions of expresses for King's Cross would be often diagrammed for a B16, especially the heavier trains.

Little changed at first during the Second World War. One B16, 925, was destroyed in the bombing raid on York shed in April 1942. Then, in 1943 a decision was taken to base the entire class at York as the centre of operations and to minimise the spare parts required for their maintenance. After the war, five were loaned to Stockton and a couple to Darlington, but the rest stayed at York until 1949. They were much in demand for the frequent but heavy stopping passenger trains between Doncaster and Newcastle during the difficult post-war years, especially as the 4-4-0s and 4-4-2s, all in poor state of maintenance like all other engines, were less able to cope than the slow but powerful and rugged B16s. The Rail Performance Society's archives have no B16 running logs before the war years, but there are a number of records of B16s between Leeds and York in 1940 and 1941. One locomotive prominent in those records is the first Gresley rebuild, 2364, which was recorded five times between April and August 1940 completing the 25.5 miles in times varying from 32 minutes 45 seconds to 36 minutes 57 seconds, with loads between 220 and 250 tons. 840 had a ten-coach Leeds-Hull train in December 1941 which was badly delayed by signals over the first twelve miles but averaged exactly 60mph over the four miles from Gascoigne Wood to Thorpe Gate before the Selby stop.

The York engines worked also to Woodford and Banbury with through trains via the GC line to the former GW lines and there was one York overnight parcels diagram which took a York B16 (usually a B16/3) to Marylebone every night – out one night and back the next. Sometimes a York B16 would replace a V2 on freight or parcels service on the GN main line to Peterborough or even King's Cross. 1458 was noted on the relief *Aberdonian* out of King's Cross in September 1946 and in July and August 1953 there were several sightings at King's Cross including 61476 on a Cambridge buffet train service and 61420 on a King's Cross-Leeds express, returning from Grantham on the up *White Rose.* On 10 August 1953, five were seen in the King's Cross area – three on down goods trains, one on empty stock and one light engine.

Yet another mass murmuration of B16s occurred in 1949 when forty-one of York's allocation descended suddenly on Neville Hill and Hull Dairycoates. Then off flew

B16/2 2364 near Dinting with a freight from the Manchester area towards Sheffield, 15 June 1945. MLS Collection

B16/3 1454 rebuilt in December 1944, near Darlington with a down parcels train, August 1947. Photomatic/ MLS Collection

the Dairycoates engines back to York again, then some migrated to Neville Hill to join the flock there. By 1952 York had 35, Leeds Neville Hill 33 and Scarborough a lone one, now 61445. The Leeds/York split was:

Neville Hill:	61410-61415, 61422, 61424-61429, 61431-61433, 61440, 61442, 61446, 61447, 61452, 61458, 61460, 61462, 61465, 61466, 61469-61471, 61473, 61474, 61478
York:	61416-61421, 61423, 61430, 61434-61439, 61441, 61443, 61444, 61448-61451, 61453-61457, 61459, 61461, 61463, 61464, 61467, 61468, 61472, 61475-61477

York's allocation included all the rebuilt B16/2s and B16/3s, with Neville Hill's fleet being unrebuilt B16/1s only. In 1955, ten B16/1s were transferred to Heaton and a couple went to Selby and Leeds Starbeck. The Heaton engines were used, amongst other duties, for freight and summer Saturday specials on the Newcastle-Carlisle route. Between 1955 and 1958 summer traffic to Filey and Scarborough was heavy and the B16s were very involved. The York engines worked to Scarborough and stopping trains to Darlington. In the summer of 1955, whilst holidaying at Whitby, I spent a day trainspotting at York, and travelled on a midweek *Scarborough Flyer* with A8 69890 to Malton where I picked up the full train from Scarborough headed by York's B16/3 61472 (formerly 843, 1403 then renumbered to avoid duplication with the B1s). Whilst at York I decided to take a trip out to Thirsk and just missed B16/3 61434 on the northbound stopping service, getting a V2 in both directions instead.

A Newcastle-Birmingham express unusually sported a B16/3 in 1954 which gave a creditable account of itself:

Darlington-York
61434 – B16/3
10 chs 318/330 tons
4 August 1954

Miles	Location	Times	Speeds	Gradients	Schedule
0	Darlington	00.00			T
3.5	Croft Spa	04.50	51		
5.1	Eryholme Junction	07.54	53	1/391 R	
10.2	Danby Wiske	13.10	63½/60	1/650 F	
14.0	Northallerton	16.50	61	L	
17.3	Otterington	20.03	72	1/629 F	
21.8	Thirsk	23.43	69	L	
26.0	Sessay	27.20	68	L	
27.8	Pilmoor	29.17/36.47	sigs stand		
31.5	Raskelf	41.40	50		
33.6	Alne	43.59	58½	L	
35.0	Tollerton	45.25	61		
39.3	Beningbrough	49.20	67½	L	
	Skelton Junction	-	sigs		
44.0	York	57.48	(45 net)		13 L

This is the only record I've seen where a B16 reached 70mph and the net time, which was exactly the schedule, the only run where a mile-a-minute start-to-stop performance was all but recorded. In contrast to this, the same engine was recorded on the 2.15pm York – Birmingham between York and Rotherham where such high speeds are less usual, and time would have barely been kept without the final signal checks.

York-Rotherham
61434 – B16/3
8 chs, 237 tons
4 February 1955

Miles	Location	Times	Speeds	Gradients	Schedule
0	York	00.00			¼ L
3.8	Copmanthorpe	07.36	44	L	
7.7	Bolton Percy	12.38	48	L	
10.9	Church Fenton	16.26	51/45		3½ L
12.9	Sherburn-in-Elmet	19.01	53	L	
16.8	Burton Salmon	23.45	pws 30*		6 L
19.4	Ferrybridge	27.12	50		
21.4	Pontyfract	30.06	39½	1/122/152 R	2¼ L (Recovery time)
24.1	Ackworth	33.47	52½	1/156 F	
28.4	Moorthorpe	38.59	44/53/pws 20*	1/150 R,1/150 F	3¼ L
	Frickley	-	29½	1/150 R	
33.7	Bolton-on-Dearne	46.54	53	1/150 F	3¾ L
35.2	Mexborough West Jn	48.41	38* sigs		3¾ L

York-Rotherham
61434 – B16/3
8 chs, 237 tons
4 February 1955

Miles	Location	Times	Speeds	Gradients	Schedule
36.2	Swinton	50.31	18* sigs		3¾ L
	Parkgate	-	13*/ sigs cont		
42.3	Rotherham	62.48	(53½ net)		9 L

The performance of a B16/1 was recorded in 1957 between Scarborough and York and is shown below and is probably typical of B16 performance on the Leeds – Scarborough services.

During 1958 and 1959, J.N. Proudlock was a regular traveller between Leeds and York and timed the runs and kept meticulous records. I have analysed twelve eastbound and four westbound logs with five different B16/1s and three different B16/3s and find that on the whole they kept poor time. Most trains stopped at Crossgates and Church Fenton and usually dropped a minute or two on each section arriving at destination over five minutes late – more if signal checks were incurred. Eastbound on the 1 in 162 climb out of Leeds to Crossgates, the B16/1s with 10 coaches sustained the low 30s – the B16/3s had lesser loads but on the one run with ten coaches 61472 held 38mph on the climb. The B16/1s did not exceed 60mph on the 1 in 133/1 in 145 descent from Micklefield to Church Fenton and were usually in the 55-58 range, but the B16/3s were more free running and achieved 65-68mph. One B16/1, 61415, was priming badly and could only make 22mph on the climb to Crossgates and dropped over ten minutes on the whole journey. In the other direction one B16/1, 61411, was on a non-stop service and would have kept time with a 200 ton load but for signal checks approaching Leeds. 61411's crew went out of York hard and achieved 72mph at Ulleskelf on the level equalling the maximum speed on the Darlington-York run above though it was a much lighter load. Interestingly, most of the B16/1s performed better than the one solitary B16/3 westbound service. Again B16/1 61415 seems to have been in poor condition and dropped six minutes without checks with 250 tons. It could manage no more than 47mph out of York on the level before the climb after Church Fenton.

Although the three subgroups were often used indiscriminately, the B16/1s began to be withdrawn from 1958, the first to go (apart from the war victim) being 61474 (ex 845).

2.10pm Scarborough-York-Leeds
61411 – B16/1
9 chs
Sunday 1 September 1957

Miles	Location	Times	Speeds	Gradients	Schedule
0	Scarborough	00.00			1¼ L
3.0	Seamer	06.15	47/53	1/220/255 F	
7.9	Ganton	11.29	57	L	
12.8	Heslerton	16.49	55	L	
16.7	Rillington	21.02	54/59	1/352 R: 1/569 F	
21.0	Malton	26.24			1¾ L
0		00.00			1 L
2.8	Huttons Ambo	05.49	41/39	1/630 R	
5.4	Castle Howard	10.04	38		
	Kirkham Abbey	-	33	1/464 R/ L	
9.6	Barton Hill	16.09	50/48	1/289 R	
12.0	Flaxton	18.56	54	1/310 F	
14.6	Strensall	21.39	61		
17.0	Haxby	23.56	64	L	
	Bootham Junction	-	sigs 20*		
21.0	York	30.41	(29½ net)		3¾ L

B16/1 61412 storms up the 1 in 160 to Crossgates with a Manchester Exchange – Scarborough summer Saturday relief formed of ex-LMS coaches, 6 August 1958. A.C. Gilbert/ MLS Collection

Another Scarborough Saturday relief formed of a motley collection of LNER rolling stock climbs Crossgates bank out of Leeds behind Neville Hill's B16/1 61425, 15 June 1957. B.K.B. Green/ MLS Collection

A third Neville Hill B16/1, 61428, climbs out of Leeds to Crossgates with a Scarborough relief train composed of some non-corridor LNER stock, 1 April 56. The driver is clearly expecting the photographer and is putting on a show.
B.K.B. Green/MLS Collection

Another Neville Hill B16/1, 61471, on the 8.50am Stalybridge-Filey Holiday Camp and Scarborough at Market Weighton on the 1 in 95/100 climb to Enthorpe summit, 25 August 1956.
A.C. Gilbert/MLS Collection

Six more went in 1959 and twelve in 1960, after many had been in store at their home depots. Four B16/1s (61411, 61414, 61416 and 61447) were suddenly transferred in November 1960 to Mirfield between Leeds and Huddersfield, a new home for the class, replaced by four B16/3s (61461, 61464, 61468 and 61476) in September 1961 when all other remaining B16/1s were condemned. The Mirfield engines were mainly working coal trains, although they still appeared on summer Saturdays on Leeds-York-Scarborough trains. The Gresley and Thompson rebuilds lingered on, gradually diminishing in number until June/July 1964.

One of the odd things about their operation seems to have been sudden decisions to move whole swathes of the class to new depots rather than the usual occasional reallocation of single examples. I have been unable to fathom the rationale behind such decisions apart from the wartime concentration which was to minimise the holding of stores and parts for those engines at a time when the country needed to preserve metal resources for the war munitions.

York's B16/3 61467 descends the bank to Market Weighton with the 10.50am SO Fliey Camp-Derby, 25 August 1956. A.C. Gilbert/MLS Collection

Neville Hill's B16/1 61447 passing York Helgate with an unfitted goods train for Dringhouses Yard, c1956. Real Photographs/ MLS Collection

B16/1 61431 takes a 'breather' at Torside Signalbox as the fireman contacts the signalman with a train of eastbound mineral empties, c1956. Torside Reservoir is below. MLS Slide Collection

B16/3 61468 waits with a train at the north end of York station, c1956. MLS Collection

A Stephenson Locomotive Society/ Manchester Locomotive Society joint *Tees-Tyne* railtour from Darlington around the Hartlepool area at Wellfield station, 2 September 1956. It was headed by B16/1 61443 of York for most of the tour although G5 67284 was involved at Bishop Auckland and 70033 brought the connecting train from Manchester. N. Fields/ MLS Collection

B16/3 61463 pulls out of York on a summer Saturday train from Scarborough to Sheffield, c1962. The large group of enthusiasts on the platform (and track!) are examining something unidentified but of interest on the adjacent platform. It looks to me like the low lying brake tender of a new Class 37 diesel fitted also with snow plough. Any better ideas? J. Davenport/ MLS Collection

A York B16/3, 61420, ambles through Doncaster with an up goods, 23 May 1959. J.D. Darby/MLS Collection

B16/3 61467 passes through Doncaster with an up freight, 1959.
David Maidment

B16/3 61418 taking water at Newcastle Central with the SLS/MLS/King's College Durham Railway Society railtour, 13 October 1962. V3 tank 67636 had worked the special from Durham to West Auckland Colliery where 61418 took over for the rest of the tour to Stockton, Sunderland, Newcastle, Consett and back to Durham. Late running and a failed express on the main line and the stalling of 61418 on the 1 in 36 to Consett eventually caused the special to end the day three hours late.
A.C. Gilbert/MLS Collection

Chapter 4

THE GREAT EASTERN 4-6-0s

The GE 1500 class (LNER B12) – 1911

After 1901 the expresses of the Great Eastern Railway Company were in the hands of the competent 'Claud Hamilton' 1900 4-4-0s introduced the previous year, but like everywhere else in the country, train loads were increasing as large numbers of the population became more prosperous and travelled both socially and for business purposes. This posed problems for the Company as its track permitted only restricted axleweights and its turntables restricted locomotive lengths.

The Locomotive Superintendent, James Holden, led the Stratford Drawing Office in the design of a 4-6-0 that not only had to be powerful enough to cope with the increasing loads for trains like the continental expresses, but met the size and weight limits. In 1908, authority was given for the design of such a 4-6-0, identified as order number S69, and the basic 'Claud Hamilton' was enlarged with 20 rather than 19 inch diameter

Great Eastern 'Claud Hamilton' 4-4-0, No.1828, in the Company's blue livery, the precursor to Holden's proposed 4-6-0, built with Belpaire firebox in 1909. This became LNER D15 8828, and BR 62579, being withdrawn in the early 1950s still in its original D15 condition. H. Gordon Tidey/MLS Collection

cylinders, boiler size increased, a Belpaire firebox provided and coupled wheel diameter reduced from the 4-4-0's 7ft to 6ft 6in to increase tractive effort. With the use of the standard GE short tender, the wheelbase was contained to 48ft 3in and thus just fitted on the routes' turntables. The first five locomotives, numbered 1500-1504 were delivered from Stratford Works between December 1911 and May 1912, their key dimensions being:

Cylinders (2 inside)	20in x 28in
Coupled wheel diameter	6ft 6in
Bogie wheel diameter	3ft 3in
Stephenson's valve gear	10in piston valves
Boiler pressure	180psi
Heating surface	1,834.2sqft (incl 201.6sqft superheating)
Grate area	26.5sqft
Axleload	15 tons 13 cwt
Weight – Engine	63 tons
– Tender	38 tons 6 cwt
– Total	101 tons 6 cwt
Water capacity	3,700 gallons
Coal capacity	4 tons
Tractive effort	21,969lbs

Holden 4-6-0
1501 running in on a stopping train shortly after its construction, 1912. It is in the GE lined dark blue livery.
MLS Collection

Holden 4-6-0 1505 at Liverpool Street on an express for Norwich, 1912. It is in the GE lined dark blue livery which would be replaced by plain grey after the beginning of the First World War. MLS Collection

These dimensions, particularly the low axleload for a powerful 4-6-0, gave the engine a wide route availability, a capability that would become very useful beyond the boundaries of the GE in future years. The success of the new engines led to further orders, with Stratford Works building 1505-1514 between February and June 1913, 1515-1519 in November and December, 1520 - 1529 between April and September 1914 and 1530-1535 from November 1914 to March 1915. The last one, 1535, was officially a replacement for 1506 which was condemned as beyond repair after a collision at Colchester in July 1913. A further five engines were ordered from Stratford and 1536-1538 were built in May and July 1915, but the use of Stratford Works for munitions and war supplies delayed the building of 1539 and 1540 to the summer of 1917. After the war leisure travel increased rapidly and more 4-6-0s were needed rapidly so while Stratford engaged in the building of 1561-1570 between March and June 1920, orders were placed with W. Beardmore & Co. of Glasgow to build 1541-1560, which were delivered between June 1920 and June 1921. Full details of construction dates and the weight diagram are in the Appendix, where it will be noted that by some quirk, 1548 and 1549 were built out of order, at the end of the series of Beardmore engines.

The engines were right-hand drive and were fitted with Westinghouse air-brakes as was standard for the Great Eastern. They were equipped with the Schmidt superheater initially, though two, 1513 and 1514 were tested with the Robinson superheater and this was then fitted to 1536 onwards and eventually to all the B12s as the LNER classified these GE 4-6-0s. Because of the coal strike in 1921, 1525 was equipped to burn oil, but this was short-lived. At first, the 1500 class locomotives were painted in the GE dark blue with red lining livery, but those built after the start of the First World War were painted plain grey. The twenty Beardmore constructed engines were also grey but lined in white. The cab numberplate was replaced by large yellow numerals on the tender. After the Grouping they were painted in the LNER lined apple green livery, 1534 in 1923 being one of the early engines turned out in the proposed livery for inspection by the directors. The grey livery lasted on some engines until 1929. All GE locomotives had 7,000 added to their number. From 1929 the number was displayed on the cabside with the tender inscribed LNER.

After the 1926 strikes and poor supply of quality fuel, the need for more engines of sufficient power on the LNER's GE section was vital and at first this was met by the transfer of twenty Gresley GN K2 moguls. Doncaster had the designs of the B17 'Sandringham' class in hand and a proposed 2-6-4T for the Southend line, but the derailment of the Southern's 'River' 2-6-4T at Sevenoaks in 1927 created doubts about the suitability of tank engines for express work. As a short term solution therefore, the LNER

B12 1534E repainted in the LNER lined apple green livery in 1923 before renumbering – at the Grouping ex GE engines were identified with the letter 'E' after their number until in 1924 7,000 was added to all the numbers of GE locomotives. Note the initial inscription L&NER on the tender – the '&' was soon dropped. MLS Collection

8549, the former 1549, now repainted and renumbered in the LNER livery, at Stratford, c1925. F. Moore/ MLS Collection

ordered ten more B12s from Beyer, Peacock & Co. with Lentz poppet valve gear and slightly extended smokeboxes. The Company quoted £5,975 per locomotive and although this was not the lowest tender, only Beyer, Peacock could deliver in the timescale required. In fact, the contract ran into difficulties with late delivery causing legal arguments over penalty clauses and counter claims from the Company that the railway had made considerable alterations to the drawings. In the end, the claims cancelled out each other and the ten locomotives were delivered between August 1928 and October of that year and numbered 8571-8580, the GE engines at the Grouping being renumbered 8500-8560 with the gap of 8506 as the withdrawn number 1506 was not filled. The 1928 engines were classified B12/2s, the original design therefore B12/1s.

Before this, Gresley had been experimenting with methods to improve heat retention and in 1926 fitted 8509 with a Worthington-Simpson feed pump and heater, removed in 1929. In 1927 he tested A.C.F.I. feed water heating apparatus as developed in France (Gresley had taken great interest in continental steam locomotive development). This equipment, mounted on the boiler behind the chimney, was fitted at first to 8505, 8517 and 8523 and was successful and between 1931 and 1933 an additional fifty B12s were fitted numbered:

> 8500, 8501, 8503, 8504, 8507-8515, 8518-8522, 8524, 8526-8532, 8534-8540, 8542-8544, 8546, 8548, 8549, 8553, 8554, 8556, 8560, 8563, 8564, 8567-8570, 8577.

However, from November 1937 the equipment was removed as the maintenance costs were not offset by the savings. This was done as new boilers were fitted. Two sets removed from other engines were used on 8551 and 8552 in 1934, so with the three initial experimental engines, some fifty-five were equipped with this unsightly apparatus and the converted engines were nicknamed 'Hikers' as their feed water heaters looked like back packs – others, particularly on the GE, called them 'Camels'.

The Beyer, Peacock Company constructed Lentz poppet valve gear B12/2, 8575 in Works photographic grey, as built, 1928. MLS Collection

B12/2 8571 in LNER livery in service, c1929. F. Moore/MLS Collection

8517, one of the first three B12s that Gresley equipped with ACFI feed water heating apparatus in 1931 at Stratford in that year. MLS Collection

One of the B12s fitted with ACFI equipment between 1931 and 1933, 8520 at Gorton, 30 July 1933. MLS Collection

ACFI fitted 8536 in a later version of the LNER livery, c1935. MLS Collection

In 1930, Gresley, under pressure from Thompson at Stratford, applied the learning of the benefits of long travel valves to a B12, having modified his Pacifics after the 1925 locomotive exchange with a GWR 'Castle'. 8579 was the engine chosen and a decision was made to remove the Lentz gear from 8571-8580 and rebuild with Stephenson gear and long travel valves. Also by this time renewal of GE routes with heavier track enabled the use of engines with greater axleloads and this meant that the B12s could be rebuilt with larger boilers. 8579 was provided with a larger boiler with round top firebox at the same time as its valve gear was modified in May 1932. Revised dimensions of the rebuilt engines, classified as a B12/3 were:

Boiler barrel diameter	5ft 6in (compared with 5ft 1½ in of B12/1)
Heating surface	1,874sqft incl 315sqft superheater surface
Grate area	31sqft (compared with 26.5sqft)
Engine weight	69½ tons (an increase of 6½ tons)
Axleload	17 tons (compared with 15 tons 13 cwt)

8579, the first B12 reboilered and with long lap valve travel and reclassified from B12/2 to B12/3 in May 1932, seen here after its next heavy overhaul at Stratford, 26 May 1935. MLS Collection

The rebuilding was clearly successful and fifty-four were rebuilt between 1932 and 1944, leaving the remaining B12/1s whose low axleweight was of great value on the of the LNER's Scottish lines. The engines rebuilt were:

1932:	8516, 8576, 8578-8580
1933:	8569, 8571-8575
1934:	8517, 8525, 8540, 8557, 8577
1935:	8509, 8518, 8519, 8523, 8527, 8535, 8542, 8544, 8554-8556, 8558, 8564, 8567
1936:	8541, 8545, 8550, 8559, 8566
1937:	8510, 8512, 8522, 8533, 8538, 8547, 8553, 8561, 8565
1938:	8514, 8515, 8530, 8546, 8562
1939:	8537
1940:	8520
1941:	8568
1943:	8570
1944:	8549

From 1941, some of the remaining B12/1s retained for work in Scotland were reboilered to current LNER standards, acquiring a new round-topped boiler and firebox in place of the Belpaire box. Four of fifteen designed in 1941 were put on 8508 in 1943, 8505 and 8507 in 1944 and 8504 in 1948. Many of the new boilers went to Stratford's J20 0-6-0s but more were built and 1511 and 1524 were equipped in 1946, 1500 in 1947 and 1526 and 1532 in 1948. These engines were reclassified as B12/4s. The 25A boilers for these engines had a heating surface of 1,699.1sqft including 201.6sqft superheater surface. Engine weight was just under two tons heavier than the B12/1s and axleload was heavier by 6 cwt which did not preclude them from the Scottish secondary routes in the north east of the country.

8514 went into the Works at the end of 1938 and was rebuilt as a B12/3 early the following year. It is here at Stratford ex-works, 7 May 1939. MLS Collection

B12/1 61536 ex-works from Inverurie and repainted in LNER lined green with BR number and lettering at Keith, 30 July 1948. MLS Collection

B12/1 61563 at Ballater still in LNER lined apple green livery but renumbered and early BR tender lettering, 18 July 1949. J.D. Darby/ MLS Collection

B12/4 61507 with the round topped new boiler at Keith shed, 2 September 1952. A.C. Gilbert/MLS Collection

B12/1 61543 on the turntable at Elgin (note – not much room to spare!), 15 June 1951. This photo and that of 61507 and 61563 appear to be lined out on tender and boiler rings only with no lining of the cab, in contrast to the photo of 61536 in 1948. J.D. Darby/MLS Collection

B12/1 61539 has been repainted in the BR mixed traffic lined black livery with the small 'lion & wheel' icon on the tender. It stands in Ballater shed with steam up ready for action, 2 September 1952. N.R. Knight/MLS Collection

A B12/1, 1534, was withdrawn in 1945 and 1548 in 1946 and six further withdrawals in 1947 including four B12/3s. Seventy-two engines – fifteen B12/1s, seven B12/4s and fifty B12/3s were taken into BR ownership and after reverting to their former GE numbers in the LNER 1946 renumbering scheme, became BR 61500-61580 at nationalisation in 1948. However 1500, 1509, 1510 and 1517 were withdrawn in 1948 and 1949 before displaying their BR number. The Scottish based B12/1s and B12/4s were gradually replaced by LNER B1s and BR standard engines. The last B12/4 was withdrawn in 1953, and B12/1s 61502 and 61539 lasted until 1954. The withdrawal of the B12/3s took place steadily in the 1950s and nearly all had gone as the Brush Type 3 diesels came onto the GE section in 1958. The last of the GE built engines was 61535 withdrawn in December 1959. Seven of the LNER built engines were withdrawn that year with just 61572 surviving into the 1960s, only being withdrawn in September 1961 before ultimate preservation.

B12/3 61576 rebuilt from the 1928 B12/2, in plain black BR livery with large 'lion & wheel' emblem on the tender at Yarmouth South Town, May 1951. J. Davenport/MLS Collection

B12/3 61512 stands at Liverpool Street at the head of a semi-fast train for Shenfield and Southend Victoria, c1953. Some B12s were painted plain black. Others, like this one, in the BR lined mixed traffic livery. Another B12/3 is also awaiting departure on one of the platforms on the eastern half of the station. It bears an express headcode and is probably heading a train for Chelmsford, Colchester and Ipswich. MLS Collection

B12/3 61558 in plain black livery but with unpainted beaded splashers as many ended their days. 61558 was one of the last to be withdrawn in 1959 and the author found it at the head of the down *Fenman* (4.36pm Liverpool Street – King's Lynn) in the spring of 1958, though by then it had the full mixed traffic livery in excellent condition. It is illustrated here at Stratford earlier, 26 July 1953. MLS Collection

One of the GN main line based Grantham B12/3s 61565, in lined black at its home depot taking water, 3 April 1955.
MLS Collection

B12/3 61573 awaiting repair at Stratford, c1955. It was not withdrawn until January 1959.
MLS Collection

Operations

The first batch of the 1500s was based at Stratford and Norwich for the main expresses between London and the Norfolk city and for the London-Harwich continental boat trains.

The performance of these low axleload 4-6-0s was exceptional especially on the heavy boat trains and caused much favourable comment in the pages of the *Railway Magazine.* Some of the best prior to the Grouping are tabled below.

		8.30pm Liverpool Street-Harwich (Parkeston Quay)											
		1501			**1567**			**1565**			**1566**		
		325/345tons			**325/345 tons**			**388/420 tons**			**388/415 tons**		
Miles	**Location**	**Times**	**Speeds**		**Times**	**Speeds**		**Times**	**Speeds**		**Times**	**Speeds**	
0	Liverpool St	00.00			00.00			00.00			00.00		
1.1	Bethnal green	03.15			03.25			03.10			03.25		
4	Stratford	07.55	sigs 25*	T	08.25	sigs	½ L	07.35	50	½ E	07.50		¼ E
7.3	Ilford	12.50			12.50	50		12.05	48½		11.55		
10	Chadwell H'th	16.05		1 L	15.55		1 L	15.00		T	14.50		¼ E
12.4	Romford	18.50	54		18.40	53½		17.40	54		17.25	55	
15	Harold Wood	21.50	55		21.45			20.35	56		20.15	58/sigs	
18.2	Brentwood	26.00			26.10			24.40			24.25		
19.3	Ingrave Box	27.55	33		28.10	31½		26.40	33		26.25	33 (1/103R)	
20.2	Shenfield	29.05		1 L	29.25		1½ L	27.55		1 E	27.40		1¼ E
	Ingatestone	-	70½		-	70½		-	67		-	71½	
29.7	Chelmsford	38.05		T	38.35		½ L	36.50	54	1 ¼ E	36.30	55	1½ E
35.9	Hatfield P'vl	44.25	61		45.15	50		43.25	60		42.50	62	
38.6	Witham	47.00	68	1 E	47.55	68	T	46.05	65	2 E	45.35	66	2½ E
42.3	Kelvedon	50.25			51.20			49.40			49.10		
	Hill House Bx	-	55		-	55		-	50		-	54 (1/222R)	
46.6	Marks Tey	54.55			55.45			54.30			53.40		
50.4	Lexham Box	58.30	64½		59.10	68		58.10	67		57.05	70½	
51.7	Colchester	60.20	pws	¾ E	60.35		½ E	59.30		2 ½ E	58.25		3½ E
54.1	Parsons H'th	64.20			63.30	43½		62.20	44½		61.40	40 (1/144R)	
	Dedham Box	-	pws 5*		-	60		-	65		-	68	
59.5	Manningtree	71.30		1½ L	69.55		1 E	68.20		1 ¾ E	67.20		2¾ E
61.2	Mistley	76.00			73.05			71.35			70.15		
65.1	Wrabness	80.50	sigs		77.45	54/66		76.20			75.20	easy	
68.9	Parkeston Q.	86.00		4 L	82.05		T	81.05		1 E	80.15		1¾ E
		(81½ net)			(81 net)			(81 net)			(80 net)		

The climb to Ingrave Box starts with just over two miles of 1 in 103 after Harold Wood, a half mile at 1 in 85 after Brentwood and a final half mile at 1 in 155 to the summit. Cecil J. Allen was on the footplate of the fourth run above with Driver Chapman and recorded the maximum output for a 1500 in original condition on the tight schedule with the heavier load as far as Colchester. After that as they were nearly four minutes ahead of schedule, the engine was eased. These runs were the more remarkable in that the fireman had an unusually long distance between the firehole and the front of the tender – some eight feet compared with the more usual 5-6 feet. The grate, however, was flat for the first half and then sloping which meant that coal did not need to be thrown right to the front as the coal would shake down. Having the engines allocated to regular crews helped.

6.32am Parkeston Quay-Liverpool Street

		1518			1567			1505			1566		
		272/285 tons			272/285 tons			272/285 tons			324/340 tons		
Miles	**Location**	**Times**	**Speeds**		**Times**	**Speeds**		**Times**	**Speeds**		**Times**	**Speeds**	
0	Parkeston Q	00.00			00.00			00.00			00.00		
3.6	Wrabness	08.55	27		08.55	27		08.25			07.10	(1/134R)	
7.7	Mistley	13.40	pws		13.50			13.05			11.25		
9.4	Manningtree	16.30		2½ L	16.10		2¼ L	15.15		1¼ L	13.25	sigs 10*	½ E
12.9	Ardleigh	23.40	27		22.15	34		21.50	26½		20.05		
17.2	Colchester	29.40		4¾ L	26.55		2 L	27.00		2 L	24.50		¼ E
22.3	Marks Tey	37.45	pws		33.25			33.30			30.55	51/43	
26.6	Kelvedon	42.40			38.00			38.15			35,25	66	
30.3	Witham	46.15	64	5¼ L	41.25	65	½ L	41.50	64	¾ L	38.40	67	2¼ E
33	Hatfield Pvl	49.15			44.40			44.50			41.25	58/65	
39.2	Chelmsford	55.45		3¾ L	51.05		1 E	51.10		¾ E	47.20	60/sigs 40*	
45.3	Ingatestone	63.10			58.40			58.10			54.35		
48.7	Shenfield	67.30			62.45			62.20			58.30	55	
49.6	Ingrave Box	68.55	41		64.00	38		63.35	41½		59.40	48½	
50.7	Brentwood	70.25			65.35			65.00			60.50		
53.9	Harold Wood	73.15	71½		68.35	69		68.00	69		63.35	76½	
58.9	Chadwell H	78.15		3¼ L	78.00	sigs	3 L	73.05		2 E	73.30	sigs	1½ E
64.9	Stratford	85.00		2 L	85.20	sigs		80.10		2¾ E	80.30	sigs	2½ E
68.9	Liverpool St	92.40	sigs	1¾ L	94.20	sigs	3¼ L	87.35		3½ E	93.00	sigs	2 L

Chapman's effort with 1566 and the heavier load (with the encouragement of Cecil J. Allen) was in a superior locomotive performance class to the other runs, although it paid for its exuberance with severe delays after Harold Wood and thus finished a couple of minutes late, whereas 1505 running closer to time at that point ran in unchecked and arrived early. Below is a further run from the same period on a Norwich express with a 12 coach load to Ipswich, reduced thereafter.

8.30am Liverpool Street-Norwich/Lowestoft
1527
12 chs, 345 tons
7 chs, 200t from Ipswich

Miles	**Location**	**Times**	**Speeds**		**Gradients**
0	Liverpool St	00.00		T	
	Stratford	09.25			
10	Chadwell Heath	16.55	52		
19.3	Ingrave Box	29.25	28½		1/84 R
20.2	Shenfield	30.50		2L	
30	Chelmsford	40.20			
38.6	Witham	49.40	64½	½ L	
46.6	Marks Tey	58.20			
51.7	Colchester	65.45	(64 net)	¾ L	
0		00.00		1¼ L	

8.30am Liverpool Street-Norwich/Lowestoft
1527
12 chs, 345 tons
7 chs, 200t from Ipswich

Miles	Location	Times	Speeds		Gradients
7.8	Manningtree	-	64½/ sigs		
13.5	Belstead	-	45		1/145 R
17	Ipswich	23.00	(22½ net)	1 ¼ L	(Detach 5 coaches)
0		00.00			
2.3	Bramford	04.20			
11.75	Stowmarket	14.30	Spl stop SO		
0		00.00			
2.3	Haughley	04.10	45½		1/148: 1/131 R
5.9	Finningham	08.40			
14.2	Diss	16.50	66½		
19.7	Tivetshall	22.55			
32.2	Trowse Upper Jn	36.10	sigs stand/sigs stand		
34.25	Norwich	46.05 (50 net from Ipswich without spl stop, schedule 56 mins)			

1520 on the 3.10pm Liverpool Street-Ipswich with 9 coaches, 290 tons, got a bad signal check at Stratford and then dragging brakes until stopped and released at Gidea Park. It then accelerated to 44 at Brentwood, fell to 30½ at Ingrave summit and passed Shenfield nine minutes late. With 68 at Margaretting, 67 at Witham, the lateness had been reduced to five minutes at Colchester. A final 67 at Manningtree and 47 on Bentley Bank saw 1520 complete the 48½ miles from Shenfield-Ipswich in 52 minutes 50 seconds (50 net).

In the reverse direction, 1516 had a full 15 coach 430 ton load on the up *Norfolk Coast Express* completing the 130 miles from North Walsham to London in 154 minutes, arriving five minutes early in the capital. It had gained 50 seconds to Tivetshall and did the 31¾ miles on to Ipswich in 32 minutes 40 seconds. The 17 miles from the Ipswich stop to passing Colchester took 21 minutes 10 seconds and the 13.2 miles onto Witham gained a further couple of minutes, but there was a two minute signal stand before reaching Chelmsford. Speed reached the low 70s on the descent from Brentwood and despite constant checks from Chadwell Heath, engine and crew were still gaining time.

1521 on the 11.33am Norwich - Liverpool Street knocked nearly four minutes off the 54 minute schedule to Ipswich with a top speed of 76½ at Haughley, but with only seven coaches. At Ipswich four coaches were added and 1521 left with 11 coaches, 300 tons. The run up from Ipswich is tabled below.

Ipswich-Liverpool Street
11.33am ex Norwich
1521
11 chs, 300 tons

Miles	Location	Times	Speeds	Schedule	Gradients
0	Ipswich	00.00		2 L	
3.75	Belstead	07.35	35½		1/120 R
	Manningtree	13.40	68		1/157 F: L
17	Colchester	22.20	44½		1/165: 1/128 R

Ipswich-Liverpool Street
11.33am ex Norwich
1521
11 chs, 300 tons

Miles	Location	Times	Speeds	Schedule	Gradients
	Marks Tey	-	62		
30.2	Witham	36.15	65		L
39	Chelmsford	45.40			
	Ingatestone	-	50		L
48.6	Shenfield	56.40	47½		
	Ingrave summit	-	44		1/136 R
50.75	Brentwood	59.10	77		1/103 F
	Romford	-	72		1/380 F
58.8	Chadwell Heath	66.05	70½		
61.4	llford	69.05/69.50		3 E	
	Stratford	-	sigs stand		
68.75	Liverpool Street	85.00	(79 net)	1 L	

The 1500s also worked on the Cambridge route, where substantial loads were carried. Three runs from 1913 recorded in the 1914 *Railway Magazine* are shown below.

Cambridge-Liverpool Street

		1509		**1509**		**1520**		
		10chs/270 tons		**12 chs/300 tons**		**13 chs 365 tons**		
Miles	**Location**	**Times**	**Speed**	**Times**	**Speed**	**Times**	**Speed**	
0	Cambridge	00.00		00.00		00.00		
3.3	Shelford	05.40	54/46	05.50	53/43	05.49		1/276 R
10	Gt Chesterf'd	13.10		13.40		13.26		
14	Audley End	18.10	sigs	19.15	58	18.46		1/135 R
20.1	Elsenham	28.40		26.55	40	25.46		1/176 R
25.3	B'.Stortford	34.45	(31¼ net)	33.15		31.34		3 ½ E
0		00.00		00.00		00.00		
5.9	Harlow	08.25		09.00		08.24		
13.3	Broxbourne	16.10		16.30		15.28		
17.6	Waltham	21.05		21.15		19.50		
24.6	Tottenham	29.00	sigs	29.05	sigs	26.36	sigs	
30.4	Liverpool St	43.45	(40 net)	44.55	(40 net)	42.41	(37 ½ net)	

1520 had brought 250 tons to Ely with a top speed of 66mph, made up to 365 tons at the latter station. It then covered the 14.7 miles on to Cambridge in 22 minutes 13 seconds arriving on time.

The GE engines were economical compared with their other pre-Grouping LNER 4-6-0s. GE engines cost 9.6d per mile, GNR Atlantics 9.7, GC engines 10.8 and NER 11.8

The GE figures were similar to LNWR and LSWR engines, but the Midland and GWR both recorded just 8.5d per mile for their passenger engines of the same period.

1501 running in on a stopping train composed of six-wheelers shortly after delivery from Stratford Works, 1912.
MLS Collection

Newly delivered 1503 heads a 'Claud Hamilton' round-topped boiler 4-4-0 (LNER D14) on a Great Eastern express, 1912.
MLS Collection

1510, now painted the wartime plain grey is accelerating hard on a heavy GE express, c1914. H. Gordon Tidey/MLS Collection

The allocation at the end of 1921 after all seventy locomotives had been delivered was as follows:

Stratford:	28
Norwich:	7
Cambridge:	9
Parkeston:	5
Ipswich:	19
Yarmouth:	2

Continental traffic grew considerably in the 1920s and in 1925 the LNER added two Pullman cars to the formation so that the B12s were faced with regular loads of around 465 tons gross, though the schedule was eased to 87 minutes for the 68.9 miles.

Two B12s were tested on passenger and perishable freight services from Leeds Copley Hill and Doncaster immediately after the Grouping (1552 and 1561) in the period when the LNER management was trying to assess the best distribution of the assets absorbed from the pre-Grouping companies, but this experiment was short-lived. However, in 1926 8526 was tested on the LNER's routes in the north-east

1536E identified as a former GE engine immediately after the Grouping and before the application of 7,000 added to ex-GE numbers, leaving Colchester with a heavy 13-coach express, 1923. H. Gordon Tidey/MLS Collection

The day *Hook Continental* on a date when the bookings could be contained in a five coach set. 8535 heads the boat train passing Charlton, c1925. W. Potter/MLS Collection

8566, renumbered by the LNER in 1924, heads a GE express formed of two six-wheel non-corridor coaches and eight bogie coaches, c1925. MLS Collection

8570, the last of the Stratford built B12s delivered in June 1920, with a heavier Harwich boat train, climbing Brentwood Bank during the quadrupling engineering work, c1925. MLS Collection

8532 finds itself on humble freight duty hauling an unfitted goods train up Brentwood Bank, c1928. F.R. Hebron/ MLS Collection

of Scotland where the G.N.S. 4-4-0s had been the only permitted power because of the route weight restrictions. The test was a success, although no immediate follow-up was implemented as the GE section was short of power until Gresley's B17s became available to replace some of the B12s there.

Another area outside the GE where the B12s were active was the former Great Central line to Manchester when in 1927 the former Harwich-York boat train acquired a Manchester and Liverpool portion. Gorton's GC fleet and Ipswich's B12s shared the through working on alternate days, but as the GC engine had to come off at March and be replaced by a D15 (because of height restrictions) a B12, 8557, was transferred to Gorton and worked this turn for a year until joined by 8538 in 1928. This engine worked the Gorton diagram until 1929 when a new B17 became available.

In 1928 the ten B12/2s were delivered to the GE section and because of route strengthening and new rolling stock developments the B12s and B12/2s were widely used throughout East Anglia. The 1931 allocation was:

Stratford:	29
Ipswich:	17
Cambridge:	12
Norwich:	6
Parkeston:	7
Colchester:	7
Yarmouth:	2

Performances on the Harwich boat trains and Norwich expresses were compared with the new 'Sandringhams' in the 1929/30 period with very little difference to show. Three runs to Ipswich and one as far as Manningtree on a Harwich boat train are shown on next page.

		Liverpool Street-Manningtree-Ipswich											
		8580	**(B12/2)**		**8535**			**8515**			**8501**		
		294/315 tons			**347/365 tons**			**417/445 tons**			**438/470 tons**		
		Boat Train			**4.55pm L.St**			**3.10pm L.St**			**3.10pm L.St**		
Miles	**Location**	**Times**	**Speed**		**Times**	**Speed**		**Times**	**Speed**		**Times**	**Speed**	
0	Liverpool St	00.00			00.00			00.00			00.00		
1.1	Bethnal Gn	03.45			03.45			-			-		
4	Stratford	08.15			08.15			08.25			08.30		
7.3	Ilford	12.10	56		12.51			12.40			12.50		
10	Chadwell H.	15.00	57		15.44			15.40	54		15.55	52	
12.4	Romford	17.30			18.17			18.30			18.45		
15	Harold Wood	20.15	61		21.10	56		21.40	49		22.00	48	
18.2	Brentwood	24.05			25.15			26.25			27.05		
19.3	Ingrave Box	26.05	34		27.05	31		28.55	26		29.45	24	
20.2	Shenfield	27.15	70		28.18	sigs		30.15	70		31.15	68	
23.6	Ingatestone	30.45			33.37	62		33.45			34.45		
29.7	Chelmsford	36.20	eased		40.02			42.25	sigs		40.35		
35.9	Hatfield Pev.	42.50			46.48	50		50.35			47.25		
38.6	Witham	45.55			49.39	64		53.30	62		50.15	65	
42.2	Kelvedon	49.45			53.11	57		57.30			54.00		
46.6	Marks Tey	55.05			57.42	51/63		63.00			59.20		
51.7	Colchester	60.30			62.43			68.40			65.00		
54.1	Parsons Hth	63.10			65.23	45		-			67.35		
56	Ardleigh	65.15			67.50			74.20			70.10		
59.5	Manningtree	69.00	pass	1 E	71.45	61		78.15	60		73.50	65	
63.2	Bentley				71.45	36½		82.25			78.10		
65.2	Belstead				79.10			84.50			81.15		
68	Halifax Jn				82.55			87.50			85.00		
68.7	Ipswich				84.41 (82 net)		3 ½ E	89.30 (85 ½ net)		½ E	87.05		3 E

One regular commuter between Broxbourne and London between 1931 and 1934 timed services in both directions – a couple of morning up trains and three down services in the evening peak hours. He logged 8520 fourteen times, 8521 thirty-three times and 8527 seven times as well as other locomotives less frequently. In the down direction speed on the gradually rising gradient normally reached the mid-upper 50s with 250-300 tons, with 60mph being topped a couple of times. However, in the up direction 60mph was usual and the recorder noted 8527 reaching 68mph one day with (quote) 'a mad driver'. However, the run was ruined by signal checks after Tottenham.

As well as traffic on the main lines to Cambridge and Norwich, the Stratford engines also worked the faster trains to Southend Victoria after the 1933 timetable accelerations, some which divided at Shenfield with the front five coaches running non-stop to Prittlewell, 20.7 miles, booked in 22 minutes over the undulating road with its 1 in 100 gradients. B12/1 8551 which was transferred to Scotland in 1939 was timed with 5 coaches, 145 tons gross, achieving even time between Shenfield and Rayleigh, 12.9 miles in 12 minutes 35 seconds, start to pass, and arriving at Prittlewell in 19 minutes 55 seconds. This involved high speeds of 86mph through Wickford, 56 at the

8571, the first of the Beyer, Peacock Lentz poppet valve gear B12/2s, at work on an East Anglian express, c1929. F. Moore/MLS Collection

8521, now fitted with the boiler-mounted ACFI water feedwater heating equipment, passing Copper Mill Sidings Box, c1932. Photomatic/ MLS Collection

summit of 1 in 100 to Rayleigh and another 80 at Rochford. 8571, a Lentz B12/2, had 170 tons and beat the 22 minute schedule by half a minute with 74 at Wickford 53½ minimum at Rayleigh and 75 at Rochford. The same B12/2 took 330 tons gross on the 8.15am from Southend in the harder direction with 34 on Hockley bank, 72 after Rayleigh, 45 minimum after the four miles of 1 in 100 to Billericay and 68 afterwards before the 20mph slowing through Shenfield. The Brentwood stop was reached half a minute under the tight 29 minute schedule for the 21.7 miles despite the load. 8551 worked the non-stop 265 ton 9.13am Prittlewell - Liverpool Street in 52 minutes exactly, 40.9 miles, (48 net after two p-way slacks) with 75 after Rayleigh, 42 at Billericay, 72 before Shenfield and 71 through Chadwell Heath.

When sufficient B17s were available for Cambridge, three B12s were transferred to March and at last some B12s were available for the Scottish routes. 8500-8504 went north in 1931 and six more in 1933, a further one in 1937 and a final batch of seven unrebuilt B12/1s in 1939. Then because of wartime increase of traffic in the north of Scotland with the navy fleet based in Scapa Flow, six more were sent in 1940 augmented by a further two in 1942. The twenty-five unrebuilt engines that finished in Scotland were:

8500-8505, 8507, 8508, 8511, 8513, 8521, 8524, 8526, 8528, 8529, 8531, 8532, 8536, 8539, 8543, 8548, 8551, 8552, 8560, 8563.

They worked from Aberdeen-Elgin via Keith, the coast route and the Ballater branch, working passenger, parcels, fish and freight trains indiscriminately. Although initially unpopular, especially with firemen because of the distance between the firehole door and the coal in the tender, once mastered by the crews they performed very competently and were not displaced until B1s were available in the early 1950s. Between 1941 and 1943 a number of B12s worked out of Edinburgh at both Haymarket (8500, 8503, 8521) and St Margaret's (8526) but inexperience with the class caused problems and they returned to the former GNS section.

From 1932 a number of rebuilt B12/3s became available but most remained at their former depots. They frequently worked in the same diagrams as the B17s, but whilst the B12s were preferred for acceleration and hill climbing when short bursts of power were required, the B17s were preferred for the Norwich expresses. The heavy *Hook Continental* remained a B12 turn. One of the stars in the 1930s (and also at Richard Hardy's Ipswich in the 1950s) was 8535 and Cecil J Allen published a 43½ minute net run for the 46.3 miles from Ipswich to Norwich which included the highest recorded speed for a B12 - 90mph. The full log is shown below.

Ipswich-Norwich
8535
280/305 tons

Miles	**Location**	**Times**	**Speeds**	**Gradients**
0	Ipswich	00.00		
2.3	Bramford	04.35	50	L
4.7	Claydon	07.05	60	
8.3	Needham	10.30	65	1/337 R
11.75	Stowmarket	13.35	72	
14.1	Haughley	15.38	61/58	1/131 R
17.7	Finningham	19.12	70	1/248 F
22.5	Mellis	23.05	79	
25.4	MP94 ¼	25.05	90	1/132 F
26.2	Diss	25.59/29.19	sigs stand	
28.6	Burston	33.39	50	1/260 R
35.3	Forncett	40.26	74	1/138 F
37.75	Flordon	42.26	84	1/136 F/1/134 R
40.74	Swainsthorpe	44.49	75/81/sigs	1/148 F
46.2	Norwich	52.29	(43½ net)	

The maximum power output was 1,102 hp on accelerating from the Diss signal stop and 1,312 when reaching 84mph at Flordon.

However, during the Second World War, despite the needs in Scotland, an even greater priority for their use became apparent. Because of their light axleload and consequent wide route availability, the B12s became the mainstay of the heavy ambulance trains and two of

Rebuilt B12/3 8574, previously one of the Lentz gear B12/2s, near Ipswich with the all-Pullman *Eastern Belle*, c1935. Colling Turner/ MLS Collection

B12/3 8566 at Yarmouth South Town station, 4 September 1938. MLS Collection

A war-worn and neglected Scottish B12/1, 8526, pilots GNS D41 6901 at Keith Junction with a down express, 4 August 1945. N. Fields/ MLS Collection

the Scottish B12/1s (8521 and 8531) went south to assist the B12/3s. 8535 (renumbered 7449 in 1942), 8509, 8510, 8516, 8519, 8525, 8530, 8547, 8549, 8555 and 8557 were assigned to them for the American troops based in East Anglia and operated from there all over the country, being also equipped with the necessary air-brake system. The other B12/3s and the two B12/1s transferred worked passenger trains loading up to 500 tons on the GE section as many military personnel - British and American - were based there.

In 1944, the two GE B12/1s from Scotland plus 8534, the only one that had remained on the GE, worked the East Suffolk line from their Ipswich base. At the end of the war in 1945, 8534 became the first GE B12 (apart from the accident victim 1506) to be withdrawn and 8521 and 8531 returned to Scotland. Some of the GC B17/4 'Footballers' were transferred to the GE section and as B1s also became available, the B12s were concentrated at Stratford and were used on all the faster Southend services as well as slower services to Cambridge, Colchester and Ipswich.

At nationalisation in 1948, the B12/3s were allocated to:

Stratford:	37
Ipswich:	7
Colchester:	4
Norwich:	1
Yarmouth:	1

B12/1 61539 at Ballater with the 8.07pm to Aberdeen, 18 July 1949. J.D. Darby/MLS Collection

One of the Scottish reboilered B12/4s, 61504 double-heading B12/1 61513 on an up fish train near Dyce, July 1949. J.D. Darby/MLS Collection

B12/1 61563 leaving Dinnet with the 3.30pm Ballater-Aberdeen, July 1949. J.D. Darby/ MLS Collection

B12/4 61507 approaching Cantur D'May with the 5.50pm Ballater-Aberdeen 18 July 1949. J.D. Darby/ MLS Collection

B12/4 61508 entering Inverurie with the 12.25pm Keith-Aberdeen, 20 July 1949. J.D.Darby/ MLS Collection

B12/1 61528 at Fraserburgh with the 2,58pm to Aberdeen, 18 June 1951. J.D. Darby/ MLS Collection

B12/1 61532 at Torphin with the 3.18pm Aberdeen-Ballater, 1 June 1953. MLS Collection

B12/1 61502 with an up goods train at Tillynaught, 3 June 1953. A.C. Gilbert/MLS Collection

B12/3 61564 at Woodbridge on the East Suffolk line, c1949. Eddie Johnson Collection

Later in the year B12/3s were allocated to work on the former Midland and Great Northern Railway (M&GN), Yarmouth Beach as opposed to the South Town shed receiving 61520, 61530 and 61545, while South Lynn had 61533, 61537, 61540 and 61547. Most were displaced when BR built ex-LMS Ivatt moguls took over much of the M&GN work in 1954/5, but Yarmouth Beach continued to use 61530 and 61533 almost until their withdrawal in 1959.

In 1954, Grantham received an allocation for working to Lincoln and stopping services on the main line to Peterborough and Doncaster, including 61553, 61554 and 61565, which on occasions took over from ailing Pacifics on the GN main line, such as 61553's exploit in 1950 with a fourteen coach southbound express when it had to replace a failed A3. In 1955/6 61538, 61554, 61558, 61565 and 61567 moved to Peterborough Spital Bridge working to Rugby and Northampton. They also appeared on the cross-country Cambridge-Oxford route sharing that work with the dwindling number of 'Claud Hamilton' 4-4-0s.

A smart 61554 at Lincoln on a train bearing an express headcode but formed of non-corridor coaches, 29 September 1950. J.D. Darby/ MLS Collection

61562 arrives at Beccles with a parcels train, 19 May 1951. H.D. Bowtell/ MLS Collection

61561 pilots B17/4 61649 *Sheffield United* near Woodbridge, c1951. Eddie Johnson Collection

61580 departs from Retford with a Grantham – Doncaster stopping train, July 1954. T.K. Widd/MLS Collection

61542 arrives at Lowestoft with an express from Liverpool Street, 1955. N. Harrop/MLS Collection

61574 near Retford with a Doncaster – Grantham stopping train, 7 August 1956. B.K.B. Green/ MLS Collection

In the 1950s, until electrification in December 1956, the B12/3s were the mainstay of the Liverpool Street-Southend Victoria services, although B17s and B1s also shared the work. The fast and semi-fast trains ran over the Anglia main line to Shenfield and then a further 21.3 miles to Southend via Billericay and Wickford. There were 1 in 100 two mile banks to Billericay and past Rayleigh but harder work was required in the up direction with a two-and-a-half 1 in 100 climb soon after the start from Rochford to Hockley and four miles of 1 in 100 to Billericay. There were fast commuter services in the morning and evening peaks that were allowed 68 minutes in the 1950s for the 41.5 miles with two or three intermediate stops. A typical down run in August 1953 with a 9 coach train had unusually Yarmouth's 61533 (after Stratford repair?). It departed Liverpool Street two minutes late

61576 at Wickford with a Southend Victoria-Liverpool Street train, 5 August 1955.
MLS Collection

and was on time at Billericay, with 52mph at Forest Gate, 33 minimum after Brentwood and 60 after Shenfield, some two minutes less than scheduled. The timetable was observed meticulously thereafter and the arrival at Prittlewell was one minute early. Once the line was electrified, a proportion of the fleet of Stratford's B12s became redundant and eleven were withdrawn in consequence early in 1957 – 61512, 61538, 61541, 61545, 61550, 61557, 61565, 61569, 61574, 61578 and 61579. Although these included one Ipswich and four Grantham based engines, some of the lower mileage Stratford engines became available as replacements. A B12, 61555, appeared on a down Clacton interval buffet car express and 260 tons in the mid-1950s and kept time comfortably at all points without exceeding 68mph anywhere.

The last route on which the remaining B12s regularly appeared was the Norwich-Cromer line, which had an allocation of five in 1958. However, sixteen were still extant in 1958 despite the early dieselisation of the Anglia routes and often appeared at Liverpool Street alongside the B17s, B1s and Britannias. The Scottish B12/1s and B12/4s had gone by 1954 and all but 61572 of the B12/3s had been withdrawn by the end of 1959. 61572 lingered on at Norwich on mainly parcels train work, but it also worked railtour specials and after withdrawal in September 1961, was purchased privately for preservation.

I am fortunate to have had some experience of the class at work. In 1950 as a twelve-year-old I was sent to stay with relatives at Chelmsford and during my stay I was taken to see a West End Show. I can't remember the motive power up to London – I suspect a B1 – and we returned on the fast 10.30pm mail train, first stop Chelmsford. I must have been anticipating a 'namer' because I remember my disappointment and surprise that it

61578 cuts off from the train on which it has arrived from London at Southend Victoria while the passengers make their way to the exit, 5 August 1955. MLS Collection

61546 passing Stratford with a Liverpool Street-Southend Victoria train, 27 May 1956, 27 May 1956. MLS Collection

was 'only' a plain black B12. Little did I know then that my steed was none other than one of Dick Hardy's precious and pampered B12s, 61535, and I remember being surprised at the rapidity with which we were transported back to Chelmsford. The following year my cousin (a primary school teacher) collected me at Liverpool Street and again to my disgust put me on a semi-fast hauled by 61566 instead of one of the fast services with a new Britannia. In subsequent years I got my due fill of Britannias in several family visits, and now I look back with pleasure that I had runs with two of the Ipswich prized B12s.

Then, in 1958, as a student at University College London, I used to repair frequently to Liverpool Street after lectures and before evening engagements. As I only had £47 a year available from my grant after paying for my lodging and Woking-Waterloo season ticket, I was unable to venture too far – Tottenham, Broxbourne, or even Bishop's Stortford or Shenfield if I had economised during the week. The attraction was a possible run behind one of the B17 'Sandringhams' in their last year of GE line operation, and I could check what was available before deciding what ticket I could afford as the 4-6-0s brought the empty stock in of preceding trains before backing on to their appointed services. If I was 'flush' and lectures finished at 4pm, I could see the engine for the 4.36 *Fenman*, and I travelled several times to its first stop, Bishop's Stortford, behind B2s and B17s. However, two weeks running in the spring of 1958 I discovered B12s, 61580 and 61558, on the turn and despite the penalty of going without my main meal for the next day or so, bought return tickets to Bishop's Stortford to enjoy both on top link operation. Regrettably I had not yet started the habit of timing every train. Early the following year, on a London University Railway Society visit to Stratford Works, we caught 61580 actually moving onto the depot to rest as it completed its last run before withdrawal and storage to await scrapping.

Ipswich's pride, 61535, as it appeared at the head of the author's mail train at Liverpool Street in the summer of 1950. David Maidment from a photo by Brian Morrison

61546 at Shenfield at 10am with a Liverpool Street-Southend train, 6 September 1951, taken during the author's trainspotting trip whilst staying with relatives in Chelmsford. The photo was taken with a £12 Kodak folding 'Brownie' camera, fixed 1/25 speed and f8 aperture. David Maidment

61549 on the turntable at Liverpool Street station, 4 April 1953. The author gained first prize in the Charterhouse School Railway Club 1953 photographic competition with this study. David Maidment

61549 backing out of the platform at Oxford station having arrived with a train from Cambridge, 4 March 1957. The photograph was taken during one of the author's visits to attempt to get a scholarship to a university college there (unsuccessful). David Maidment

61580 at Stratford having just been withdrawn from Cambridge depot and stabled pending scrapping. The photo was taken during the London University Railway Society visit to Stratford Works, 25 February 1959. David Maidment

Preservation

61572

8572 was built by the Beyer, Peacock Company in August 1928 as a B12/2 with Lentz valve gear and was rebuilt by Gresley as a B12/3 in 1933. It was initially withdrawn from Norwich shed in 1959 with cracked cylinders but the shedmaster, Bill Harvey, managed to get it repaired and it was not officially withdrawn until 20/9/1961. It was bought by the Midland & Great Northern Society in 1962 for £1,500 and stored at Devons Road depot. It was enabled to be one of the first privately owned engines to run a tour on the main line (the *Wandering 1500* tour of 5 October 1963) and moved to March depot, then to the North Norfolk Railway at Sheringham in 1967. It was in poor condition, but was cosmetically restored for display.

An appeal for £20,000 to restore the engines was made in 1977 and the tender was being restored by volunteers. A local boilersmith tackled the boiler. However, progress was slow. The project restarted in 1984 but the firm then contracted for the boiler was bankrupt and a Dutch Company contracted to take the boiler to Holland for repair and the frame and tender sub-contracted to an East German company at Kloster Mansfield near Leipzig. That company was then bought out by its employees who were initially reluctant to complete the repair but eventually the boiler and parts were reunited and the completed locomotive was returned to the UK in December 1994. It was steamed and then re-commissioned in March 1995 and repainted as 8572 in LNER apple green livery. It was in traffic on the North Norfolk Railway until withdrawal for overhaul in 2007, in the meantime having operated on a number of other heritage railways (and the LT *Steam on the Met* repainted in BR lined black). It was overhauled by Riley & Son and returned to the North Norfolk Railway in 2012 in LNER livery and in operation until its boiler certificate expires in November 2020. (For photographs, see Colour Section.)

Chapter 5

GRESLEY'S B17 'SANDRINGHAMS' & 'FOOTBALLERS'

B17/1 – 1928

Design and construction

In the mid-1920s, the Great Eastern Section of the LNER was suffering a crisis in the motive power department. The B12s were the mainstay but all engines were struggling with poor coal supplies following the 1926 General Strike. Locomotive power for the Cambridge and Southend lines was insufficient for the growing traffic and stopping services throughout the GE section were in great trouble. Gresley was required by the Board to remedy the situation urgently and a 4-6-0 with at least 25,000lbs tractive effort was specified with the proviso that it must meet the section's length limitations and have no more than a 17 ton axleload (the B12's tractive effort was just under 22,000lbs). In the meantime, the GE power requirement was partially met by the transfer of some of Gresley's K2 moguls that met the restrictions and after some abortive efforts of the Doncaster drawing office to meet the Board's and Gresley's requirements, the Board lost patience and authorised a further ten B12s as outlined in the previous chapter.

Throughout 1927 and 1928, Doncaster and Gresley made further attempts to meet the stringent specification, envisaging a three cylinder engine and looked at design aspects of the D49 4-4-0 and the NE B16 to see how they could be modified to fit the required engine, basically to be a more powerful B12 but no heavier or longer. First efforts gave a locomotive weighing 71 tons with a bogie axleweight of 20 tons which was unacceptable. Modifications to the design extended its length which was unacceptable to the Locomotive Running Department. At the same time, Doncaster was designing a 2-6-4 tank for the Southend services, but the Southern Railway accident involving the derailment of the company's 'River' 2-6-4T gave management fears about the instability of such a tank engine required to run at express speeds.

In the end, Gresley and the Board decided to contract out the design work and a proposal by the North British Company of £7,280 for each of an order for ten locomotives was accepted, with delivery due in the summer of 1928. The North British Company had experience of building some Gresley A1 pacifics in 1924 and followed the boiler design of the K3 mogul and O2 2-8-0. After perusal of the initial design, some modifications were required to achieve the needed power output (by enlarging the cylinder diameter by half an inch), and to increase the grate area, causing the frame to be extended. Although fitted with the short wheelbase GE tender, the result was a longer engine than specified and an axleload of 18 tons restricting the class from some of the GE lines, though the main routes would be available. After all these trials and tribulations, 2802 was delivered in November 1928, somewhat incongruously followed by 2801 and then the other eight, 2800 and 2803-2809, in December. The main dimensions of the new B17 'Sandringhams' were:

Cylinders (3)	17½in x 26in
Coupled wheel diameter	6ft 8in
Bogie wheel diameter	3ft 2in
Walchaerts/Gresley conjugated gear with 8in piston valves	
Boiler pressure	200psi
Heating surface	2,020sqft (incl 344sqft superheating)
Grate area	27.5sqft
Axleload	18 tons
Engine wheelbase	27ft 9in
Tender wheelbase	12ft
Length over buffers	58ft 4in (9in more than the B12)
Weight – Engine	76 tons 13 cwt
– Tender	39 tons 8 cwt
– Total	116 tons 1 cwt
Water capacity	3,700 gallons
Coal capacity	4 tons
Tractive effort	25,380lbs

Initial experience with these North British built engines was not propitious. They experienced steaming problems, cured by altering the blastpipe dimensions and within a year they were suffering frame fractures with nine of the ten locomotives in Stratford Works in the early part of 1930. The frames were light to keep within the axleload limit, but various modifications to the springing became necessary and it was 1935 before the problems with these early ten were resolved. Despite these experiences, a dozen more were ordered simultaneously to be constructed at the LNER's own Darlington Works and 2810-2821 were delivered in 1930, incorporating some of the lessons re springing learned from the earlier failures. Westinghouse air brakes were fitted to 2800-2815 for the engine and train although they had a vacuum ejector for alternative braking, but 2816 onwards were equipped only with vacuum brakes.

Darlington continued to build further members of the class and 2822-2836 were delivered in 1931, 2837-2842 in 1933 and 2843-2847 in 1935. Despite some plans to allocate engines of the class to the North East, and then Scotland, a decision was made to retain them entirely within the LNER's Southern Division.

The prototype, 2800 *Sandringham* as built in 1928 by the North British Company in Works Grey. F. Moore/MLS Collection

2816 *Fallodon* as built new at Darlington, seen here at Stratford, 1930. It was rebuilt by Thompson in 1945 as a two-cylinder B2. Note the cylinder casing painted black. MLS Collection

2837 *Thorpe* *Hall*, constructed and delivered to Norwich depot in March 1933. The cylinder casing of the later builds were painted lined green. MLS Collection

2839 ***Rendlesham Hall***, constructed in May 1933 and renamed after football team *Norwich City* in January 1938. It was rebuilt as a B2 in 1946. MLS Collection

2846 ***Gilwell*** *Park*, was built in 1935. The vacuum reserve reservoir on the back of the tender is clearly visible. MLS Collection

A rear view of North British built 2805 *Burnham Thorpe*, with a good view of the GE tender detail, seen at Liverpool Street, 1936. It was renamed *The Lincolnshire Regiment* in April 1938. MLS Collection

B17/4 – 1936

In March 1935 a further raft of twenty-five engines was ordered, the first fourteen at Darlington numbered 2848-2861 and the order for the last eleven was transferred to Robert Stephenson & Co in February 1936. 2862-2872 were delivered in 1937. The earlier engines had originally been classified B17/1, B17/2 and B17/3, so the 1936/7 locomotives were classified B17/4. However, as the springing and frame modifications of 2800-2847 were modified and standardised, all of these were reclassified as B17/1s. The main difference of the B17/4s was their equipping with longer wheelbase standard LNER tenders holding 4,200 gallons of water and 7½ tons of coal. As it was intended to use these engines on the Western Section of the LNER's Southern Division (the former Great Central main line), the length limitations did not apply. Whereas all the

GE tender engines had been named after stately homes located throughout the LNER system, the B17/4s were named after football teams also located on the railway. When later some were renamed, the football names were transferred to a couple of B17/1s (2830 *Tottenham Hotspur* and 2839 *Norwich City*). The splashers were painted with the teams' colours and included the half-surface of a football.

The key dimensions of the B17/4s were identical to the B17/1s apart from the tender which weighed 52 tons instead of the GE tender's 39 tons 8 cwt and its wheelbase – 13ft 6in compared with 12ft. Then, in September 1937, the LNER introduced the *East Anglian* named express between London and Norwich and, with streamlining the vogue on the East Coast main line, two B17/4s, 2859 and 2870, were streamlined in the style of the A4s and renamed *East Anglian* and *City of London* respectively, their football names passing to the two B17/1s. The streamlining increased their weight to 80½ tons and the tender weight to 52 tons 13 cwt. A further build of B17/4s had been envisaged in 1937 but this was dropped in favour of the V2 2-6-2 design. When 2858 *Newcastle United* was renamed *The Essex Regiment* in June 1936 a month after its construction, it exchanged tenders with 2847 as management wished to retain the renamed engine in Anglia, so 2847 then became in effect a B17/4.

2848 *Arsenal*, the first of the B17/4s constructed in March 1936, seen here at Doncaster, c1938. Real Photographs/ MLS Collection

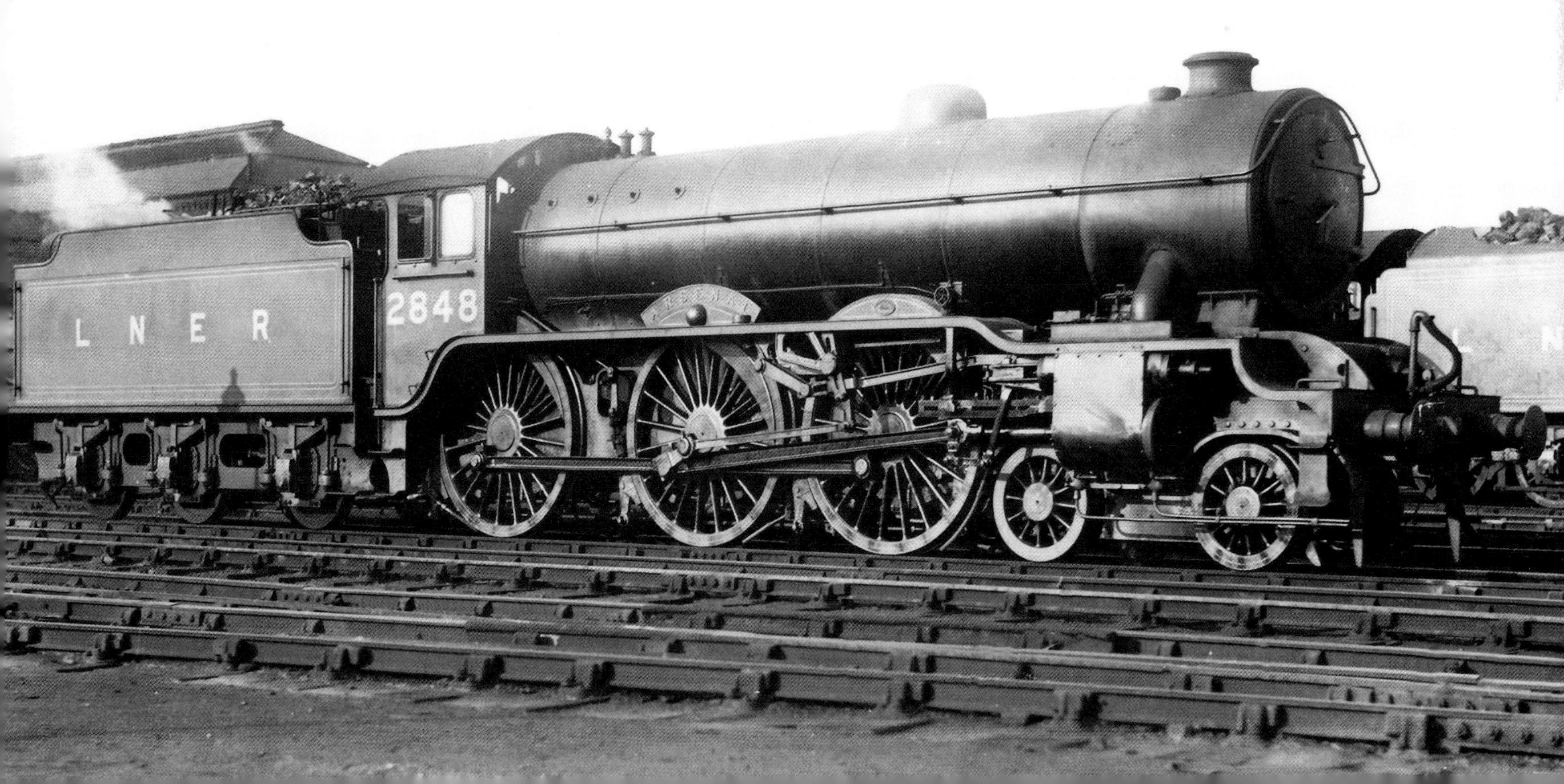

2859 *Norwich* *City*, constructed in 1936, in Doncaster Works being streamlined for the new *East Anglian* service and being renamed *East Anglian,* 19 September 1937. MLS Collection

The completed transformation of 2859 as a B17/5 together with the Gresley *East Anglian* train set posed for an official photograph, September 1937. F. Moore/MLS Collection

Formal portrait of the other B17/4 converted to B17/5 2870, formerly named *Manchester City* when built in May 1937 and changed immediately to *Tottenham Hotspur*, streamlined and renamed again in September 1937 as *City of London*. Real Photographs/ MLS Collection

B17/6 – 1947

During the Second World War, the boiler pressure was dropped from 200 to 180psi to achieve maintenance savings but was restored after the war. However, Edward Thompson had developed the successful 225psi 100A boiler for his B1 class introduced in 1942 and between December 1947 and April 1958 fifty-five of the B17/1s and B17/4s were fitted with this boiler and the engines were reclassified B17/6s. The engine weight increased slightly to 77 tons 3 cwt and tractive effort increased significantly to 28,553lbs. Grate area increased to 27.9sqft, although the total heating surface reduced slightly to 2,005sqft. In August 1945 Thompson had rebuilt 2871 as a two-cylinder engine and it lost its *Manchester City* football club name, becoming *Royal Sovereign* and acting as the royal engine. Nine more were similarly rebuilt between then and 1949 and classified as the B2 class (see Chapter 7 for the full description of Thompson's 4-6-0 rebuilds).

Finally, after draughting tests at Swindon with V2 60845, two (61633 and 61669, formerly 2833 and 2869) had modified blastpipe dimensions. The experiment was successful and a further twenty-six engines of the class were so modified despite the fact that some had already been withdrawn from service.

B17 (General)

All were originally liveried in the standard LNER apple green with black and white lining. 2800-2809 had their numbers on the tender but subsequently they and all further engines had cabside numbers and LNER on the tender. They were renumbered 1600-1672 in the 1946 renumbering scheme and 61600-61672 at nationalisation when they received the BR Brunswick green passenger lined livery. The two streamlined engines were painted in the same style as the A4s but green rather than blue with black skirting. Both lost their streamlining in 1951. The B17/1s and B17/4s were put into

BR's '4P' category, the same as the B12s, while the B17/6s with the higher boiler pressure and tractive effort were classified '5P', as were the rebuilt B2s.

Despite the reboilering and redraughting, the first B17/6, 61628, was withdrawn as early as September 1952, presumably after a serious flaw, probably cracked frame. Two others followed in 1953, unmodified B17/1, 61624, and another B17/6, 61604. Then there was a prolonged gap without any withdrawals until dieselisation came early to East Anglia (the D55XX Brush Type 2s in particular) and eighteen were withdrawn in 1958, all bar four being B17/1s or B17/1s rebuilt as B17/6s. Twenty-four were condemned in 1959, leaving just six of the 'Sandringhams', five of which were withdrawn in January 1960, and the last survivor of the GE tendered engines, 61608 *Gunton,* in March. Only four of this batch were B17/1s at their withdrawal – 61624 condemned in 1953, 61601 in 1958 and 61625 and 61629 in 1959. Only two B17/4 'Footballers' were not rebuilt with 100A boilers, 61667 withdrawn in 1958 and 61660 *Hull City* which was one of the four survivors withdrawn in June 1960. B17/6s 61657 and 61664 were also withdrawn in June 1960, leaving just 61668 *Bradford City* which survived for just another two months when the class became extinct.

B17/1 1645 *The Suffolk Regiment*, constructed as 2845 and named in 1935, seen here at Ipswich, c1947, in the wartime LNER plain black livery and renumbered in September 1946, a livery it retained until 1949. J.D. Darby/MLS Collection

B17/4 E1664 *Liverpool*, still in wartime black livery but given the prefix 'E' and with BRITISH RAILWAYS painted on the tender, at Stratford, 7 February 1948.
H.C. Casserley/MLS Collection

B17/1 ***Naworth*** *Castle*, in the initial Eastern Region post nationalisation livery applied to the B17s, lined apple green but with BR number 61629 on cabside and smokebox and BRITISH RAILWAYS on the tender, at Woodbridge, c1950.
Eddie Johnson Collection

61604 *Elveden,* constructed by the North British Company in 1929 with Westinghouse air brake and pump and rebuilt in 1951 with a B1 type 100A boiler to be re-designated B17/6, in the post 1952 BR Brunswick green livery with the 'lion & wheel' emblem on the tender, at Woodbridge, c1952. This was one of the early withdrawals the following year, 1953. Eddie Johnson Collection

B17/1 61618 *Wynyard Park*, a long-time resident of Cambridge shed, ex-works in the Brunswick green BR passenger livery, and still with the original B17 boiler, at Doncaster, 18 January 1953. MLS Collection

61613 ***Woodbastwick*** *Hall*, constructed at Darlington in 1930, one of the first fifteen equipped with the Westinghouse air-brake, but rebuilt in 1951 with a 100A boiler as a B17/6, at Stratford, its home depot, 1957. M.L. Boakes/ MLS Collection

B17/5 61659 *East Anglian* was rebuilt with a 100A boiler in 1949 but was not de-streamlined until 1951, when it was classified as a B17/6. It is parked here at Liverpool Street station along with B1 61254, 14 September 1956. G.A. Coltas/ MLS Collection

B17/1 61634 *Hinchingbrooke* spent its early years at Gorton, one of the few that operated there for any length of time with the short GE tender. It returned to the GE section after the war and was rebuilt as a B17/6 as late as January 1957 being withdrawn just eighteen months later. It is seen here c1956. R.C. Riley/ MLS Collection

Cambridge's Westinghouse fitted B17/6 61608 *Gunton* backs onto a train in the western side of Liverpool Street station as Britannia 70037 *Hereward the Wake* stands waiting release after arriving with a Norwich express, and 61637 *Thorpe Hall* backs out of platform 8, 1958. 61608 was the last of the B17s constructed for the GE section to survive and one of the original ten North British built engines. It was withdrawn in March 1960. A.G.W. Goff/ MLS Collection

61657 *Doncaster* *Rovers*, a B17/4 reboilered as a B17/6 in 1950, at March depot, 4 May 1958. MLS Collection

Operations

The first ten engines being built by the Glasgow North British Works were run in on stopping services between Glasgow and Edinburgh, although by early January 1929 they were appearing on the key Liverpool Street – Cambridge expresses. The initial allocation was:

Stratford:	2800, 2801, 2808 (2802 added in March 1929)
Ipswich:	2806, 2807
Parkeston:	2803, 2804, 2805
Gorton:	2802 (replaced by 2809 in March 1929)

The Stratford engines worked to Cambridge and Ipswich, the Parkeston engines worked the continental boat trains and the Ipswich and Gorton engines worked the important Ipswich-Manchester *North Country Continental* boat trains. A Parkeston B17 would haul the service from Harwich to Ipswich and a Gorton engine from Manchester to Liverpool. The *Railway Magazine* of April 1929 recorded a couple of early runs over the Trans-Pennine route with the Ipswich and Gorton allocated engines.

Manchester-Sheffield, 1929
Manchester-Harwich *North Country Continental*

		2802 *Walsingham*-Gorton 225/240 tons			**2807 *Blickling*-Ipswich 218/230 tons**			
Miles	**Location**	**Times**	**Speeds**		**Times**	**Speeds**		**Gradients**
0	Manchester (Central)	00.00			00.00			
1.5	Throstle Nest Junction	04.20	sigs		03.55			
3.1	Chorlton	07.05	49		06.35			
4.2	Wilbraham Road	08.55			08.40	pws		
6.9	Levenshulme	12.20			13.10	pws		1/108 & 1/133 R
9.8	Fairfield	16.30	40½		18.00	37/34		
11.1	Guide Bridge	18.45	sigs	1 ¾ L	20.10	40	3¼ L	
14.4	Godley Junction	24.20			24.55	43		1/143 R
18	Dinting	29.30	47		29.45	49		1/100 R
21.4	Torside Crossing	35.00	35/37½		35.00	37½		
23.3	Crowden	38.00			38.10	38		1/117 R
25.3	Woodhead Tunnel	41.25		2½ L	41.30	28 slipping	2½ L	1/201 R
28.5	Dunford	46.30	38	2½ L	47.20		3¼ L	
34.5	Penistone	53.15	67	2¼ L	54.06	65	3 L	1/124 F
38.6	Wortley	58.55	pws		58.40			1/120 F
42.5	Oughty Bridge	64.00	sigs		62.50	sigs		
47.4	Sheffield	71.10	(66¼ ne)	5¼ L	70.00	(67 net)	4 L	

Neither run was particularly impressive in these early days, hardly surpassing the GC 4-4-0s and 4-6-0s or the B12s. Both runs would have struggled to maintain the schedule without the checks and both with relatively lightweight trains.

Early experience of the new engines was favourable on the Cambridge route, but less so on the line through Colchester with the need to lift heavy expresses up the gradient of Brentwood Bank to Ingrave summit. The early series suffered initial steaming problems and as stated earlier, was remedied by alteration of the blastpipe diameter.

The next batch of dual-fitted brake engines, 2810-2815, were all allocated to Stratford, 2816 replaced 2809 at Gorton (it moved to

2800 ***Sandringham*** heads a Norwich express at Liverpool Street, 1929. B12 8516 can just be spied in the background. G.M. Shoults/MLS Collection

2803 ***Framlingham*** climbs Brentwood Bank with a heavy continental express for Parkeston Quay, 1929. F. Moore/ MLS Collection

2807 ***Blickling*** of Ipswich on the Harwich-Manchester boat train at Woodhead, 1929. It appears to be fitted with a different style of chimney, probably part of the blastpipe variations which were carried out to attempt to improve the B17s' steaming problems. MLS Collection

Stratford also) and 2817-2819 were the first allocated to Cambridge shed. These three gained a good reliable reputation with their Cambridge crews. They could also appear at King's Cross on the Cambridge 'buffet car' expresses. 2820 and 2821 went to Ipswich to replace 2806 and 2807 on the Manchester workings and these two remained at Ipswich for semi-fast duties to London or Norwich. Colchester received its first allocation of B17s with 2822-2824 working to Clacton, but this was short-lived and they soon were transferred to Parkeston where there was more suitable work. 2825 and 2826 went to Ipswich and 2827 – 2831 to Stratford. Then in 1931 three – 2832, 2833 and 2835 – were allocated to Doncaster for working passenger and fish trains via Sheffield and the GC line to Banbury and the Great Western. 2834 was allocated to Gorton and 2836 to Parkeston.

The Gorton allocated 2834 *Hinchingbrooke* departing from Manchester Central with the 3.50pm for Sheffield and Marylebone, 7 August 1933. R.D. Pollard/ MLS Collection

Parkeston's 2822 *Alnwick Castle* with the down *Flushing Continental* near Ipswich, c1935. Colling Turner/ MLS Collection

2811 *Raynham* *Hall* with a down express near Romford, c1935. MLS Collection

Gorton's 2816 *Fallodon* with a local stopping train formed of six-wheel coaches at Marple, 2 May 1936. N. Fields/MLS Collection

It seems strange that no allocation of B17s was made to Norwich until 1933 when the first of the next batch, 2837-2839, were allocated there. Although the Stratford, Ipswich and Parkeston engines were not universally popular on the Colchester route, the Norwich men, like their Cambridge colleagues, took to them well and did good work with them. Finally Gorton got a larger allocation with 2840-2842 and this allowed that depot to use them on ex-Great Central expresses to Leicester and Marylebone as well as the *North Country Continental* trains. This was not universally popular as the GC men valued their 'Director' 4-4-0s and compared the new B17s unfavourably with them for the first few months. In 1935 Norwich got two more, 2843 and 2844 and 2845-2847 were allocated to March, although 2845 was exchanged with 2821 when it was decided to name 2845 *The Suffolk Regiment* and therefore based at Ipswich.

After the delivery of all the initial batch of B17s (the B17/1 class) the allocation in 1935 was:

Stratford:	2800, 2802, 2803, 2808-2815, 2828-2830
Parkeston:	2801, 2804, 2805, 2822, 2823, 2826, 2827, 2831, 2836
Ipswich:	2806, 2807, 2820, 2825, 2845
Norwich:	2837-2839, 2843, 2844
Cambridge:	2817-2819
March:	2821, 2846, 2847
Doncaster:	2832, 2833, 2835
Gorton:	2816, 2841, 2842
Neasden:	2824, 2834, 2840

Despite the large number now allocated to the former GE section, they didn't eliminate the B12s from top link work, especially as many of the latter had now been effectively rebuilt as class B12/3s. The influx of the 'Sandringhams' did, however, release a number of the unrebuilt B12/1s to move to Scotland as outlined in the previous chapter. For example, the Cambridge depot top link diagrams required six 4-6-0s and therefore comprised the three allocated B17s and three B12/3s, with other B12/3s replacing any of the top link engines when unavailable. Although the Parkeston boat trains were often worked by the depot's B17s, B12/3s still made appearances, especially on the heavy down *Hook Continental*. Ipswich depot used its B12/3s on its main London services in preference to the B17s although the latter always worked the Harwich-Manchester trains.

A number of tests had been carried out with the B17s in both 1931 and again in 1936, when the first batch of B17/4s was delivered. 2800 (one of the best of the Stratford B17s) was tested in December 1931 on a Liverpool Street-Cambridge excursion and then a couple of weeks later on an excursion to Norwich, and finally on a Southend-Liverpool Street booked fast service. Logs are available from the March 1932 *Railway Magazine* and from the archives of the Railway Performance Society.

Liverpool Street-Cambridge, 13 December 1931
2800 *Sandringham* – Stratford
222/235 tons

Miles	Location	Times	Speed	Gradients
0	Liverpool Street	00.00		
3	Hackney Downs	08.05	pws	
6	Tottenham	13.53	pws	
7.7	Angel Road	15.42	65/50* sigs	
12.8	Waltham Cross	20.54	64½	
17.1	Broxbourne	24.51	66	
20.1	Reydon	27.35	65	
24.5	Harlow	31.44	62½	1/374 R
26.7	Sawbridgeworth	33.47	66	
30.4	Bishop's Stortford	37.35	30*	
33.4	Stansted	41.31	58½	1/124 & 1/107 R
35.6	Elsenham	43.54	53	
39.9	Newport	47.55	71	1/176 F
41.7	Audley End	49.33	64	1/130 R
49	Whittlesford	55.48	77	1/135 & 1/320 F
52.4	Shelford	58.71	70	
55.7	Cambridge	62.37	(59½ net)	

Whilst quite good, there was nothing more spectacular as a result of the engine not steaming freely. However, a couple of weeks later 2800 fared much better on a Sunday excursion to Norwich.

Liverpool Street to Norwich & return, December 1931
2800 *Sandringham* – Stratford
10 chs, 277/295 tons

Miles	Location	Times	Speeds	Gradients	Miles	Times	Speeds
0	Liverpool Street	00.00			51.7	56.53	
1.1	Bethnal Green	03.20	22/pws 23*		50.6	53.00	20*
4	Stratford	09.20	45/33*		47.7	48.50	33*
5.3	Forest Gate	11.07	54		46.4	47.13	58
7.3	Ilford	13.38	45* sigs		44.4	45.04	51* sigs
10	Chadwell Heath	16.24	60		41.7	42.38	66
12.4	Romford	18.45	62		39.3	40.22	57* sigs/62
18.2	Brentwood	24.47	47	1/84 R	33.5	35.23	66/83
19.3	Ingrave Box	26.12	39	1/103 R	32.4	34.19	53
20.2	Shenfield	27.13		1/136 F	31.5	33.21	57
23.	Ingatestone	30.13	75/70	1/224 F	28.1	29.57	55/62
	Margaretting	-	78			-	64
29.7	Chelmsford	35.27	29*		22	23.20	44*
35.9	Hatfield Peverel	42.16	63/58	1/143 & 1/181 R	15.8	17.20	57/65
38.6	Witham	44.45	71	1/178 F	13.1	14.43	70
42.2	Kelvedon	48.00	68/60	1/222 R	9.5	11.24	68
46.6	Marks Tey	52.25	32*		5.2	07.12	62/58
48.6	Stanway Box	55.47/56.50	sigs stand				
	Lexden Box	-	56			-	47/45
51.7	Colchester	60.44	37*		0	00.00	
					17	19.03	
54.1	Parson's Heath	63.33	47	1/144 R		-	65
56	Ardleigh	65.28	63	1/134 F	12.7	14.15	54
59.5	Manningtree	68.25	80		9.2	10.48	74/60
63.2	Bentley	71.28	69	1/145 & 1/157 R	5.5	07.37	47/68
68	Halifax Jcn	75.40		1/130 F			
68.7	Ipswich	76.56	(69¼ net)		0	00.00	
0		00.00			46.3	50.53	
2.5	Bramford	04.05	55	L	43.7	47.15	62
4.9	Claydon	06.20	68		41.4	45.03	69
5.4	Needham	09.33	66	1/337 R	37.9	41.52	68
11.9	Stowmarket	12.40	70		34.4	38.53	77
14.2	Haughley	14.45	63/58	1/131 R	32.2	36.57	68
17.9	Finningham	18.17	68		28.4	33.10	62/52
22.7	Mellis	22.17	80	1/248 & 1/132 F	23.6	27.58	50
26.3	Diss	25.05	78		20	24.15	66
28.8	Burston	27.05	68	1/260 R	17.5	22.00	67
31.8	Tivetshall	29.53	62/75		14.5	18.57	51
38	Flordon	34.55	78	1/136 F	8.3	12.32	65
41	Swainsthorpe	37.27	67/76	1/134 R &1/143 F	5.3	08.55	50
44.2	Trowse Upper Jcn	40.32	23*		2.1	04.44	35/29*
46.3	Norwich Thorpe	44.40	(113 net non-stop)		0	00.00	

The Ipswich-Norwich section on the down run was remarkable in achieving calculated drawbar horse power figures of over 1,200 in the acceleration away from Ipswich, 1,300 between Finningham and Diss and 1,188 on the brief rise before easing after Flordon. The third and final element of the trial took place on a normal service train, the 9.17am Southend Victoria-Liverpool Street and 5.22pm return. The up journey was allowed 60 minutes for the 41.5 miles including a stop at Prittlewell just over half a mile from Southend. It left Prittlewell 12 minutes late and with a clear run completed the journey in 45 minutes 39 seconds plus just under two minutes for the short run from Southend, arriving at Liverpool Street exactly on time.

Prittlewell-Liverpool Street, December 1931
9.17am Southend Victoria-Liverpool Street
2800 *Sandringham* – Stratford
10chs, 277/295 tons

Miles	Location	Times	Speeds	Gradients
0	Prittlewell	00.00		
2.2	Rochford	03.32	57	1/150 F
4.7	Hockley	06.35	43	1/100 R
7.8	Rayleigh	10.05	62/79	
11.9	Wickford	13.30	68/73	
16.5	Billericay	18.21	45/70	1/100 R
20.7	Shenfield	22.42	22*	
21.6	Ingrave Box	24.30	45	1/136 R
22.7	Brentwood	25.55	60/78	1/103 & 1/84 F
28.5	Romford	30.56	65*	
30.4	Chadwell Heath	32.54	74	
33.6	Ilford	35.10	65*	
35.6	Forest Gate	37.03	67	
36.9	Stratford	38.47	35*/52	
39.8	Bethnal Green	42.47	20*	
40.9	Liverpool Street	45.39		

The return evening commuter train was even more spectacular. With the same load, 2800 topped Ingrave summit at 50mph despite a slight signal check before Brentwood. Then it tore down the 1 in 100 from Billericay at a full 92mph and was still doing 90 before the Rayleigh stop – which it failed to make, finishing a clear train length beyond the platform!

One of the early diagrams for the B17/4s allocated to the GC route in 1937 was the Sheffield-Swindon service with the Sheffield engine and crew working throughout. Local driver Skelton with brand new 2863 decided that if the GW Castle could time the *Cheltenham Flyer*, then he and his steed could match its times, at least as far as Didcot. Three runs with the same engine and driver in the summer of 1957 had the incentive of a late start from Swindon.

Swindon - Oxford, 9.05 pm Swindon-Sheffield

		2863 *Everton* 7 chs, 201/215 tons 11 June 37			**2863 7 chs, 243/260 tons 17 June 37**			**2863 8 chs 278/295 tons 27 May 37**		
Miles	**Location**	**Times**	**Speed**		**Times**	**Speed**		**Times**	**Speed**	
0	Swindon	00.00		4½ L	00.00		4 L	00.00		7½ L
3	MP 74 ¼	04.24	62		05.11	58		04.38	57	
5.7	Shrivenham	06.43	75		07.38	70		07.04	68	

		Swindon - Oxford, 9.05 pm Swindon-Sheffield								
		2863 *Everton*			**2863**			**2863**		
		7 chs, 201/215 tons			**7 chs, 243/260 tons**			**8 chs 278/295 tons**		
		11 June 37			**17 June 37**			**27 May 37**		
Miles	**Location**	**Times**	**Speed**		**Times**	**Speed**		**Times**	**Speed**	
10.8	Uffington	10.14	83		11.44	78		11.12	77½	
13.4	Challow	12.25	86 ½		13.42	80 ½		13.12	79	
16.9	Wantage Rd	14.49	88		16.17	82		15.47	81	
20.8	Steventon	17.30	87	2 E	19.09	81	1 E	18,42	80	2¼ L
23.6	Foxhall Jn	21.16	18*	2¼ E	22.47	20*	1½ E	22.22	22*	2 L
24.3	Didcot N Jn	23.59		1½	24.17		2 E	23.40	26*	1¼ L
26.6	Culham	27.25	36		29.11	33		27.24	48	
28.8	Radley	30.44	43		32.44	41		29.54	55½	
30.5	Kenn'gton Jn	34.28	51/sigs		36.16	53/sigs		32.30	62	
33.9	Oxford	38.53		1½ L	40.27		2½ L	36.22		2 L

After Didcot the first two runs eased right down, whether to avoid signal checks or to recoup steam pressure after the earlier exertion is uncertain. The third run which pressed on found the 12 minute schedule from Didcot North Junction to the Oxford stop (9.6 miles) too tight. Bearings were checked at Oxford in all three runs and were found to be still cold.

2870 *Tottenham Hotspur* heads an unfitted freight on the GN main line a couple of months before being streamlined and renamed *City of London* to work the new *East Anglian* London-Norwich express service, July 1937.
MLS Collection

In September 1937, the GE timetable incorporated a new prestige service, the named *East Anglian* express, leaving Norwich at lunchtime and arriving at Liverpool Street at 2.10pm, calling at Ipswich only, and returning from London at 6.40pm. 2859 and 2870 were streamlined for the service and both engines worked the train regularly, each working the service in one direction balanced with another Norwich-London train, although if either of the streamlined engines was unavailable, the diagram was adjusted for the remaining engine to work the *East Anglian* in both directions. The November 1939 *Railway Magazine* published a number of logs of the express and I select three of the early afternoon up runs together with a heavier Sunday 3.45pm Norwich express hauled by 2858, built as a B17/4 but with a GE shorter tender because of its renaming and GE allocation.

Norwich – Liverpool Street, 1937-9

		2870			**2870**			**2859**			**2858**		
		City of London			***City of London***			***East Anglian***			***The Suffolk Regiment***		
		220/230 tons			**220/230 tons**			**220/230 tons**			**349/370 tons**		
Miles	**Location**	**Times**	**Speeds**		**Times**	**Speeds**		**Times**	**Speeds**		**Times**	**Speeds**	
0	Norwich	00.00			00.00			00.00			00.00		
2.1	Trowse U Jn	04.38			04.30			04.50			05.20	23	
5.3	Swainsthorpe	08.28			08.20			08.45			10.13		
8.3	Flordon	11.35	pws		11.28	71		11.50	71		14.20	61	
10.9	Forncett	14.05	pws		13.47	64		14.10	64/68		17.03	54	
14.5	Tiverton	21.27		3½ L	17.02	64	1 E	17.25	65	½ E	20.43	56½	
20	Diss	26.29	75		21.40	75		21.53	80½		25.25	77	
23.6	Mellis	29.33	64½		24.45	63		24.42	68		28.23	64	
28.4	Finningham	33.53	70/66		29.10	68½/63		28.48	74/70		32.45	69/64	
32.1	Haughley	37.10	60*	2¼ L	32.33		2½ E	31.55	61*	3 E	36.00	sigs slight	
34.4	Stowmarket	39.07		2 L	34.32	74	2½ E	33.58		3 E	38.10	81/ sigs 40*	
37.9	Needham	41.53			37.20			36.52			41.48		
41.4	Claydon	44.35	79		40.03	80		39.40	75		44.45	75	
45	MP70	47.20			42.56			42.35			47.40	sigs	
46.3	Ipswich	49.25		1½ L	45.15		2¾ E	44.30		3½ E	51.55		1 L
0		00.00		1 L	00.00		T	00.00		T	00.00		3 L
3.5	MP 65 ¼	05.57	44		06.05	41½		05.52	47		06.43	36½	
9.2	Manningtree	11.28	75/58*	1 E	11.40	74/ pws	2 E	11.15	74/63*	2¼ E	12.40	70	
12.7	Ardleigh	15.10	53½		18.12	48/69		14.55	54/70		16.30	50/69	
17	Colchester	20.57	pws/48	½ E	22.32	50*	T	19.12	46*/pws	2¾ E	21.00	pws 20*	
22.1	Marks Tey	28.00	pws		27.58			25.38			28.03		
26.5	Kelvedon	32.02	72		31.47	77		29.33	77		32.10	71	
30.1	Witham	35.00	74	T	34.38	76	1½ E	32.25	75	3½ E	35.10	73	
32.8	Hatfield Pev.	37.20	66		37.00	64		34.47	65		37.33	63½	
36.6	New Hall	40.27	75		40.12	73		37.55	75½		40.50	71	
39	Chelmsford	42.45	45*	1¼ E	42.40	40*	2¼ E	40.15	36*	4¾ E	43.12	46*	
45.1	Ingatestone	51.30	sigs		49.20	58		47.18	56		50.05	52	
48.5	Shenfield	55.30		½ L	52.42		3¼ E	50.50	60	5¼ E	53.52	56½	
49.5	Ingrave Box	56.33	53		53.42	55 ½		51.52	54		54.57	52	
53.7	Harold Wood	60.30	pws		57.10	79		55.30	77		58.35	81	

Norwich – Liverpool Street, 1937-9

Miles	Location	**2870** *City of London* **220/230 tons** Times	Speeds		**2870** *City of London* **220/230 tons** Times	Speeds		**2859** *East Anglian* **220/230 tons** Times	Speeds		**2858** *The Suffolk Regiment* **349/370 tons** Times	Speeds	
58.7	Chadwell H'th	66.07	pws	1 L	61.43		4¼ E	59.48	pws	6¼ E	62.40		
61.4	Ilford	68.25			64.17	pws		64.05	pws		65.00	pws/SL	
64.7	Stratford	73.50	pws	2¾ L	72.05	pws/sigs	T	71.05	pws	1 E	71.35	pws	
68.7	Liverpool St	80.45		1¾ L	80.15		¼ L	79.30		½ E	79.50		1¼ E
	(Net times)	(45 + 72¼)			(45¼ + 72¼)			(44½ + 72)			(48¼ + 74¾)		

All three *East Anglian* services got time in hand – or attempted to – in anticipation of the succession of pre-electrification permanent-way slacks approaching Liverpool Street. The fourth log with the significantly heavier load was excellent and matched the lighter expresses once up to speed from rest. I now show four runs on the down 6.40pm Liverpool Street *East Anglian*, all with the regulation load of 220 tons tare, 230 gross.

Liverpool Street-Norwich *East Anglian*, 1937-9

Miles	Location	**2870** Times	Speeds		**2859** Times	Speeds		**2859** Times	Speeds		**2870** Times	Speeds	
0	Liverpool St	00.00		T	00.00		T	00.00		T	00.00		T
4	Stratford	09.50	pws		07.20			07.35			07.10		
7.3	Ilford	-	pws		-	pws 5*		-			-	pws 5*	
10	Chadwell H'th	15.50	49	¼ E	13.10	62	2¾ E	12.35			13.00		
15	Harold Wood	25.53	66		21.47	pws 20*		21.40	easy		21.23	64½	
18.2	Brentwood	29.05	51½		27.50			26.05			24.45		
19.3	Ingrave Box	30.20	49		29.23	43		27.48	39		26.07	45½	
20.2	Shenfield	31.20		2¼ L	30.28		1½ L	28.58		T	27.50	sigs	¼ E
23.6	Ingatestone	36.23	sigs		33.28	76		31.58	80		31.10	77	
29.7	Chelmsford	44.45	sigs	6¾ L	38.37		½ L	37.05	42*	1 E	36.28	44*	1½ E
32.1	New Hall	47.45			41.15			40.00			39.13		
35.9	Hatfield Pev.	51.05			44.28	75		43.23			42.33		
38.6	Witham	53.15	81	6¼ L	47.50	pws	¾ L	45.40	77	1 ¼ E	44.52	75	2 E
42.2	Kelvedon	58.20	sigs		51.20	67 ½		48.32	70		47.47	74	
46.6	Marks Tey	63.20			55.12	65		52.15			51.23	65	
49	Stanway	65.20	77		57.10	76		54.20	77½		53.23	73	
51.7	Colchester	68.15	pws 20*	8¼ L	60.55	pws	1 L	56.55		3 E	57.38	pws	2½ E
56	Ardleigh	73.50			67.55			61.55			63.18		
59.5	Manningtree	76.45	79/64*	¾ L	71.33	65	2½ L	65.20		3 ¾ E	66.25	64.8	2½ E
	MP64 ¾	81.36	63/75		76.28	75		71.16	easy		71.28	sigs	
68.7	Ipswich	86.00		6 L	80.50		¾ L	76.40		3 ¼ E	78.00		2 E
0		00.00		6 L	00.00		1 L	00.00		T	00.00		T
2.5	Bramford	03.50			04.05			03.52			04.10		
4.9	Claydon	06.00			06.25			06.10			06.35		

Liverpool Street-Norwich *East Anglian*, 1937-9

		2870			**2859**			**2859**			**2870**		
Miles	**Location**	**Times**	**Speeds**		**Times**	**Speeds**		**Times**	**Speeds**		**Times**	**Speeds**	
8.4	Needham	08.58			09.42			09.17			09.55		
11.9	Stowmarket	11.50	75	4¼ L	12.47	71	¼ L	12.15	73	1 ¼ E	13.12	67	¼ E
14.2	Haughley	13.47	63		14.52	56		14.15	61		15.22	53	
17.9	Finningham	17.07	77		18.33			17.43			19.13		
22.7	Mellis	20.52	81		22.30			21.43			23.12		
26.3	Diss	23.35	82		25.15	81		24.25	82		25.57	81	
31.8	Tivetshall	28.00	69	2 L	29.40	71	1¼ E	34.10	pws (long)		30.22	69	
35.4	Forncett	30.52	78½		32.29	80		37.37			33.17		
	Flordon	-	80		-	85		-	82		-	78	
41	Swainsthorpe	35.17	70/75		36.45			42.02	80		37.48	77	
44.2	Trowse U Jn	38.03			39.40	18*		44.40			41.00	sigs	
46.3	Norwich	42.00		T	44.00		3 E	48.20		¼ L	45.55		2 E
	(Net times)	(70¼ + 42)			(7 ¾ +44)			(76¾ + 42½)			(71¾ + 44½)		

By the end of 1938 and the delivery of the B17/4s, and the allocation of many of these to the former Great Central main line, the distribution of the entire class was as follows:

Stratford	2800-2804, 2807-2815, 2863 (15)
Parkeston	2822, 2823, 2827, 2828, 2830, 2831, 2836, 2858 (8)
Ipswich	2805, 2806, 2820, 2825, 2845 (5)
Norwich	2816, 2826, 2832, 2835, 2837-2839, 2843, 2844, 2859, 2870 (11)
Cambridge	2817-2819, 2824, 2833, 2840-2842 (8)
March	2821, 2829, 2846
Gorton	2834, 2860, 2862, 2864, 2869, 2871, 2872 (7)
Neasden	2857, 2866
Woodford	2847, 2850, 2855
Leicester	2848, 2849, 2851-2854, 2856, 2861, 2865, 2867, 2868 (11)

Initially the B17/4s performed well on the Marylebone-Leicester, Sheffield and Manchester services although they had to be worked harder there than on the GE services and weaknesses in the design were revealed that caused rough riding. In consequence by 1939 the GC line received Gresley V2s and some Pacifics and some of the large tender B17s went to the GE section, the main sheds now having longer turntables. They also replaced the Ivatt Atlantics on the Cambridge-King's Cross buffet car trains. However, before their removal from the GC route (virtually completed by 1940), I show below a couple of examples of their best work on the Leicester-Marylebone line, recorded in the December 1939 *Railway Magazine.*

Leicester-Marylebone, 1939

		2867 *Bradford* – Leicester **11 chs, 369/405 tons** **8.51am (Sat) Leicester**			**2848 *Arsenal* – Leicester** **13 chs, 437/465 tons** **(incl 4 chs off Immingham boat)**		
Miles	**Location**	**Times**	**Speeds**		**Times**	**Speeds**	**Gradients**
0	Leicester	00.00		1½ L	00.00		
4.7	Whetstone	07.53			07.45	50	1/176 R
9.2	Ashby	-	sig stand (32 secs)		13.55	42	
13.1	Lutterworth	23.12	78½		18.59	73½	1/176 F
19.9	Rugby	29.12	69		25.12	63	1/176 R

		Leicester-Marylebone, 1939 2867 *Bradford* – Leicester 11 chs, 369/405 tons 8.51am (Sat) Leicester			2848 *Arsenal* – Leicester 13 chs, 437/465 tons (incl 4 chs off Immingham boat)		
Miles	**Location**	**Times**	**Speeds**		**Times**	**Speeds**	**Gradients**
24.6	Braunston	32.56	78½		29.23	70	1/176 F & L
27.9	Staverton Rd	35.43			32.42		1/176 R
31.6	Charwelton	39.44	49		37.17	44	1/176 R
34	Woodford	42.14		6¾ L	39.53		
37	Culworth	44.50	73½		42.40	69½	1/176 F & 1/176 R
40.6	Helmdon	48.02	64		45.58	60	
43.8	Brackley	50.42	85		48.46	79	1/176 F
48.6	Finmere	54.20	74½		52.37	69	1/176 R
54.3	Calvert	58.20	90/82		57.03	80½/ 72	1/176 F & L
56.3	Grendon U.Jn	59.52	84/eased	5 L	58.45	63*	
59	Quainton Rd	62.12		4¾ L	61.14		
65.2	Aylesbury	67.37	60	4 L	66.37	69	L
67.4	Stoke M'ville	70.11	36		68.49		1/117 R
69.8	Wendover	73.45	34		71.54		1/117 R
71.9	MP 31 ½	77.21	34		75.05	43	1/117 R
74.3	Gt Missenden	79.59	74	5½:L	77.37	71	1/125 F
79.5	Amersham	84.39	59		82.33	55	1/160 R
81.5	Chalfont	86.27	76	5 L	84.26	80	1/105 F
85.0	Rickmansworth	90.24		4½ L	88.11		
89.4	Northwood	95.08	44/66		92.45	46/pws	1/176 R & 1/145 F
93.9	Harrow	99.55		4½ L	98.47		
98	Neasden Jn	103.58	71	4 L	103.12	68	1/91 F
100.1	Brondesbury	106.03			105.21	49	1/90 R
103.1	Marylebone	110.20	(104¾ net)	2¾ L	110.06	(109 net)	

2867's run is remarkable for the high speed between Woodford and Grendon Underwood Junction, but performance tailed off on the climb from Aylesbury to the summit beyond Wendover suggesting that boiler pressure was suffering. Cecil J Allen in his article described 2848's performance with this very heavy load as the finest ever seen with a locomotive of this class (remarkable indeed for a locomotive that in BR days was only classed as a 4P, prior to rebuilding with a 100A1 boiler and becoming a B17/6). Such strenuous efforts, however, do seem to have reaped consequences and the B17s' reputation for rough-riding was well founded. Earlier some high speeds were recorded on the 23 mile racing stretch between Leicester and Nottingham, B17/1 2816 reaching 83 ½mph with 250 tons, completing the 23.4 miles in even time (23 ¼ minutes). Two B17/4s, 2853 and 2849, in their first months of operation both touched 85mph through Loughborough and then 86 ½ and 87mph respectively at Ruddington, completing the journey in exactly 23 minutes.

The *Railway Magazine* of July 1939 recorded the logs of four B17s between Sheffield and Manchester, two with the lone Gorton B17/1, 2834, and two with B17/4s.

Leicester's 2861 *Sheffield Wednesday* heads a Great Central line express near Ecklands, c1938. A.C. Gilbert/MLS Collection

2860 ***Hull** City* with a foxhunting special, with vans for hounds and horses immediately behind the engine. It is passing Staverton Road signalbox near Rugby, c1938. G.A. Coltas/ MLS Collection

2862 *Manchester United* heads a York – Swindon cross-country via Woodford express displaying the chalked GW train identification number on the smokebox door at Staverton Road near Rugby, c1938.
G.A. Coltas/MLS Collection

Sheffield-Manchester London Road, 1938/9

		2834			**2852**			**2834**			**2848**	
		Hinchingbrooke			***Darlington***			***Hinchingbrooke***			***Arsenal***	
		175/180 tons			**207/215 tons**			**241/250 tons**			**341/360 tons**	
Miles	**Location**	**Times**	**Speed**		**Times**	**Speed**		**Times**	**Speed**		**Times**	**Speed**
0	Sheffield	00.00			00.00			00.00			00.00	
1.2	Neepsend	-			03.02			02.58			03.36	
2.9	Wadsley Bdge	-			05.36	41½		05.36	42½		06.31	36
4.9	Oughty Bdge	07.43	47		08.18	43½		08.17	44½		09.35	39½
7.9	Deepcar	11.46	45½		12.38	42		12.30	43½		14.15	40
8.8	Wortley	12.54	47½		13.54	40		13.43	45		15.37	40½
12.9	Penistone	17.56		1 E	19.46	44	¾ L	19.04		T	21.20	45
16.7	Hazlehead	23.00	45		25.05	42½		24.13			26.38	42½
18.9	Dunford Bdge	25.58	44	1 E	28.23	42	1 ¼ L	27.16	43	¼ L	29.58	40
22.1	Woodhead	29.23	62	1½ E	32.01	57	1 L	30.46	60	¼ E	33.59	
26	Torside	32.58	68		35.35	68		34.23	66		37.33	68
29.4	Dinting	36.33	40*		39.09	45*		38.00	37*		40.49	44*
33	Godley Jn	41.25	53*		43.26	40*		42.23	50*		46.33	pws
36.3	Guide Bdge	45.12	43*	1¾ E	47.25	40*/65		46.10	30*	¾ E	50.14	30*/64
41.3	Manchester	52.14		2¾ E	54.19		¾ E	53.42		1¾ E	57.11	(56 net)

Initially, during the Second World War, the B17s left the former GC and were concentrated in East Anglia. However, with the heavy loads on the East Coast main line, the GC allocated pacifics returned there and eight B17/4s returned to Gorton – until 1944 when a return of more V2s reduced the B17s on the GC route permanently. The remaining Gorton B17s left the route in October 1946. The GE engines struggled with heavy loads during the war years and their low pressure and poor maintenance caused a significant loss of performance. Colwick retained a few, one (1647) was at Lincoln and the rest were on the GE section by the end of 1946.

Train running with post-war heavy loads and B17s in poor condition was pedestrian in the 1946-48 period, logs from this time on semi-fast ten/twelve coach trains on the Cambridge line showing at best 40-45 minute net times for the thirty miles to Bishops Stortford, with no speed higher than the mid-50s. The allocation as the fleet passed to nationalised ownership in January 1948 was:

Stratford	1605, 1606, 1609, 1612, 1655, 1658 (6)
Ipswich	1600-1602, 1604, 1618, 1634, 1645, 1649, 1668 (9)
Norwich	1625, 1626, 1629, 1644, 1659, 1670 (6)
Cambridge	1608, 1610, 1611, 1613, 1619-1624, 1627, 1628, 1631, 1633, 1637, 1638, 1640-1643, 1654, 1663, 1665, 1666 (24)
March	1630, 1635, 1636, 1646, 1648, 1656, 1660, 1671, 1672 (9)
Lincoln	1647
Colwick	1650-1653, 1657, 1662, 1664, 1667, 1669 (9)

As seen above, the majority were now based at Cambridge working to both Liverpool Street and King's Cross though shortly that work would reduce as the Thompson B1s increased. Some were so badly

Tender-first 1620 *Clumber* in typically dreadful post-war condition hauls an empty stock train from Liverpool Street to Stratford through Coborn Road station, Mile End, on 2 December 1946 just six days before the closure of the station. H.C. Casserley/MLS Collection

1600 *Sandringham* in parlous external condition on a down fast at Brentwood station, 9 August 1947. MLS Collection

Spruced up 1668 *Bradford City*, although still in wartime black livery, pauses at Woodbridge station on the South Suffolk line with a stopping train for Ipswich, c1948. Eddie Johnson Collection

run down that they were restricted to freight duties. Numbers were reduced as some were rebuilt to B2s and a further shuffle of B17s took place in the early 1950s as more B1s were allocated to the GE section. The December 1951 shed allocation was:

Stratford	61602, 61605, 61606, 61608, 61610-61613, 61648, 61650, 61651, 61654, 61655, 61660-61662, 61667, 61672 (18)
Ipswich	61600, 61601, 61604, 61618, 61634, 61645, 61647, 61649, 61668, 61669 (10)
Norwich	61609, 61629, 61664, 61665 (4)
Cambridge	61619, 61620, 61622-61625, 61627, 61628, 61636, 61637, 61640, 61642, 61643, 61652, 61653, 61657, 61663 (17)
March	61621, 61626, 61630, 61631, 61633, 61635, 61638, 61641, 61646, 61656, 61658, 61666 (13)
Yarmouth	61659, 61670

The two Yarmouth engines had just been overhauled, losing

Streamlined B17/5 61670 *City of London* near Woodbridge with a Yarmouth-Liverpool Street express, c1950. Eddie Johnson Collection

B17/5 61670 *City of London* departing from Woodbridge with a Liverpool Street - Yarmouth express, c1950. Eddie Johnson Collection

B17/5 61659 *East Anglian* at Woodbridge with a stopping train for Ipswich, c1950. Eddie Johnson Collection

Norwich based
B17/1 *Naworth Castle* leaving its home base with a train for Yarmouth, May 1951.
J. Davenport/MLS Collection

B17/6 61654 *Sunderland* near Woodbridge heading the *Easterling*, a Yarmouth – Liverpool Street express, c1951.
Eddie Johnson Collection

***Above left*: B17/4 61649** *Sheffield United* standing at Woodbridge with a stopping train for Ipswich, c1950. Eddie Johnson Collection

***Above right*: Train crew** of B17/6 61665 *Leicester City* during a halt a Woodbridge, c1951. Eddie Johnson Collection

their streamlining in the process, and did excellent work between Ipswich and Yarmouth and Ipswich B17s hauled the *Easterling* through London service. The defrocked 61670 shone once when a Britannia failed just before hauling the 6.45 pm from Norwich, and with eight coaches, 280 tons gross, maintained the schedule to Ipswich, stopping at Diss and Stowmarket, top speeds 74 at Burston, 76 at Haughley and 73½ at Claydon. Three p-way checks between Ipswich and Chelmsford meant that the express passed the latter town six minutes late, but 57½mph minimum at Ingrave Box and 72-75 sustained from Harold Wood to Ilford recouped all but two minutes.

However, the main GE services were in the hands of Britannia pacifics after 1951 with B1s as standbys and with Gresley pacifics, V2s and B1s on the former Great Central, the B17s were relegated to secondary services with the B12s, despite many increasing their tractive effort with the higher pressure B1 boilers. 61627 *Aske Hall* left Cambridge with an 8-coach buffet car express thirteen minutes late in October 1952 and managed to recover two minutes to King's Cross inclusive of a couple of short signal stops with maxima of 60 before the Royston stop, 67 at Baldock, 40 at Woolmer Green and a final 71 at New Barnet. A recorder in 1950 timed B17/1 61625 *Raby Castle* on an up Cambridge buffet express commenting on a 'commendable trip', but it was a lightweight six coaches only and reached 70mph only once at Baldock. B17/4 61650 *Grimsby Town* with 8 coaches (280 tons gross) on the 1.36pm Liverpool Street-Clacton interval service in 1953 dropped three minutes on the 32 minute schedule to Shenfield with nothing over 46 before Harold Wood and falling to 27mph at Ingrave summit. It had regained schedule by Witham without exceeding 58mph. It eventually arrived at Clacton a minute early without having exceeded 65mph anywhere (down the 1 in 128 before Colchester).

In March 1952 a very run-down 61613 *Woodbastwick Hall* of Stratford worked the 6pm Liverpool Street-Cambridge with nine coaches, and kept time to Bishop's Stortford (½ minute early on a 45 minute schedule) without exceeding 57mph. It managed the climb from Stansted to Elsenham, culminating in a mile of 1 in 107 at 42mph and reached 63 on the three-mile descent to Newport. After the Audley End stop it just managed 60mph on the long eight mile favourable grades to Shelford and despite a slight signal check outside Cambridge, arrive ¼ minute early. The regular recorder marked this as a 'good run'.
I found an interesting comparison compiled by Mr B. Nathan of a B17, B2 and L1 on Cambridge-King's Cross buffet expresses and I give the broad outlines of the logs on next page:

B17/4 61649 *Sheffield United* approaches Shenfield with an up express, 11 April 1953. M.L. Boakes/MLS Collection

Miles	Location	Cambridge-King's Cross 61619 *Welbeck Abbey* (B17/6) 8 chs, 245 tons 5 March 1952 Times	Speed		61671 *Royal Sovereign* (B2) 8 chs, 275 tons 13 March 1953 Times	Speed		67746 (L1 2-6-4T) 8 chs, 285 tons 13 June 1953 Times	Speed		
0	Cambridge	00.00		T	00.00		T	00.00			T
2.5	Shepreth B. Jn	05.26	41		04.54	43/36*		05.25	40/35*		
6.9	Foxton	10.58	61		10.35	60		11.04	55		
12.9	Royston	17.15	62/48		17.16	55/47		18.00	57/45	1/120 R	
21.2	Baldock	26.17	68		26.16	68		27.51	58	1/197 F	
23.2	Letchworth	28.37		1 ½ E	28.30		1½ E	30.23			½ L
0		00.00		T	00.00		½ E	00.00			1 L
2.7	Hitchin	06.27	43/sigs	1½ L	05.15		¼ E	05.00			1 L
0		00.00		T	00.00		3 L	00.00			2 L
3.35	Stevenage	06.52	40		06.11	48		05.57	46	1/200 R	
6.85	Knebworth	13.01	pws 20*/45		10.06	55		09.41	58		
9.9	Welwyn North	16.34	62	3 L	13.15	62		12.42	68		
11.6	Welwyn-G-C	18.51		3 L	15.27		2 ½ L	14.53			2 L
0		00.00		3 L	00.00		3 L	00.00			¼ E
2.6	Hatfield	03.55	54/52		03.58	55/52		04.08	53/52		
7.6	Potters Bar	09.16	62		09.21	57		09.43	53		
11.2	New Barnet	12.35	70		12.53	65		13.21	63		
17.8	Finsbury Park	18.44	64		19.13	64		20.09	56/ sigs		
20.2	King's Cross	23.09		1½ L	24.54		3 L	26.15			1 L

61619 was reputed to be one of the best of the Cambridge B17s. 61671 was kept as the royal engine used for the Sandringham trains. The L1 matched the 4-6-0s by good acceleration and hill climbing although maximum speeds were lower. The L1 was presumably covering for a 4-6-0 failure.

O.S. Nock had a footplate pass for the 11.03am Liverpool Street-Yarmouth (undated) with B17/6 61669 *Barnsley* and 9 coaches (282 tons tare). The train left Liverpool Street four minutes late and with 20 per cent cut-off and full regulator accelerated from 45mph through Stratford to 50 at Forest Gate before a 20mph p-way slack at Ilford. It then sustained a succession of signal checks onto Harold Wood, recovering with full regulator and 30per cent cut-off to 47mph before Brentwood, and advancing the cut-off to 35 per cent fell to 33½mph at Ingrave summit. Passing Chelmsford five minutes late at 62mph, it fell to 57 at New Hall but raced away to 77mph after Witham (full regulator, 15 per cent cut-off). It was 5¾ minutes late at Colchester after a 10mph signal check at Marks Tey, fell to 47 at Ardleigh, touched 76 before Manningtree and was back to five minutes late at Ipswich, passed in 78 minutes. With 72 below Wickham Market, 43 on the 1 in 89 before and 71 in the dip after Darsham, it was nearly on time at Beccles and left on time (station allowance – 5 minutes) but was 3 minutes late at Great Yarmouth after a p-way slack between Haddiscoe and St Olave's.

By 1953, the Britannias had total command of the key GE line expresses. The B17s and the B12s had a few semi-fast and stopping services on the Cambridge and Southend lines, but the opportunity for noteworthy performances was rare. In fact, the first B17/6 to be withdrawn, 61628 *Harewood House,* had gone in September 1952 and 61604 (another B17/6) and 61624 (a B17/1) were condemned in March 1953. 61624 had been logged in March 1952 on the 8.05pm King's Cross-Cambridge semi-fast, dropping six minutes to Hitchin before signal checks before Letchworth caused the train to be 16 minutes late there and with further loss by the engine, Cambridge was reached 18 minutes late. The recorder described the run as 'pretty awful'. March's 61621 with 300 tons on the Liverpool-Harwich on 3 January 1952 took over at Lincoln, lost eleven minutes to Sleaford, another six minutes to Spalding and further problems to March where it was replaced. The engine was clean, but was slipping, exhausting steam constantly from the cylinder cocks and the valves were 'all over the place'. It was recorded again six months later on the same train and kept time without exceeding 57mph. 61622 took the 10.38am Caistor-Liverpool Street holiday express over at Ely in the summer of 1952 with 286 tons and kept time on an easy schedule with just a brief 62mph descending from Stansted. 61625 had the 7.45pm Liverpool Street – Cambridge with 255 tons and dropped eight minutes on the 80- minute schedule, just about offsetting the signal checks at Broxbourne and Audley End.

No more withdrawals were made until 1958 and then the condemnation and scrapping of the B17s accelerated as the new Brush Type 2 diesels (class 31) eliminated the need for the 4-6-0 classes within a couple of years. At the end of

B17/4 61660 *Hull City* on the turntable at the Liverpool Street engine stabling point, c1957. 61660 was one of two B17/4s that were never rebuilt with the 100A boiler. MLS Collection

B17/1 61637 *Thorpe Hall* pilots B12/3 61535 into Ipswich with a down stopping train, c1956. MLS Collection

B17/6 61600 *Sandringham* at Wickford with a Shenfield – Southend Victoria train, 5 August 1955. A.C. Gilbert/ MLS Collection

B17/6 61602 *Walsingham* arrives at Southend Victoria with the 2.50pm from Liverpool Street, 5 August 1955. An impatient passenger has already opened a door to alight before the train has come to a stand.
A.C. Gilbert/MLS Collection

An early casualty – B17/6 61604 *Elveden* eases a Southend-Liverpool Street train past Stratford in early 1953 just a few months before its withdrawal in August.
MLS Collection

B17/1 61611 *Raynham Hall,* a Stratford engine, at Manchester London Road presumably running in after overhaul at Gorton Works, c1955.
MLS Collection

B17/6 61623 *Lambton Castle* with one of the M&GN based LMR 4MT 2-6-0s coupled inside arriving at King's Lynn with a stopping train from Cambridge, c1958.
R.C. Riley/MLS Collection

1957 and during 1958 I frequently spent a couple of hours at Liverpool Street between the end of college tutorials at 4 o'clock and evening society or sports events and sought runs, if my finances permitted, to Broxbourne, Bishops Stortford or Shenfield if a B2, B12 or B17 backed on to a suitable train. Back in 1950, I had spent three weeks at the house of a friend near Doncaster and had not seen a single B17 during that period. I saw an occasional one at King's Cross during London 'spotting' trips in the mid-1950s and managed a trip out to Finsbury Park behind 61653 on a stopping train to Cambridge. A couple of week visits were spent with a cousin in Chelmsford in 1951 and 1952, which included a day at Shenfield during both weeks and periods trainspotting at Chelmsford, and saw plenty of Britannias, B1s and B12s but hardly any B17s – just a couple at Shenfield on Southend trains and a B2 after turning down a succession of B1s on the last trip home, settling for 61639 *Norwich City*.

I was luckier in 1958. I meandered out to Tottenham past Hackney Downs and Clapton Marshes with 61601, 61623, 61630, 61634, 61636 and 61672, usually returning somewhat faster behind an L1 or N7 tank. When a little more flush, I ventured out to Broxbourne with 61609, 61611, 61618 and B2 61607, returning with a B1 or Brush Type 2, or Shenfield with 61608, 61660 (after B2 61632 failed) and 61661 returning with 61655, 61663 and 61613, the latter giving me my fastest B17 speed, descending Brentwood bank at 79mph, but on arrival in London, displaying a scorched and glowing smokebox door.

During my first trainspotting trip to London in May 1950, my schoolfriend took this photograph from the end of platform 8 at King's Cross capturing in the yard B17/1 61625 *Raby Castle*, N2 69506, an L1 67746 and just visible the tender of New England A2/3 60513 *Dante*. Cedric Utley/David Maidment's Collection

Then, in the spring of 1958, I was tempted several times by the 4.36pm Liverpool Street-King's Lynn *Fenman* and after a couple of B2s and, surprisingly, B12s, I had two runs to Bishop's Stortford with Cambridge B17s that looked in good condition. I was particularly pleased to get 61625 *Raby Castle*, the first B17 I'd seen back in May 1950 during my earliest London trainspotting trip on the turntable that could be viewed from the end of platform 8 at King's Cross. My pleasure turned to disappointment as 61625, still a B17/1, never looked like maintaining the schedule and ran the thirty miles mostly in the mid-40s. A week later I tried again with B17/6 61627 *Aske Hall*, which was a great improvement and timed the *Fenman* comfortably. On both occasions I returned to London behind a Britannia.

I did no serious train timing myself until 1960, so have no records other than memories of these journeys, but have unearthed a couple of runs during the 1950s on Southend trains that show the lack of ambition in the secondary service schedules compared with the pre-war period. Both were on the 5.33pm Liverpool Street-Southend, an important commuter service of nine coaches stopping at Billericay, Wickford, Rayleigh and Prittlewell and allowed 62 minutes running time for the 40.8 miles to the latter point just short of Southend. B17/6 61604 *Elveden* could only maintain 44mph from Ilford to Chadwell Heath, where it was a minute down, managed 52mph before Harold Wood and fell to 29mph on Brentwood bank. A final 62 after Shenfield brought the train to a stand at Billericay just ½ minute late, in 37 minutes 26 seconds for the 24.3 miles.

B17/6 61655 *Middlesborough*, one of the 'Footballers' that I caught back from Shenfield on one of my evening trips, here arriving at Witham with an up semi-fast train, c1956. MLS Collection

It kept the seven minute schedule to Wickford (4½ miles), top speed 60mph, dropped a half minute onto Rayleigh and was a minute late into Prittlewell where the recorder, Mr E.R. Davies, alighted. B17/6 61651 *Derby County* kept time more comfortably, gaining over a minute to Billericay with 53 at Chadwell Heath, 54 at Harold Wood, 32 at Ingrave summit. It raced away to 71mph on the short downhill section to Wickford but lost a couple of minutes onto Rayleigh because of a permanent way slowing. 72mph after Hockley recovered one of those minutes. A good performance but humdrum compared with the exploits of the 1937-1939 period.

My overall conclusion? Excellent engines at their zenith, especially on the Great Central route immediately before the Second World War, but they became very rough-riding as mileage was accumulated and were overshadowed by the B1s and then the Britannias in the post-war period and the few locomotives which did not receive the B1 100A1 boiler all too often demonstrated why they were only given the BR 4P power category.

Preservation

61662

A North British Locomotive Preservation Group was founded in 1990 and in 2008, having discovered N.B. Company drawings of the B17 in the National Railway Museum, researched a project to build one of the R. Stephenson & Co. constructed B17/4s and chose 61662 *Manchester United* with the belief that the football club and supporters would help fund the scheme. In 2012 the project team planned to build the locomotive in five years, but in February 2019 the directors of the project issued a statement, of which extracts are:

'No.61662 *Manchester United* is currently a full size 'mock-up' representing the cab, boiler, smokebox and bufferbeam with a planned completion date of 2019. The representation does not include wheels, frame or motion at the present time.'

A former LNER standard tender has been obtained and the possibility of constructing an operational locomotive is for future consideration.

61673

The original proposal was to build two B17s, one operational and one a full size mock-up (61662 above). After the national financial problems of 2008, the project slipped and in 2010 the B17 Steam Locomotive Trust was set up as a registered charity and in September 2012 members decided to build a B17 to be numbered 61673 and named *Spirit of Sandringham.* Anticipated cost was £2.7 million and frames were built by the Boro' Foundry in Lye (West Midlands) in 2015 and delivered to the Llangollen Railway workshops where further construction was to be undertaken. Further work on the frame was completed in 2018 and the plan is to have a rolling chassis and boiler by 2027. Planned completion date is 2028 with the locomotive certified and running by 2029, the hundredth anniversary of the building of the class.

Chapter 6

THOMPSON'S B1s – 1942

Design & construction

Edward Thompson succeeded Nigel Gresley when he died in office in 1941. Thompson, a workshops man at heart, was keen to develop greater standardisation on the LNER following the examples of Churchward and Stanier, and in contrast to Gresley's policy of designing locomotives for very specific roles which led to a multitude of classes of comparatively small sizes. Thompson proposed a 4-6-0 based on the B17 but with 6ft 2in driving wheels, two cylinders and a higher boiler pressure of 220psi. The intention was to cover the work undertaken by all the previous 4-6-0s, the D49 and D11 4-4-0s and the remaining Atlantics, and K2 and K3 moguls. Amendments to the design were carried out in 1942, but initially Thompson concentrated on boiler design, raising the pressure to 225psi and in the autumn of 1942 ten new standard 100A boilers were constructed. Thompson instructed the drawing office staff to keep it simple and authority was given by the LNER Board for the building of ten B10s, rapidly changed to B1 necessitating the re-categorisation of the ex-Great Central engines of that description. The prototype, numbered 8301 and named *Springbok* was completed at Darlington Works in December and sent to Doncaster for inspection before being released to traffic on 19 December 1942. After running in and ensuring the new engine met specification 8302 was constructed at Darlington in June 1943 and the remaining eight followed slowly, 8310 not appearing until June 1944. The dimensions of the new standard mixed traffic 4-6-0 were:

Cylinders (2 outside)	20inx 26in
Coupled wheel diameter	6ft 2in
Bogie wheel diameter	3ft 2in
Walchaerts valve gear with 10in piston valves	
Boiler pressure	225psi
Heating surface	2, 020 for first ten, then 2,005sqft (incl 344sqft superheating)
Grate area	27.9sqft
Axleload	17 tons 15 cwt
Weight – Engine	71 tons 3 cwt
– Tender	52 tons 10 cwt
– Total	123 tons 13 cwt
Water capacity	4,200 gallons
Coal capacity	7 tons 10 cwt
Tractive effort	26,878lbs

With their 6ft 2in coupled wheels and 225psi boiler pressure, they were appreciably more powerful than the LNER's previous 4-6-0s, and slightly more powerful than the LMS 'Black 5s' and slightly less than the GW 'Halls'. The naming was said to have been influenced by the recent visit of the South African General Smuts and the following nine were all named after the African species of antelope. 8301-10 were renumbered 1000-1009 in the LNER 1946 scheme and thirty more were ordered from Darlington (1010-1039) and delivered between November 1946 and December 1947, while a contract was placed with the North British Locomotive Company for 100, built rapidly between April 1946 and April 1947, numbered 1040-1139. The N.B. Company received a new order for a further 150 built between May 1947 and September 1948 (numbered on delivery as 1190 – 1287, E1288- E1303 and 61304-61339). The LNER Works and the

8304 ***Gazelle*** built in November 1943, and repainted from wartime unlined black to LNER lined green for royal train duties from Cambridge shed, ex-works at Darlington, 1945.
Colling Turner/MLS Collection

1002 ***Impala*** still in wartime black livery but renumbered from 8303 in 1946, at Perth, 20 April 1946.
MLS Collection

The prototype B1, 8301 *Springbok*, renumbered 1000 and painted LNER apple green at Stratford in 1947. MLS Collection

N.B. Company could not keep pace with the demand and fifty were constructed by Vulcan Foundry (1140-1189) between April and August 1947. The British Transport Commission gave authority for the continuing build of the B1s whilst its own mixed traffic designs were being prepared and Darlington built 61350-61359 (July-October 1949) and 61400-61409 (March-June 1950), Gorton built 61340-61349 (November 1948-July 1949) and the North British Company got a final order of 61360-61399 (March 1950-April 1952). The last B1 was therefore not 61409, but 61399 delivered nearly two years later. The series 61400-61409 required the renumbering of the first ten ex NE B16s as 61470-61479. The North British 250 locomotives cost £14,895 each and the Vulcan engines £15,300. The contract for the final fifty North British engines had inflated to £16,190.

The first of the North British built B1s, 1040, constructed in April 1946 and the only N.B. engine named after a species of antelope, *Roedeer*, as new in works grey at the North British factory in Glasgow, April 1946. Loco Publishing Co./ MLS Collection

1044 as delivered new from the N.B. Works to the LNER in May 1946, in unlined black livery, apart from the lining of boiler bands and cylinder casing. MLS Collection

The first forty all (bar one) received antelope names which tested the publicity department's wildlife knowledge (there several duplications – *Oryx & Gemsbok, Wildebeeste & Gnu, Topi & Sassaby, Impala & Pallah, Oribi & Ourebi, Stembok & Steinbok, Chiru & Jairou* and one triplication – *Reitbok, Reedbuck and Umseke.*) Two of the latter are misspelt as well – *Reitbok* should be *Rietbok* and *Umseke* should be *Umziki,* the Zulu variation. Most are Afrikaans or Bantu variations of the same animal. Other B1s received the names of the LNER Directors to honour them just before nationalisation, but these were on seemingly random locomotive identities, *Ralph Assheton* emerging from the antelopes, 1189, 1215 and 1221 were also selected and then a rush of 1237, 1238 and 1240-1251 in the autumn of 1947 before their Board disappeared. 1239 was allocated *Rupert E Beckett* which for some reason was never used. The fitting of these last nameplates took place in December 1947 as a last gesture before they became British Railways' property. One final ceremony took place in July 1951 when one of the latest North British locomotives, 61379, was named *Mayflower* as a link between the town of Boston in Lincolnshire and the city of Boston in the USA.

The full set of B1 names were:

1000	*Springbok*
1001	*Eland*
1002	*Impala*
1003	*Gazelle*
1004	*Oryx*
1005	*Bongo*
1006	*Blackbuck*
1007	*Klipspringer*
1008	*Kudu*
1009	*Hartebeeste*
1010	*Wildebeeste*
1011	*Waterbuck*
1012	*Puku*
1013	*Topi*
1014	*Oribi*
1015	*Duiker*
1016	*Inyala*
1017	*Bushbuck*
1018	*Gnu*
1019	*Nilghai*
1020	*Gemsbok*
1021	*Reitbok*
1022	*Sassaby*
1023	*Hirola*
1024	*Addax*
1025	*Pallah*
1026	*Ourebi*
1027	*Madoqua*
1028	*Umseke*
1029	*Chamois*
1030	*Nyala*
1031	*Reedbuck*
1032	*Stembok*
1033	*Dibatag*
1034	*Chiru*
1035	*Pronghorn*
1036	*Ralph Assheton*
1037	*Jairou*
1038	*Blacktail*
1039	*Steinbok*
1040	*Roedeer*

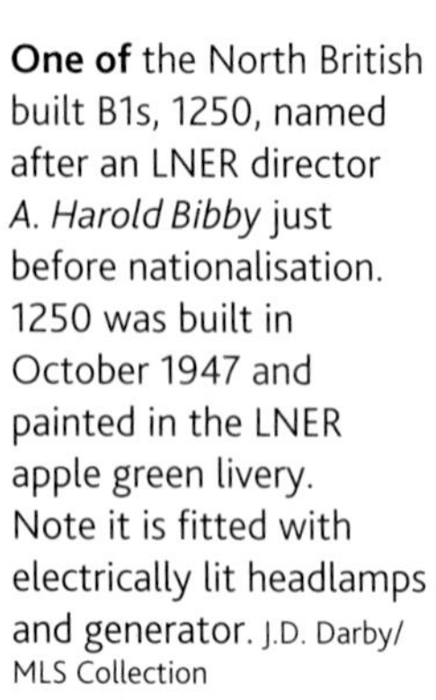

One of the North British built B1s, 1250, named after an LNER director *A. Harold Bibby* just before nationalisation. 1250 was built in October 1947 and painted in the LNER apple green livery. Note it is fitted with electrically lit headlamps and generator. J.D. Darby/ MLS Collection

61189	*Sir William Gray*
61215	*William Henton Carver*
61221	*Sir Alexander Erskine-Hill*
61237	*Geoffrey H Kitson*
61238	*Leslie Runciman*
61240	*Harry Hinchcliffe*
61241	*Viscount Ridley*
61242	*Alexander Reith Gray*
61243	*Sir Harold Mitchell*
61244	*Strang Steel*
61245	*Murray of Elibank*
61246	*Lord Balfour of Burleigh*
61247	*Lord Burghley*
61248	*Geoffrey Gibbs*
61249	*Fitzherbert Wright*
61250	*A Harold Bibby*
61251	*Oliver Bury*
61379	*Mayflower*

8301-8310 appeared in black wartime livery with LNER shaded transfer numerals on the cabside and just NE on the tender. 8304 was repainted LNER apple green livery with black and white lining for royal train duties diagrammed to Cambridge engines. In 1947 it, 1000 and later 61002 were also painted LNER green. 61001 and 61009 were given trial BR black liveries and emblems, but neither were adopted as standard. 1040-1093 built by the North British Company were painted black with red lining, though the LNER Works at Doncaster, Darlington and Glasgow Cowlairs repainted fifteen LNER apple green during their first overhauls, in the latter half of 1947 and early 1948. From November 1946 both the Darlington built engines (1010-1039) and the North British engines from 1094 to 61339 received the LNER lined apple-green livery, with the letters LNER on the tender until E1288 which was the first to bear the letters 'BRITISH RAILWAYS' and numbered with the prefix '6' from 61304 onwards. The first to appear in the new BR standard mixed traffic livery of black with red, cream and grey lining was Darlington overhauled 61084 in May 1948, followed quickly by

Thirty more B1s were built at Darlington simultaneously with the delivery of the NB order. 1032 *Stembok* was constructed in August 1947 and painted LNER lined apple green livery. It is seen here at Darlington, August 1947. Photomatic/MLS Collection

The LNER engines were initially identified with the letter 'E' before the LNER number before renumber in the 60,000 series. E1290, built in February 1948 is shown here at Darlington five months later, 4 July 1948. MLS Collection

61012, 61014 and 61071. Stratford repainted 61040, 61048 and 61057 in June. From November 1948 the Gorton, Darlington and North British built locomotives all bore the BR standard mixed traffic lined black livery.

The LNER Civil Engineer was concerned about the hammer blow of the two cylinder 4-6-0s compared with the three-cylinder B17s, which led Thompson to reduce the reciprocating balances from 60 per cent to 36 per cent, but unfortunately this led to poor riding quality, increasing the fore and aft movement and accelerating the wear in the horns, motion and side rod bushes. Mileage between main overhauls averaged 78,396 in 1953 (better than the Stanier Black 5's 56,969 but short of the WR Hall's 87,942). Like the B17s, the B1s earned a reputation for rough riding as their mileage between overhauls rose. Because of these problems 61035 was involved in an experiment to restore the 60 per cent reciprocating balance by fitting additional balance weights on the coupled wheels in 1954. Tests proved that an improvement was made and some other B1s were similarly fitted.

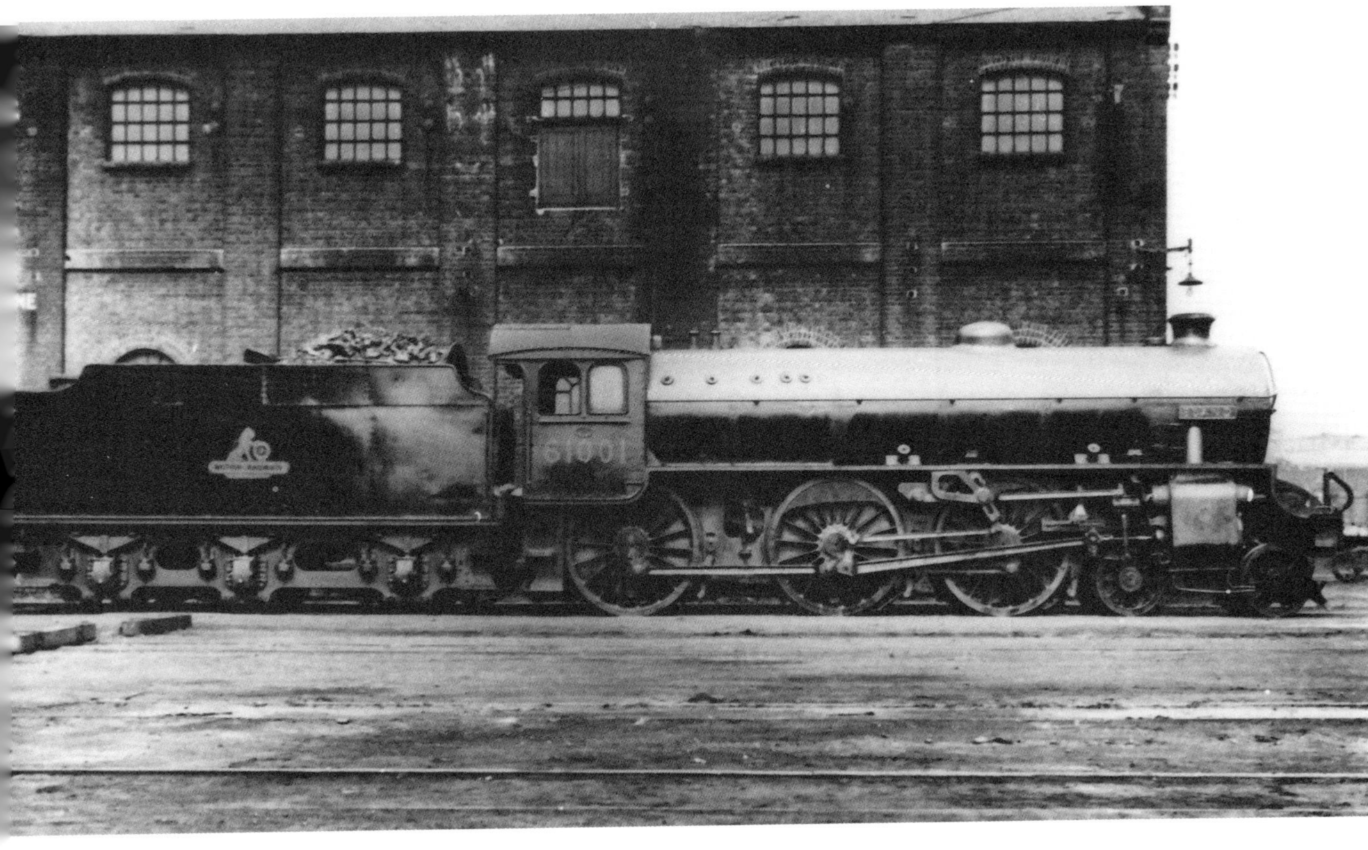

British Railways tested various liveries and emblems in 1948 and 61001 *Eland* is shown here in plain black livery but experimental tender emblem, a forerunner of the chosen 'lion & wheel' motif, 1948. MLS Collection

Some of the B1s were equipped with electric lamps and cab lighting. 1010-1017 and 1049-1139 had part of the equipment for the lamp holders but 1018-1034 and 1140-1189 were fully equipped when built. The alternator mounted on an extension to the rear bogie axle gave problems and from 1947 steam generators were used instead. 1035-1039 and 1190-61339 were fitted with the cab instrument lighting when new, the wiring to the headlamps being provided later. 61340-61399 were fully equipped from the start but 61400-61409 were not equipped with electric lighting at all. The lighting on many of the engines with alternators was not replaced when that equipment was removed and some of the steam generators were also removed and not replaced.

AWS equipment was not provided until 1956 when 61331 was fitted and tested. The remaining B1s were fitted as they went through Works up to 1959, but the programme then ceased and not all B1s received the AWS system.

The B1s were fitted with the standard LNER 4,200 gallon tenders holding 7½ tons of coal, though there were minor detailed variations. Four engines were equipped with coal weighing tenders for testing coal consumption, reducing the water capacity to 3,750 gallons. The first two were attached to 61210 and 61086 in 1951. 61075 and 61140 received the other two in 1952. The tenders were subsequently fitted to different locomotives, the others receiving them at different times being 61069, 61095, 61139, 61172, 61203, 61258, as well as four K1 moguls. Three ex North Easter tenders from withdrawn C7 and C9 atlantics were also utilised and fitted to 1038, 1039 and 61013 after 61039's withdrawal in January 1964 until its own condemnation in May 1966. 61057, built in July 1946, was involved in a collision with a freight train when working a night mail train from Ipswich to London in dense fog on 7 March 1950 and was cut up a month later when it was found uneconomic to repair the badly damaged locomotive.

***Above left*: The Ipswich** allocated B1 that was involved in a collision in March 1950, 61057, seen here shortly before the mishap at Woodbridge, 1949. Eddie Johnson Collection

***Above right*: The damaged** hulk of 61057 after the accident, awaiting the decision of official condemnation, 1950. MLS Collection

The B1s were often nicknamed 'Bongos' especially when run down and rough-riding. Here is the engine that gave rise to that epithet, 61005 *Bongo,* photographed at Colwick, c1960. WD 90438 is alongside. Real Photographs/ MLS Collection

The duplicate of 1032 *Stembok* illustrated on page 247, 61039 *Steinbok,* in standard BR mixed traffic lined black livery, at Darlington, May 1955. T.K. Widd/MLS Collection

The B1, 61036, which was named *Ralph Assheton* after an LNER director amid the antelopes in November 1947, here at Doncaster, 13 May 1956. L. Hanson/ MLS Collection

A Scottish based B1, 61221, named after LNER director *Sir Alexander Erskine-Hill* at Edinburgh Haymarkt depot with a couple of J37 0-6-0s, c1958. A.G.W. Goff/MLS Collection

One of the B1s that survived to 1967 based at Dundee, 61262, seen here at its home depot, c1961. Note the electric generator on the running plate beside the smokebox. 61262 also sports the later BR tender emblem. Bill Gwyther Collection/ MLS Collection

The B1 61379 constructed by the NB Company in June 1951, was named *Mayflower* as part of the twinning between Boston Lincolnshire and Boston USA and bore a plaque on the cabside explaining this. 61379 is seen at Immingham in June 1961. It was withdrawn in August 1962 and the name transferred to the preserved 1306 many years later. Real photographs/MLS Collection

A self-weighing tender was built to enable coal consumption figures on test to be measured and analysed. It is here on 61210 at Retford in 1951, the two photos showing each side of the tender modification. J.D. Darby & A.C.Gilbert/MLS Collection

Scottish based 61340 at Perth, 22 August 1964. It was a 1967 survivor. MLS Collection

The last general repairs for the B1s were authorised at Stratford Works in May 1960 and thereafter only casual light repairs were carried out. Apart from 61057, the first withdrawal occurred in November 1961 when 61085 was condemned. No fewer than 119 of the remaining 408 B1s were withdrawn in 1962, including 16 built between 1950 and 1952. 61391 and 61395 only just made ten years in traffic. Withdrawals continued regularly throughout 1963, 1964 and 1965 and at the beginning of 1966 just 90 were left. The last 27 B1s were withdrawn in 1967, numbers:

61002, 61012, 61019, 61021, 61030, 61072, 61102, 61115, 61123, 61173, 61180, 61189, 61199, 61216, 61238, 61255, 61262, 61278, 61289, 61306, 61309, 61337, 61340, 61347, 61354, 61388, 61407.

The last survivor was 61306, withdrawn in September. Mileages ranged from 308,084 (61383) to 701, 531 (61069) by October 1963 when engine miles ceased to be recorded. It is estimated that the maximum

The last survivor, 61306, withdrawn in September 1967 and purchased for preservation, at Carnforth after withdrawal and awaiting confirmation of fate, 2 June 1968. MLS Collection

reached by any B1 that lasted to 1966 or 1967 is unlikely to have exceeded 800,000 miles, although it would be interesting to establish the final mileage of the oldest 1967 surviving example, 61002, built as 8303 in September 1943.

Operations

After running in from Darlington 8301 went to the GE section and after successful running there 8302 and 8304-8307 followed. 8303 went to Scotland and in the autumn of 1943 was tested over a number of lines, including the West Highland line and routes radiating from Aberdeen. 8308 was also allocated to Scotland in 1944 and 8309 and 8310 were tested in the North East around Newcastle and Darlington. The route availability of the class was good, the only area where a B1 was initially prohibited was in Scotland where a bridge near Craigellachie would not take the weight, although it was due for strengthening. However, at first the turntables at Ballater, Elgin, Fraserburgh, Keith and Peterhead were considered to be too short. The equipping of Scottish B1s with a 3,500 gallon tender was mooted, then a test on an equally short turntable at Boston was satisfactorily completed and after the bridge strengthening, the B1s were able to replace the ex G.N.& S. 4-4-0s and the B12/1s that had been the heaviest passenger engines previously permitted.

In May 1944, the B1s were tested throughout the system and performance compared with the various classes they'd been designed to replace. Acceleration from rest was good and the boiler was free steaming but there was some criticism when the cut-off was linked up to 25 per cent or less. Drivers therefore tended to regulate power and speed with the regulator position rather than using the screw reversing gear mechanism.

The two North East based engines joined the six on the GE section and the first twenty of the 1946 batch, 1040-1059, all went to the GE section and took over the main expresses from the B17s and B12/3s. Some then went to the Great Central main line and to King's Cross and Hitchin to enable the remaining Ivatt Atlantics to be withdrawn. The 100 North British built locomotives were distributed to the Southern Area GN & GC lines: fifty-one engines, GE section: twenty-three engines, North East: eleven engines and Scotland: fifteen engines. The remaining named Darlington built B1s (1010-1039) went to the GN & GC lines (seven locos) and the North East to York and Newcastle (twenty-three). By nationalisation, a further eighty-four engines had been delivered by the NB Locomotive Company with thirty-nine going to the GN & GC lines, thirteen to the GE, nineteen to the North East and thirteen to Scotland. The remaining sixty-six engines of this order delivered after nationalisation were distributed in similar proportion – twenty-nine to the GC & GN, eleven to the GE, eighteen to the North East and eight to Scotland.

8301 *Springbok* at Manchester London Road with an express for Sheffield and Marylebone during trials of the first ten B1s throughout the LNER system, c1945. MLS Collection

Darlington built
1017 *Bushbuck* at York with a Newcastle-Liverpool express in 1947 shortly after its construction in January of that year.
W.H. Whitworth/MLS Collection

North British built 1077 (September 1946) in LNER plain black livery climbing to Woodford Tunnel near Crowden with the 10am Manchester-Marylebone express, 27 April 1947.
MLS Collection

1228 delivered in August 1947 and painted LNER lined green at Torside on the climb to Woodhead with a Manchester United football excursion destined for Sheffield Hillsborough stadium. J.D. Darby/MLS Collection

The first record I can find of a B1 log is of 8309 working the 9.48pm York-Crewe mail and passenger service on 29 August 1944. It had a 12 coach 340 ton load and took 42 minutes 55 seconds for the 25½ miles to Leeds which included two p-way slowings and the wartime 60mph restriction on this route. Maximum speed on the level track at Ulleskelf was 53½mph, and after a 25mph slowing through Church Fenton, sustained 30mph on the 1 in 133 through Micklefield and 38 at the top of the 1 in 155 before Garforth. The recorder alighted at Leeds. Cecil J Allen in his articles on locomotive performance in the *Railway Magazine* in 1948 published some examples of running on both the GE and GC sections prior to nationalisation.

Liverpool Street-Ipswich, 1947

		1049		**1042**		
		9 chs, 300/325 tons		**12 chs, 380/410 tons**		
Miles	**Location**	**Times**	**Speed**	**Times**	**Speed**	**Gradients**
0	Liverpool St	00.00		00.00		
4	Stratford	11.20	pws	10.05	pws	
10	Chadwell Heath	20.23		19.08		
15	Harold Wood	26.40	50	25.40	50½	
18.2	Brentwood	31.27		30.12		
19.3	Ingrave Box	33.24	31½	32.50	24½	1/103 R & 1/85 R
20.2	Shenfield	34.49		34.29		
23.6	Ingatestone	38.10	73	37.58	64	1/135 F & 1/161 F
29.7	Chelmsford	43.40		43.53		
32.1	New Hall	46.15	56	46.31	58	1/344 R
38.6	Witham	52.33	73	52.58	67	1/178 F
42.2	Kelvedon	55.37		56.23		
46.6	Marks Tey	59.40	66	61.07	55	
51.7	Colchester	65.37		66.45		
56	Ardleigh	71.51		72.04	42½	1/144 R
59.5	Manningtree	75.17	77	75.40	74½	1/134 F
63.2	Bentley	78.39	54½	79.05	53	1/157 R
68.7	Ipswich	85.05	(81 net)	85.13	(82 net)	

Ipswich-Norwich, 1947

		1049		**1059**		**1048**		
		9 chs 300/325 tons		**8 chs, 283/300 tons**		**8 chs, 283/300 tons**		
Miles	**Location**	**Times**	**Speed**	**Times**	**Speed**	**Times**	**Speed**	**Gradients**
0	Ipswich	00.00		00.00		00.00		
2.5	Bramford	04.29		04.23		04.53		
8.4	Needham	10.27		10.42		11.34		
11.9	Stowmarket	13.43	67	14.18	58½	15/16	61	L
14.2	Haughley	15.59	55	16.51	46	17.44	44	1/131 R
17.9	Finningham	20.02		21.25		22.09		
22.7	Mellis	24.21	70	26.16		26.31		1/248 F
26.3	Diss	28.14	pws	29.27	71	29.28	77	
31.8	Tivetshall	35.34		35.04	55	34.26	62½	1/142 R

		Ipswich-Norwich, 1947						
		1049		1059		1048		
		9 chs 300/325 tons		8 chs, 283/300 tons		8 chs, 283/300 tons		
Miles	**Location**	**Times**	**Speed**	**Times**	**Speed**	**Times**	**Speed**	**Gradients**
35.4	Forncett	39.04		38.26		37.32		
	Flordon	-	71	-	70	-	77	1/136 F
41	Swainsthorpe	43.50		43.37		42.16		
44.2	Trowse Upper Jn	47.10		46.53		45.20		
46.3	Norwich	51.02	T	51.17	¼ L	51.09	¼ L	

1234, built in September 1947, was at the head of an 8-coach 285 ton non-stop run to Norwich in November 1948. The train was the 10am from Liverpool Street and was allowed 140 minutes for the 115 miles. The train suffered four signal checks at the start of the journey taking nearly 28 minutes to clear Romford (12.4 miles), more signal checks after Chelmsford and approaching Norwich and a p-way slack before Colchester and arrived at destination 5¾ minutes late. Ingrave summit was surmounted at 37mph, running between the Hatfield Peveral check and the Colchester slack was steady in the mid-60s and the maximum speed was 72mph through Diss. More noteworthy were a couple of runs between Norwich and Ipswich by two of the Norwich allocated B1s shortly after their delivery. 1042 completed the 46.2 miles in 47¼ minutes with a load of 245 tons gross accelerating to 66mph up the 1 in 136 to Forncett, (assessed dbhp 1,116) and touched 80mph at Diss and a final 76 at Claydon. 1043 with a heavier 325 ton gross train took 50 minutes 54 seconds including a p-way slowing at Stowmarket and a signal check approaching Ipswich (48 minutes net), with 63mph at Forncett, 72 at Diss, 53 at Mellis (1 in 132) and 77 after the Stowmarket slowing at Bramford.

The B1s were making their mark on the Great Central main line and the September 1948 *Railway Magazine* published a number of logs of the new B1s on that route. 1283 built in February 1948 left Rugby on time with 330 tons tare, 350 gross and after a 15mph p-way slack before Charwelton, touched 79mph at Brackley and stopped at Aylesbury in 48¾ minutes for the 45.3 miles (46½ net). A few days later E1299, built in March 1948, with a similar load was slower to Woodford, and reached only 70 at Brackley but ran down the 1 in 176 at Calvert at 77½mph. Time was 50 minutes 24 seconds (48 net). The best of the three logs was E1299 again on the same train and load which recovered to 42½mph after the p-way slack on the long 1 in 176 to Charwelton and then raced away to 84 at Brackley and 80 at Calvert, the time to Aylesbury being 46 minutes 23 seconds (44 net). A down run on the *South Yorkshireman* was published in the same article.

Marylebone-Nottingham, 1948 E1299 to Leicester 1179 Leicester-Nottingham 10 chs, 330/345 tons				
Miles	**Location**	**Times**	**Speed**	**Gradients**
0	Marylebone	00.00		
5.1	Neasden	09.37	52/sigs 20*	
9.2	Harrow	16.30	pws 20*	
13.1	Northwood	23.57		
17.2	Rickmansworth	28.12	pws 25*	
19.2	Chorley Wood	32.35	31	1/106 R
21.6	Chalfont	36.55	30	1/105 R
23.6	Amersham	41.03	29	1/105 R

Marylebone-Nottingham, 1948
E1299 to Leicester
1179 Leicester-Nottingham
10 chs, 330/345 tons

Miles	Location	Times	Speed		Gradients
28.8	Great Missenden	46.43	65/48 ½		1/160 F & 1/125 R
33.3	Wendover	51.40	65		1/117 F
37.9	Aylesbury	57.11		7¼ L	
0		00.00		7L	
6.2	Quainton Road	08.08	66		
8.9	Grendon Underwood	10.42	60*		
10.9	Calvert	12.40	60/63		
16.6	Finmere	18.30	51½/62½		1/176 R
21.4	Brackley	23.27			
24.6	Helmdon	26.48	56		1/176 R
28.2	Culworth	30.07	75		1/176 F
31.2	Woodford	32.37			
33.6	Charwelton	35.00	56		1/176 R
	Staverton Road Box	-	pws 20*		
40.6	Braunston	43.10	54½		1/176 F
45.3	Rugby	48.33	pws 38*		
48.9	Shawell	52.10	60		
52.1	Lutterworth	55.22	60½		1/176 R
56	Ashby	59.00			
60.5	Whetstone	62.42	75		1/176 F
65.2	Leicester	67.08	(64 net)	4 L	
0		00.00		4 L	E1299 off/ 1179 on
2.3	Belgrave	04.28	44		1/176 R
5	Rothley	07.30	65		1/176 F
9.9	Loughborough	11.28	82		1/176 F
12.9	Barnston Box	13.59	66		1/176 R
14.4	East Leake	15.16	73½		1/330 F
19	Ruddington	18.43	85		1/176 F/L
22.5	Arkwright Street	21.36			
23.4	Nottingham Victoria	23.25		½ E	

The Aylesbury-Leicester section performance was good, but the Leicester-Nottingham time with new crew and engine was exceptional.

The B1s were included in the 1948 Locomotive Exchanges ordered by the new British Transport Commission and were compared with the LMS 'Black 5s', the GW 'Halls' and the Southern 'West Countries'. 61251 *Oliver Bury* was tested on home ground on the Marylebone-Manchester route and on the competing LMS route via Derby, as well as on the GW Bristol-Plymouth line. 61292 was tested on the Highland line from Perth to Inverness. The results were mixed. The purpose seems to have been to establish which were the more economical rather than maximum power performance, and the LMS engine scored better on the LNER route and the LNER B1 was best on the Midland route to Manchester! Overall the LMS 45253 had the better coal and water consumption figures (39.21lb/mile and 30.4 gall/mile) compared with the B1's 46.92lb/mile and 35.1 gall/mile. 61292 experienced some difficulties in the early tests with shortage of steam. 61251 performed creditably over the South Devon banks, but it was, unsurprisingly, the more powerful West Country pacifics whose performance on the road stood out in the mixed traffic range albeit with the heaviest coal and water consumption.

Leicester-Manchester Central, 15 June 1948
61251 *Oliver Bury*
310/325 tons

Miles	Location	Times	Speed	Gradient
0	Leicester	00.00		11 L*
4.7	Syston	06.59	57	
9.8	Barrow-on-Soar	11.58	66	
12.5	Loughborough	14.59		10 L
0		00.00		10 L
2.8	Hathern	05.16	46½	
4.8	Kegworth	07.35	56	
7.7	Trent Junction	10.30	59*	
8.8	Sawley Junction	11.38	55	10½ L
10.8	Draycott	13.44	58	
14.8	Spondon Junction	17.55	58	
16.9	Derby	21.16		8¼ L
0		00.00		8 L
3.2	Long Eaton	06.01	48	
7.8	Belper	11.10	56	
10.4	Ambergate	14.12	32*	7 ¼ L
13.4	High Peak Jcn	18.28	55/pws 24*	
16.1	Matlock Bath	22.18	34	
17.2	Matlock	24.29		7¾ L
0		00.00		8 L
2.2	Darley Dale	04.20	51/pws 26*	
4.5	Rowsley	07.29	32	
6.4	Haddon	11.30	26½	
7.8	Bakewell	14.02	36½/ 35	
8.8	Hassop	15.50	32	
10.8	Headstone Tunnel	19.37	31	
11.6	Monsal Dale	20.45	44	
13	MP 158	23.06	29½	
14.3	Millers Dale	25.44		10¾ L
0		00.00		11 L
2.9	Tunstead	07.13	27	
4.6	Peak Forest	11.02	26 1/2	
8.3	Chapel-en-le;Frith	15.29	63/pws 27*	
10.2	Chinley	18.46		9¾ L
0		00.00		10 L
2.7	New Mills S. Jcn	04.03	66/58*	
11.8	Cheadle Heath	12.39	70	
16.2	Chorlton Junction	16.38	37*/sigs sl	
19.7	Manchester Central	28.22		13¼ L

61251 fared distinctly better than the LMS 45253, apart from the climb to Headstone Tunnel and Millers Dale where the Black 5 recovered from an earlier lacklustre performance. The B1's performance south of Leicester had been marred by permanent-way slacks and signal checks. Three days later 61251 with 335 tons gross regained 2½ minutes of lost time in a good climb on the 1 in 90 to Peak Forest, surmounted at 29mph. However, it lost it again after observing a pws before Matlock and dropped another minute on to Derby unchecked. It left Derby just over two minutes late and with four p-way slowings, took 119¾ minutes for the 99 miles to St Pancras where it was just a minute late (111 minutes net), a reasonable but not more than an 'average' performance on this route. However, the B1's performance on the Western Region was better. On 7 July it left Plymouth with 249/260 tons, and after a p-way slack to 20mph at Plympton, passed the 1 in 42 Hemerdon summit (6.7 miles) in 16¼ minutes, falling from 42mph to 13½. A couple of days later it reached Hemerdon in 14 minutes 43 seconds but the speed at the summit was not recorded. The 'Black 5' fell to 10mph at the summit and the more powerful West Country, 15mph. The B1 finally showed what it could do with a heavy load on the level stretch from Taunton to Bristol.

Taunton-Bristol Temple Meads, 7 July 1948
61251 *Oliver Bury*
475 tons

Miles	Location	Times	Speed	Schedule
0	Taunton	00.00		
2.4	Creech Junction	04.20	56½/sigs	¼ L
5.8	Durston	08.28	53	
11.6	Bridgwater	14.40	57	
14.1	Dunball	17.08	63	
17.9	Highbridge	20.49	58	¾ L
20.6	Brent Knoll	23.42	60	
25.1	Uphill Junction	28.04	62	T
28	Worle Junction	30.49	64	¼ E
32.8	Yatton	35.20	67	
36.7	Nailsea	38.48	66	
38.9	Flax Bourton	40.53	56	
41.6	Long Ashton	-	sigs/ eased	
43.8	Bedminster	47.23	sigs	
44.8	Bristol Temple Meads	50.40	(47½ net)	2¼ E

The B1 selected for the LMR and WR routes in the 1948 Locomotive Exchanges was 61251 *Oliver Bury* which was only completed in November 1947. It is seen here working a St Pancras-Manchester express via the Midland main line prior to the dynamometer test, June 1948. R.E. Gee/MLS Collection

61251 at Teignmouth with the Wolverhampton-Penzance 450 ton train on which the B1 was being tested between Bristol and Plymouth, 8 July 1948. C.H.S. Owen/ MLS Collection

61251 leaving Plymouth for Bristol with one of the test trains, July 1948. MLS Collection

The other B1 involved in the Locomotive Exchanges, the February 1948 built 61292, departing from Perth with the 4pm for Inverness, 14 July 1948. C.C. Herbert/MLS Collection

Two days later without the signal checks it completed the section in 47 minutes 32 seconds, with speed sustained in the 66-69mph range for the major part of the journey. 61292 was the B1 selected for the tests on the Highland line from Perth to Aviemore and Inverness, but its performance on the whole was below par. The load was a substantial 375 tons gross and the weather was foul, but it lost time steadily on the test of 20 July until the final climb to Dalnaspidal when it received the assistance of a Pickersgill 4-4-0 (as did all the test runs, although it is said that the Caledonian 4-4-0 found it hard to keep up with the Southern's 34006!). Inverness was reached 11 minutes late, a net gain of just over three minutes attributed mainly to the banker on the stretch from Struan to Daslnaspidal when the pair knocked six minutes off the 30 minute schedule for the 11.3 mile climb. It did better on the southbound run the next day, though with a lighter load of 265 tons gross. It gained two minutes on the 10.8 mile climb from Inverness to Daviot, falling from 32 to 17 ½mph on the 1 in 60, then recovering to 25mph. Aviemore was reached two minutes late after yet another p-way slack.

The allocation of the B1s by depot in 1947 and 1952 was:

		1947	1952
GN Lines			
	King's Cross	14	8
	Hitchin	14	8
	New England	10	13
	Grantham	4	-
	Lincoln	1	11
	Colwick	-	10
	Doncaster	19	20
	Retford	5	6
	Ardsley	2	9
	Copley Hill	2	8
	Bradford	2	8
GC Lines			
	Neasden	9	9
	Woodford	8	3
	Leicester (GC)	12	11
	Annesley	-	3
	Sheffield (Darnell)	9	21
	Gorton	15	12
	Immingham	6	22
	Mexborough	5	5
GE Lines			
	Stratford	11	29
	Parkeston	6	9
	Ipswich	9	9
	Norwich	17	16
	Cambridge	2	9
North East			
	York	9	14
	Hull (Botanic Gdns)	6	5
	Hull (Dairycoates)	-	4
	Darlington	6	18
	Stockton	5	12
	Gateshead	6	7
	Heaton	8	-
	Tweedmouth	4	4
	Borough Gardens	-	3
	Neville Hill	12	13

Scotland			
	Eastfield	8	14
	St Margaret's	-	9
	Thornton Junction	3	7
	Dundee	3	9
	Perth	2	-
	Carlisle (Canal)	3	4
	Parkhead	-	1
	Kittybrewster	8	16
	Keith	1	2

The GN line engines replaced the Ivatt Atlantics and in the Doncaster area some of the GC 4-4-0s, 4-4-2s and 4-6-0s; on the GC all the GC 4-6-0s and the B17s from express work; on the GE, the D16 4-4-0s, the B17s and B12/3s from other than Cambridge and Southend lines; in the North East, the D20 and D49 4-4-0s and in Scotland the GNof S 4-4-0s, the B12/1s on express working and the D11/2 4-4-0s. The King's Cross and Hitchin engines worked the commuter and semi-fast services from Cambridge and Peterborough to London, the Hitchin allocation often being called upon to assist failing V2s and pacifics on the main line. They also worked some main line freights and summer Saturday trains to Skegness and the Lincolnshire coast. The Immingham engines had two regular express turns from Cleethorpes to King's Cross, which they retained until Britannia pacifics became available in 1961. The Doncaster engines took over the radiating services to Leeds, Hull, Sheffield and Cleethorpes. The West Riding engines monopolised the Leeds-York-Scarborough and Leeds-Hull services.

61160 emerges from Woodhead Tunnel with a Manchester – Sheffield express, 14 May 1950.
N. Fields/MLS Collection

61184 passing Mottram Yard with a Liverpool-Hull express, 14 May 1950. N.R. Knight/ MLS Collection

61187 assists a K3 mogul with a heavy Manchester-Cleethorpes express, passing Priory Junction, 30 June 1951. B.K.B. Green/MLS Collection

A comparison of class 5 power at the south end of Carlisle Citadel station – B1 61013 *Topi* and an LMS 'Black 5' await their next turns of duty on a peak summer Saturday, 26 July 1952. E.R. Morten/MLS Collection

I've found records of a couple of runs with the late afternoon King's Cross-Cleethorpes train. The times logged for both are sketchy and it is evident that there was substantial recovery time in the schedule approaching Peterborough, with the driver of 61190 getting time in hand for the p-way slacks and the driver of 61175 taking it more easily in the knowledge of the slackness of the schedule later in the journey.

		King's Cross-Peterborough 4.15pm King's Cross-Cleethorpes 61190 - Immingham 12 chs, 410 tons tare			3.59 pm relief King's Cross-Cleethorpes 61175 - Immingham 12 chs 410/425 tons 11 September 1954			
Miles	**Location**	**Times**	**Speed**		**Times**	**Speed**		**Gradients**
0	King's Cross	00.00			00.00			
2.5	Finsbury Park	08.02	33		-			1/107 R
12.7	Potters Bar	21.13	52/47½	1¼ L	22.00	41	2L	1/200 R
17.7	Hatfield	26.12	66	¾ E	29.16	60	2¼ L	1/200 F
	Knebworth	-			-	53		1/200 R
28.6	Stevenage	37.49	59		-			1/330 R
31.9	Hitchin	42.29	78		43.37	64		1/200 F
	Three Counties	-	88		-	69		
41.1	Biggleswade	49.07	80½		-	67		1/330 F
44.2	Sandy	51.26	76	½ E	-	64		
47.5	Tempsford	54.10	74		-			L
51.7	St Neots	57.47	72		-	62		1/330 R
58.9	Huntingdon	65.30		½ L	68.46		3¾ L	
	Leys Summit	-			-	54		1/200 R
69.4	Holme	79.32	pws		-			
76.4	Peterborough	88.05	(84 net)	4 E	87.13		4¾ E	

The Cambridge buffet car services were usually in the hands of the B2s or B17s in the 1950s, but 61285 on 29 May 1954 was more sprightly than usual, covering the Welwyn Garden City-King's Cross section in 24 minutes 20 seconds including a 10mph p-way slack at Potters Bar, with a top speed of 80mph below New Southgate.

The significantly large GC allocation took over all the express services on the Woodhead and London routes plus many secondary services, although as loads increased a few Gresley pacifics were drafted in for the prestige services (although they hardly outshone the best B1 performances and never reached the popularity with crews that they retained on the East Coast main line). 61088 on the 3.20pm Marylebone-Rugby semi-fast with 7 coaches and 2 vans (300 tons gross) ran early at all sections, with a minimum of 43mph on the climb through the Chilterns to Amersham and a drop from 70 to no more than 64 up the four miles of 1 in 176 to Finmere. A footplate run on 61183 with 265 tons gross in January 1954 covered the 12.9 uphill miles from Sheffield to Penistone in 21¼ minutes with 37mph on the 1 in 132 past Wadsley Bridge increasing gradually to 43 after Wortley at the end of the five mile climb at 1 in 120. The recorder noted full regulator and 35 per cent cut-off, eased to 25 per cent, but increased to 28 per cent in the Wortley area. After 1957 all the pacifics had returned to the GN lines and the B1s remained in charge until the GC services were truncated in the 1960s and redundant LMR engines from the West Coast lines were utilised. There were so many B1s on the GC lines that they replaced the older GC engines on even the most pedestrian stopping services especially in the Sheffield, Barnsley and Manchester areas.

A Cambridge-Derby excursion on 25 May 1952 was hauled by 61301 from Cambridge to Peterborough via Ely and March. At Peterborough 61392 took over and added two coaches, the train now being 14 vehicles, 445 tons tare, 480 gross. The return 7.25pm Derby Friargate with the full 14-coach load suddenly burst into action after Grantham, the driver clearly aware that engines would be changed at Peterborough. 61392 took 12 minutes 2 seconds to clear Stoke summit at 33mph

The changing order – 61159 at Manchester London Road at the head of an eastbound express, with Woodhead route electric 26008, 30 May 1954. N. Fields/MLS Collection

The southbound *South Yorkshireman* bound for Marylebone with B1 61061 at its head, a GC 'Director' in the background with a train for Doncaster, c1954. MLS Collection

A busy scene at Manchester London Road as 61269 removes empty stock from the station, with two LMR 2-6-4 tanks, a 'Rebuilt Patriot' and a GC C14 4-4-2T in the background, 12 May 1954. B.K.B. Green/ MLS Collection

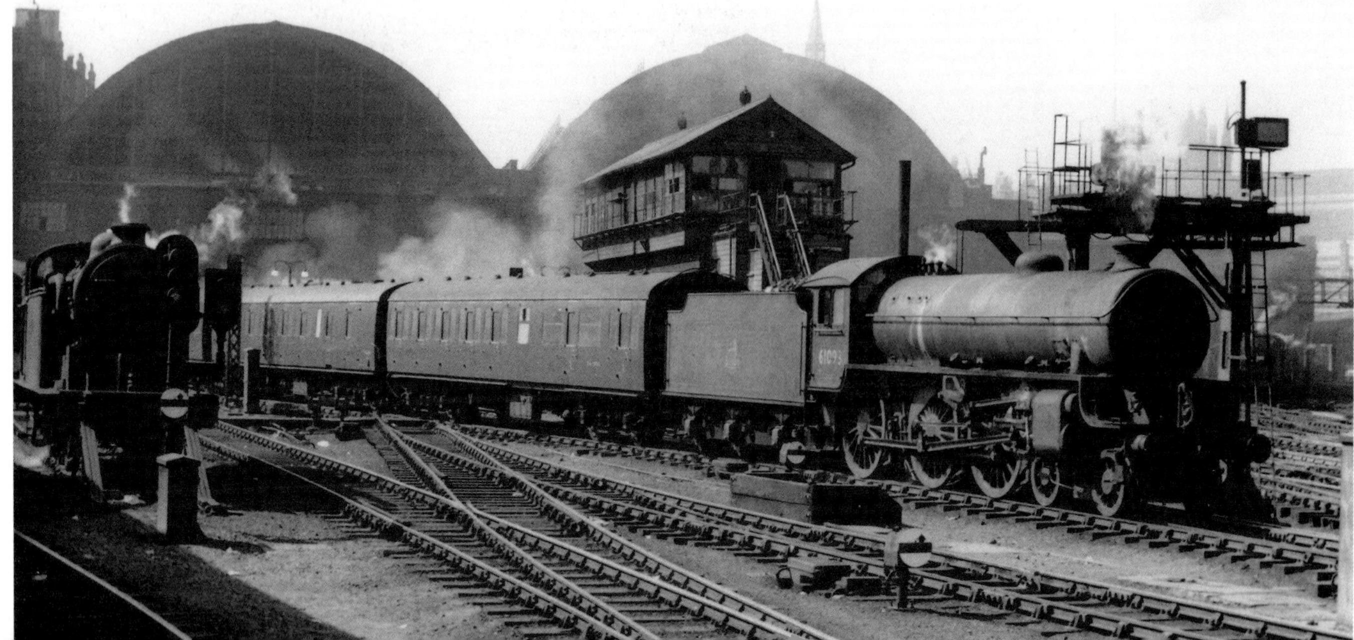

61093 removes empty stock of an outer suburban train from King's Cross past a stabled N2 0-6-2T, 2 August 1955. B.K.B. Green/MLS Collection

Top shed's 61266 hauls a fitted freight past Hadley Wood, c1954. J.D. Darby/ MLS Collection

61223 climbs to Woodhead past Thurlestone Box shortly before completion of the electrification of the route in 1955, with an up express, 19 May 1954. B.K.B. Green/MLS Collection

with this load, but steam was then left on as the B1 accelerated the train to 85mph between Little Bytham and Essendine. It was still 83 at Tallington, 78 at Helpston and the start-to-stop Grantham-Peterborough time was 32 minutes 31 seconds. 61285 took over for the run onto Cambridge.

61061 was unusually used for a relief to the *North Briton* between Newcastle and Edinburgh at Easter 1954 and was well on time at Dunbar but the last twenty-five miles were ruined by a succession of p-way and signal checks, the train eventually taking 140½ minutes for the 124½ miles (net time 125 minutes). There was nothing over 69mph before Alnmouth, but 61061 touched 75 at Chathill, 78½ at Beal and only fell to 57½mph at the summit of the 1 in 200 to Grantshouse. 80 before Dunbar was the last opportunity for any speed before the checks intervened.

The priority for the allocation of the B1s appears to have been the GE section where the wartime lack of maintenance and extra military work had taken its toll of the B17s in particular. They immediately took over the Norwich-London expresses and the Harwich boat trains and were preferred to the B17s at Ipswich, where Dick Hardy, the shedmaster, had a fine group of B12/3s and B1s kept in superb condition. The introduction of the Britannias removed them from the main Norwich-London expresses though they were the standby engines if a Britannia failed or was not available. 61046, substituting in 1952 for a Britannia with an 11-coach 390 ton gross train, was nearly 6 minutes late at Chelmsford after a p-way slack in the Romford area, working hard to sustain 31½mph at Ingrave summit. It recouped two of the minutes on to Colchester 62 at Witham, 58 at Hill House and 69 after Marks Tey. Leaving there 3¾ minutes late, it was beginning to take advantage of the 1 in 134 descent after Ardleigh, just touching 64mph, before suffering another p-way slack to 40mph, wrecking the usual high speed opportunity passing Manningtree and falling to 44mph on the 1 in 157 past Bentley, arriving at Ipswich 5 minutes late. No time could be booked against the engine, but it had no reserve with this load on a Britannia schedule. 61236 found itself in charge of the relief to the *Broadsman* in December 1952 and dashed from Ipswich to Norwich in 45 minutes net for the 46.3 miles, with 75 at Diss and 85 between Forncett and Flordon, but with six coaches (190 tons gross) only. 61051 replaced a Britannia on the *Norfolkman* on 22 July 1952 and left Ipswich 3 minutes late with 310 tons gross. It lost two further minutes on the 77 minute schedule because of signal checks preventing a fast descent on the inward journey from Brentwood. Before that it had sustained 72-74mph all the way from Marks Tey to Chelmsford with just an interruption to 66 for the two mile 1 in 178 climb from Witham to Hatfield Peverel. 61089 replaced a Britannia in 1955 on a 330 ton gross train and ran the 46.2 miles from Ipswich to Norwich in two seconds under 49 minutes including a very slow approach to the terminus, arriving three minutes early with 69 at Stowmarket, 53 minimum after Haughley and a maximum of 81mph at Diss.

The B17s featured for longer on the Cambridge-London via both GE and GN routes but 61177 with a 275 ton load cut five minutes off the 68 minute Liverpool Street-Cambridge schedule with speeds in the 60s rather than the usual 50s before Bishop's Stortford, a creditable 51 minimum at the summit of the 1 in 124/107 bank at Elsenham, 75 before Newport and 71-73 maintained between Great Chesterford and Shelford. 61302 and 310 tons gross on the fast Sunday 64 minute non-stop schedule from Cambridge was inside schedule to Tottenham with good steady running, though nothing over 72mph before a signal stop and diversion via Stratford, eventually reaching Liverpool Street 5 minutes late. When the GE section became the first Eastern Region area to be heavily dieselised the B12s and B17s went for scrap but most of the redundant B1s moved elsewhere.

In Scotland, the Edinburgh-Perth line was the first to use the B1s on a regular basis, but from 1946 they were widely used from all the former North British sheds. The Haymarket engines worked to Glasgow, Perth and Dundee and the St Margaret's B1s to Carlisle and Newcastle on secondary passenger and freight duties. Dundee and Thornton Junction engines worked Fife Coast trains to Glasgow and Edinburgh. The Glasgow Eastfield engines replaced the NB D34 'Glens' and Gresley K2 moguls on the West Highland line. In the North East of Scotland the B1s operated out of Aberdeen on passenger, fish and goods trains.

In May 1953, fourteen B1s were loaned to the Southern Region when the Bulleid pacifics were

A B1 on the Southend line – Stratford's 61363 at Wickford on the 1.49pm from Southend Victoria, 5 August 1955. MLS Collection

A Cardiff - Sheffield summer Saturday express departs from Gloucester passing the GW Horton Road depot behind 61113, c1956. MLS Collection

61240 ***Harry*** *Hinchcliffe* at Cross Gates with a Leeds-Scarborough train, 2 April 1956. B.K.B. Green/ MLS Collection

taken out of service after the failure of a driving axle on Merchant Navy 35020. Whilst Britannias and V2s covered the work of the larger pacifics on the Waterloo-Bournemouth and Exeter routes, the B1s were called on to replace West Countries and Battle of Britain light pacifics on the Southern's Eastern Section along with some LMR Black 5s and BR Standard 5s. The B1s concerned were 61015, 61041, 61050, 61109, 61133, 61148, 61188, 61192, 61219, 61273, 61274, 61329, 61338 and 61354. All were allocated to Stewarts Lane. All had returned to the Eastern, North Eastern and Scottish Regions by the end of June, as the axle examinations of the SR engines were completed. Officially the B1s were 'satisfactory' and hauled such trains as the 8.35 and 11.35am Victoria-Ramsgate. However, their use was short-lived, 61050, 61109 and 61329 returning to the Eastern Region within a week and 61041, 61188 and 61192 returning home in a fortnight. The verdict of the Southern crews was very different, mostly unprintable. 'B1' became a term of abuse and comments about their rough riding were extreme. It is of course highly probable that ER depots, ordered to send B1s elsewhere, chose their highest mileage and rundown examples.

The B1s were restricted to semi-fast services on the Cambridge and

Norwich lines in the later 1950s and shared the work on the Shenfield/ Southend line with B12s until electrification in 1956. They worked prime commuter services like the 9-coach 5.08pm Liverpool Street, first stop Billericay (24.3 miles) booked in 30 minutes and I have records of runs with 61335 and 61361 in 28 minutes without either touching 60mph. As dieselisation increased at the end of the 1950s and early 1960s, the work for the B1s reduced and many changes in allocation were forced by the construction in large numbers of the Brush Type 2s (class 31) and the English Electric Type 3s (Class 37) in particular. At the end of 1961 the remaining 408 B1s were allocated as follows:

Depot	No.	Depot	No.	Depot	No.
King's Cross	5	New England	13	Grantham	4
Lincoln	17	Colwick	21	Doncaster	24
Retford	9	Ardsley	7	Copley Hill	8
Neasden	2	Woodford	7	Leicester (GC)	10
Sheffield (Darnall)	44	Immingham	24	Mexborough	4
Langwith Junction	1	Stratford	12	Ipswich	1
Norwich	7	Cambridge	9	March	12
York	23	Hull (Dairycoates)	9	Darlington	9
Thornaby	8	West Hartlepool	3	Sunderland	2
Blaydon	7	Tyne Dock	3	Neville Hill	1
Canklow	2	Wakefield	9	Low Moor	6
Agecroft	5	Haymarket	6	St Margaret's	24
Eastfield	8	Fort William	1	Thornton Junction	11
Dundee	11	Dunfermline	3	Carlisle (Canal)	7
Parkhead	5	Aberdeen Ferryhill	4		

As seen above, the largest concentrations were at Sheffield, Doncaster, York, Immingham, Colwick and Edinburgh St Margaret's. Most of the GE section B1s had been displaced by dieselisation, a number of which were moved to March. The following depots had lost their allocations of B1s: Hitchin, Bradford, Annesley, Gorton, Parkeston, Hull (Botanic Gardens), Gateshead, Heaton, Tweedmouth, Borough Gardens, Perth, Kittybrewster and Keith. The following depots had received B1s for the first time in the late 1950s or early 1960s: Langwith Junction, March, Thornaby, West Hartlepool, Sunderland, Blaydon, Tyne Dock, Canklow, Wakefield, Low Moor, Agecroft, Fort William and Aberdeen (Ferryhill).

61313 with a local stopping service formed of LMR coaching stock at Chinley, 11 April 1964. N. Fields/MLS Collection

Carlisle Canal's 61217 stands ready to depart from Carlisle Citadel with a Newcastle train, 7 May 1959.
R.E. Gee/MLS Collection

61243 *Sir Harold Mitchell* between Haymarket and Edinburgh Waverley with the up *Queen of Scots* Pullman train, July 1959.
L. Perrin/MLS Collection

61343 shunting empty stock at Edinburgh Waverley under the Mound Tunnel, 25 July 1959. MLS Collection

St Margarets 61404 at Stirling with the 9.40am Callander-Edinburgh Waverley, 19 July 1959. A.G. Cattle/MLS Collection

61003 ***Gazelle*** passing Wath Junction with a Sheffield-Manchester train of mixed ER and LMR rolling stock, 18 August 1962. MLS Collection

61368 on a Saturdays Only Sheffield-Bournemouth train formed of SR rolling stock passes a northbound train headed by a 'Black 5' at Heath, between Nottingham and Sheffield, 12 September 1959. MLS Collection

***Above and opposite*: Three photos** of the celebrated double-headed Newcastle-Red Bank empty stock train with B1 participation in the haulage:

- 61199 and a 9F 2-10-0 at Castleton, 1965, R.S. Greenwood/MLS Collection
- 61018 (stripped of its *Gnu* nameplate) and 45020 at Mirfield, 28 June 65, MLS Collection
- 61303 and 45135 on the very last one, also at Castleton, 20 April 1966, I.G. Holt/MLS Collection

In the last year of the B1s and before the remaining BR steam was concentrated in the North West, the 27 remaining active engines of the class were based as follows:

Dundee:	61072, 61102, 61180, 61278, 61340, 61354
Thornton Jcn	61347, 61407
Dunfermline	61262
York	61019, 61021, 61123, 61173, 61189, 61199, 61216, 61238
Low Moor	61030, 61306, 61337
Wakefield	61115, 61309, 61388
Dairycoates	61002, 61012, 61255, 61289

A number of B1s were retained as stationary boilers after their withdrawal, mainly for carriage heating. They were allocated Departmental Stock numbers as following:

BR No.	Departmental No.	Withdrawn from traffic	Condemned
61050	30	2/66	4/68
61051	31	2/66	3/66
61059	17	11/63	4/66
61105	27	3/65	5/66
61138	26	1/65	10/67
61181	18	11/63	12/65
61194	28	8/65	6/66
61204	19	11/63	2/66
61205	20	11/63	1/65
61233	21	11/63	4/66
61252	22	11/63	5/64
61264	29	11/65	7/67 Preserved
61272	25	1/65	11/65
61300	23	11/63	11/65
61315	32	2/66	4/68
61323	allocated 24	11/63	11/63
61375	24	11/63	4/66

The last survivor, Low Moor's 61306, with the final steam-hauled Bradford portion of the *Yorkshire Pullman* at New Pudsey, 30 September 1967. 61306 was withdrawn after this duty and was then stored pending preservation. A.C. Gilbert/MLS Collection

The former 61050 which was withdrawn from traffic in February 1966 and became a stationary boiler, here at Royston, 9 April 1967. It was numbered 30 in the Departmental stock list and withdrawn in April 1968. N. Fields/MLS Collection

The final survivors were 61306 and 61337 which were operating in the Leeds-Bradford area and 61306 hauled the Bradford portion of the last steam *Yorkshire Pullman* in September 1967 before withdrawal and preservation.

I had many personal experiences of the B1s. I was a 12-year-old trainspotter spending three weeks at Hatfield near Doncaster with a schoolfriend in 1950, and we were both fed up with the innumerable Doncaster B1s we observed from the Doncaster station cattle dock that had by then replaced the Great Central 4-6-0s and Directors and Ivatt Atlantics previously in that area. We visited my friend's relations in Scunthorpe and joined a Leeds-Cleethorpes semi-fast at

Thorne with 61409 just two months after its construction, returning in the evening behind named Doncaster B1 61249 *Fitzherbert Wright.* The final disappointment was finding my friend's uncle putting us on a return train to London that ran in with 61167 only to find with some relief that we were in the Hull coaches that were attached to the Leeds portion headed by A1 60141. A holiday in Whitby in 1955 included a day trainspotting at York, and the return *Scarborough Flyer* was hauled as far as Malton by 61237 *Geoffrey H Kitson* (I'd had B16/3 61472 on the outward run and was hoping for another).

A return from my cousin's home in Chelmsford in 1951 produced the Norwich 61046, an engine that reappeared on the *Hook Continental* in April 1958 when I joined a party of London University German Department students for a cultural tour of Goslar and Bad Harzburg (I spent much of the time seeking 01 and 03 pacifics rather than the mediaeval treasures). 61311 had the return *Day Continental.*

My January 1952 Chelmsford visit included a day spotting at Shenfield when it snowed so hard that I got stranded on the station after letting 61201 go (I'd had it already that visit) and finding no more trains back until the station staff took pity on me and rustled up L1 67734 from the sidings and two coached to take me home – my own 'special'.

The engine that kept turning up during my Chelmsford and Shenfield spotting visits in 1951/2 when I was wanting a 'namer', 61201, though seen here far away at Godley Junction with a train of WR rolling stock on an up express, c1956. N.R. Knight/ MLS Collection

One of the many B1s seen by spotters throughout the 1950s at Doncaster, this one – 61390 – having just arrived with a stopping train from Grimsby, 23 May 1959. J.D. Darby/ MLS Collection

A photo I took of 61254 on the turntable at Liverpool Street with my folding Kodak equivalent of a 'Box Brownie' (f8 1/25 sec only) with which I won my school Railway Club photographic competition in 1953. David Maidment

In the mid-1950s I used to get an N2 out to Finsbury Park to take photos of the northbound expresses pounding through the station, and if lucky, catch one of the main line trains stopped by signals in the platform back to King's Cross. I managed an A4 and an A2, and tried my luck with named B1 61027 *Madoqua,* only to find that I was on a mystery tour (for me) to Broad Street. All of these earlier runs were before I started train timing in earnest, but I did manage to time a couple in regular traffic in their last years. I was courting a girl at the time at Nottingham University and found my return journey after spending a Saturday with her was with 61187 instead of the usual Black 5, BR Standard 5 or Royal Scot.

Nottingham-Marylebone, 2 February 1962
61187 – Leicester
5.15pm Nottingham-Marylebone semi-fast
6 chs

Miles	Location	Times	Speed	Gradients
0	Nottingham	00.00		
0.9	Arkwright St	02.40	36	
4.4	Ruddington	06.43	68/71	
	Rushcliffe	10.00	74/65	1/176 R
	East Leake	10.55	81	1/176 F
13.6	Loughborough	15.25		
0		00.00		
	Quorn	03.34	54	1/176 R
4.8	Rothley	06.33	70/68	1/264 R
7.5	Belgrave	-	75	1/176 F
9.8	Leicester	11.54		
0		00.00		
4.7	Whetstone	07.17	47/52	1/176 R
9.2	Ashby Magna	13.14	58	1/176 R
13.1	Lutterworth	18.21		
0		00.00		
	Shawell Box	-	51/71	1/176 R & 1/176 F
6.8	Rugby	08.52		
0		00.00		
4.7	Braunston	06.52	53/48/50	1/176 F & 1/176 R
11.7	Charwelton	15.50	58	1/176 R
14.1	Woodford Halse	19.16		
0		00.00		
3	Culworth	-	48	1/176 R
6.6	Helmdon	09.17	60	
9.8	Brackley	13.03		
0		00.00		
4.8	Finmere	07.07	54	1/176 F & 1/176 R
10.5	Calvert	13.16	66/50	1/176 F
12.5	Grendon Underwood	15.27	58/51	

Nottingham-Marylebone, 2 February 1962
61187 – Leicester
5.15pm Nottingham-Marylebone semi-fast
6 chs

Miles	Location	Times	Speed		Gradients
14.9	Quainton Road	18.38	61		
21.3	Aylesbury	25.42			
0		00.00			
	Stoke Mandeville	04.41	39		1/117 R
4.7	Wendover	08.09	45/50		1/117 R
9.2	Great Missenden	13.52	63		1/125 F
14.4	Amersham	20.16			
0		00.00		T	
	Chalfont	03.23	55		
	Chorley Wood	06.00	35*/50		1/105 F
6.4	Rickmansworth	09.27	25*		
9.9	Northwood	16.17	pws 5*/46		
14.4	Harrow	23.55			
0		00.00			
	Wembley Park	03.55	61		
4.4	Neasden	05.35	50		
	West Hampstead	09.46			
9.2	Marylebone	15.03		6 ½ L	

This run was more sprightly than usual for the light 6-coach semi-fast trains that ran between London and Nottingham via the GC route in the 1960s. It was on time or waiting time at each station until the very severe p-way check at Northwood. In 1961 I'd tried some South Coast-Sheffield summer Saturday trains between Rugby and Nottingham and enjoyed an excellent run on the 10.14am Hastings-Sheffield with 61138 of Darnall shed. We accelerated the 11-coach 385 ton gross load to 51mph up the 1 in 176 through Shawell and touched 75 on the descent through Whetstone.

I changed at Loughborough to the 11.38 Brighton-Sheffield and 61265 also of Darnall took its 10 coaches on to Nottingham in 19 minutes without any special effort. Then in 1963 I picked up the 8.49pm Friday night holiday Burton-Newquay (working from Newcastle) with 61167 (the engine I'd nearly had from Doncaster in 1950). 61167 hailed from Mexborough and had 12 coaches in tow, 425 tons gross. We stopped at Tamworth and I alighted at Birmingham New Street. 57mph at Wichnor Sidings and 54 at Kingsbury were the top speeds. The holidaymakers were in for a long night though I doubt if they would appreciate too early an arrival in Cornwall.

Finally, after spending a couple of days in Scotland in the summer of 1964 on the Glasgow-Aberdeen expresses with A4s, and B1 61262 on the 7.15am Glasgow Buchanan Street-Dundee (undistinguished), I returned overnight to Bristol Temple Meads. The journey south culminating with a run behind a Stafford Road Castle (5063) on a Wolverhampton-Devon holiday express, and I was somewhat surprised to be met by a former King's Cross B1, 61394, then at Canklow. It backed on to the 12.45pm 8-coach Bristol-Sheffield so I decided to take it to Birmingham New Street before returning to London from there.

Bristol-Birmingham New Street, 25 July 1964
12.45 SO – Bristol-Sheffield
61394 – Canklow
8 chs

Miles	Location	Times	Speed	Gradients
0	Bristol Temple Meads	00.00		
1.9	Lawrence Hill	03.05	27	
3.6	Fishponds	08.02	25/27	
6	Mangotsfield	11.13	47/32*	
	Westerleigh North Jn	15.23	49	
11.2	Yate	18.26	56½	
15.7	Wickwar	24.00	62	
17.7	Charfield	25.51	64	
23	Berkeley Road	-	67/62	
25.2	Coaley Junction	32.21	58	
27.5	Frocester	34.26	61	
29.2	Stonehouse	36.21	65/60	
32.2	Haresfield	-	67	
38	Gloucester Eastgate	46.06		
0		00.00		
3.2	Churchdown	07.13	44/47	
6.5	Cheltenham Lansdown	11.35	30*	
10.3	Cleeve	15.53	63	
13.7	Ashchurch	19.28	69/63	
16	Bredon	21.48	64	
18.5	Eckington	24.23	62 ½	
	Ditton	25.28	65	
24.2	Abbots Wood Junction	31.11	15*	
	Norton Junction	33.30	32*/56	
	Worcester	38.15		
		00.00		
	Fernhill Heath	06.37	pws 5*/52	
	Droitwich Spa	11.53	sigs 8*	
	Stoke Works Junction	19.34	48	
0	Bromsgrove	22.30//23.54	Attach 8401 as banker	
2.1	Blackwell	31.02	23/17/19	
3.2	Barnt Green	33.18	54	
5.8	Halesowen Junction	36.18	58	
8.3	King's Norton	39.12	54*/36*	
9.3	Bourneville	42.45	sigs 5*	
10.4	Selly Oak	45.13	sigs 10*	
13.5	Church Road	50.12	44	
15	Birmingham New St	53.09		

This train I discovered was booked for a Sheffield B1 that summer. I'd seen 61394 several times previously at King's Cross on Cambridge buffet car services or Peterborough stopping trains. It was in good external condition and was driven hard up the 1 in 69 of Fishponds Bank, but thereafter progress was fairly normal for a Saturday train. This was the last run I had behind a B1 in BR steam days. Other B1 runs would have to await the resurrections of 61264 and 61306.

Preservation

61264

1264 was constructed by the North British Company in Glasgow for £16,190 in December 1947 and allocated to Parkeston Quay depot where it remained for thirteen years. It was painted LNER lined green initially, but in the BR mixed traffic lined black livery in November 1949. In November 1960, upon dieselisation of the GE section, it moved to Colwick and on its withdrawal in November 1965, was deemed suitable to act as stationary boiler at its home depot, as Departmental No.29. Withdrawn again in July 1967, it was sold to Woodham Brothers at Barry for scrap and moved there in April 1968.

It remained in store awaiting breaking up until purchased in July 1976 by the Thompson B1 Trust and moved to Loughborough. A twenty-one year restoration costing £230,000 was undertaken there although the boiler went to Pridham Engineering in Tavistock for renewal. It returned in 1995 and was restored to the frames in 1996, was completed and in steam in March 1997, hauling its first passenger train since withdrawal on 28 March. It operated on the Great Central heritage line and ran a number of main line rail tours before withdrawal for major repairs to its boiler in 2008 – costing over £450,000. These were completed in December 2012 and 61264 in BR lined black livery was then stationed in traffic on the North Yorkshire Moors Railway where it is still operational in 2020.

I have traced a log of 61264 on a Parkeston Quay-Liverpool Street continental boat train in the Railway Performance Society's archives. The run took place on 6 July 1954, and the train was the 9.55am from the quay consisting of ten coaches 325 tons tare. The ferry was on time and the train left punctually and passed Colchester nearly four minutes early. With speeds in the mid-60s most of the way to Chelmsford, it was 5½ minutes early there, and time was in hand for a couple of planned permanent way checks either side of the Essex county town. The train was on time at Shenfield but suffered another p-way slowing on the descent of Brentwood Bank but regained speed to 63mph and with an unusually clear run in, arrived in London half a minute early.

After preservation 61264 had a period in Scotland including seasons working the *Jacobite* and on 26 September 2000 it ran a 7-coach (256 ton) special from Stirling to Perth. It fell from 51 to 39mph on the climb through Dunblane to Kinbuck and touched 73mph on the descent from Gleneagles before braking. Despite a signal stand between Forteviot and Forgandenny it arrived in Perth three minutes early.

For photo in preservation, see colour section.

61306

61306 was built by the North British Company in 1948 and was stationed at Hull Botanic Gardens. In 1959, it moved to the other Hull depot, Dairycoates and, right at the end of its BR life, to Bradford Low Moor in June 1967, when it was the last surviving B1. With steam in the North East coming to a close, it was withdrawn just two months later and was privately preserved at Steamtown, Carnforth, where it was repainted in LNER apple green livery, renumbered 1306 and named *Mayflower* after the withdrawn 61379. It was used on a number of main line special trains in the 1970s and moved to the Great Central Railway at Loughborough in 1978 where it operated until 1989.

After its ten year overhaul, it went to the Nene Valley Railway and in 2006 was sold to the Boden family who owned the Boden Rail Engineering Company at Washwood Heath. After repainting in apple green livery again in 2013 and located at Carnforth, it was sold on to David Buck in 2014 and after further overhaul was cleared in 2019 for main line operation which included regular Tuesday special runs from Waterloo to Windsor.

I was present on a railtour in June 1975 when 1306 piloted V2 4771 *Green Arrow* on a 16 coach 600 ton train from Carnforth to Ravenglass and back. The train departed from Carnforth 28 minutes late after waiting for a late running special from Nottingham hauled by *Flying Scotsman*, and my notes say that as far as Ulverston the B1 seemed to be making the major effort, accelerating the heavy train to 58mph before a slack there now only 21 late. Then it seemed to be the V2's turn and the pair eventually arrived at Ravenglass only 9 minutes late. On the return run the B1 was heroic as the V2 was in trouble for steam - its brick arch was collapsing. It regained thirteen of an eighteen minutes late start and managed to exceed 60mph at Silecroft and again before Barrow. However, as a result of its having to be thrashed to compensate for the V2's troubles, I commented in my notes that the countryside was covered with cinders thrown from the B1's chimney.

To demonstrate its versatility, it operated the *Cathedrals Express* from Huntingdon to York on 12 March 2015 and was going well on the climb to Stoke summit still doing 63 at Corby Glen with its 370 ton gross load, when unfortunately it was brought to a stand by signals at MP 99. With 77mph at Barkston South and 72 after Dukeries Junction, it was on time into Retford and with 73 at Rossington, was on time into Doncaster. In August of the same year, it was at the opposite end of the country working a

1306 *Mayflower* pilots V2 4771 *Green Arrow* at Carnforth on a railtour for Barrow and Ravenglass, as 4472 *Flying Scotsman* arrives with a special from Nottingham, June 1975. A further photo in preservation is in the colour section. David Maidment

Victoria-Weymouth railtour via Clapham, Staines, Weybridge and the Bournemouth main line. Progress was necessarily slow until the main line was regained and the B1 climbed to Milepost 31 very respectably at 54mph, took water at Winchfield and touched 77mph through Winchester. It was on time at Bournemouth and ran easily on to Weymouth with a final sprint at 71 down from Bincombe Tunnel.

Chapter 7

THOMPSON'S REBUILDS

The B7/3 proposal – 1941

Edward Thompson proposed ten new standard designs when he eventually was appointed Chief Mechanical Engineer in 1941. Several were to be two cylinder versions of Gresley's three cylinder engines, but other locomotives faced rebuilding if their frames were in good enough condition. The robust Great Central 5ft 8in B7s were one of the classes chosen and a scheme was initiated to include a 100A boiler and B1 cylinders with the following dimensions:

Cylinders (2 outside)	20in x 26in
Boiler pressure	220psi
Coupled wheel diameter	5ft 8in
Axleload	18 tons
Weight – Engine	74 tons

The GC tender would have been retained. However, in the event the proposed B1 fulfilled the LNER's mixed traffic requirement and a decision was made not to proceed with the B7 rebuilding. A diagram of the proposed B7 rebuild is in the appendix, page 345.

The B3/3 – 1943

Thompson considered a mixed traffic 4-6-0 on the lines of the LMS 'Black 5' and the GW 'Hall' was urgently needed on the LNER and after deciding not to go ahead with the B7 rebuilding, decided to rebuild one of the Caprotti B3s with a 100A boiler, B1 type cylinders and valve gear at the same time as developing the prototype new design, the key difference being the coupled wheel size, the B3 retaining 6ft 9in diameter compared with the proposed B1 6ft 2in. The reconstruction undertaken was comprehensive, retaining only bogie and driving wheels, rear part of the frame and tender. The engine chosen was 6166, formerly *Earl Haig,* and it was delivered in October 1943. The revised dimensions were:

Cylinders (2 outside)	20in x 26in
Coupled wheel diameter	6ft 9in
Walschaerts valve gear with 10in piston valves	
Boiler pressure	225psi
Heating surface	2,020sqft (incl 344sqft superheater)
Grate area	27.9sqft
Axleload	18t 3cwt
Weight – Engine:	71 tons 7 cwt
– Tender	48 tons 6 cwt
– Total	119 tons 13 cwt
Tractive effort	24,555lbs

6166 was renumbered 1497 in the 1946 LNER renumbering and was the only B3 to go into BR ownership, being renumbered 61497 in April 1948. However, the rebuilding was not a success as the old engine could not bear the strain and was in constant need of attention to cracked frames. After rebuilding 6166 was stationed at Gorton, moved back to Neasden in 1945, but ended its days in 1947 at Immingham. The other B3s were all withdrawn before nationalisation but 61497 survived until April 1949.

B3 1166 as built at King's Cross shed, 1923. F. Moore/ MLS Collection

6166 after rebuilding with Caprotti valve gear as a B3/2, repainting in the LNER livery and renumbering, December 1929. Real Photographs/ MLS Collection

6166 after rebuilding as a B3/3 by Edward Thompson in October 1943. LNER official photograph/MLS Collection

6166 at Aylesbury with a local passenger train before its last overhaul and renumbering as 1497, c1946. Colling Turner/MLS Collection

The B2 – 1945

The B17s were included in Thompson's standardisation rebuilding programme – only the GE B12s and the NE B16s were excluded from the 4-6-0 classes for treatment because of their lighter axleloads. The first drawings were completed in 1942, showing 220psi boiler and two outside cylinders, but retaining much of the Gresley outline appearance. The tractive effort was 24,310lbs and the weight, 75 tons 17 cwt. However, a number of design changes took place before an order to rebuild twenty B17s was authorised in October 1944. Boiler pressure was increased to 225psi using the B1 100A boiler. 2871 *Manchester City* in works for a heavy repair was the first earmarked, although other priorities delayed the rebuilding for nearly a year. It eventually emerged from Darlington Works in August 1945, and others followed with the following dimensions:

Cylinders (2 outside)	20inx 26in
Coupled wheel diameter	6ft 8in
Bogie wheel diameter	3ft 2in
Walchaerts valve gear with 10in piston valves	
Boiler pressure	225psi
Heating surface	2,005sqft (incl 344sqft superheating)
Grate area	27.9sqft
Axleload	18 tons 12 cwt
Weight – Engine	73 tons 10 cwt
– Tender	52 tons 10 cwt (LNER)
	44 tons 2 cwt (NER)
	51 tons 8 cwt (ex P1)
– Total	126 tons (with LNER tender)
Water capacity	4,200 gallons (LNER)
	4,125 gallons (NER)
	4,700 gallons (ex P1)
Coal capacity	7 tons 10 cwt (LNER)
	5 tons 10 cwt (NER)
	7 tons (ex P1)
Tractive effort	24,863lbs

They were reclassified B2s necessitating the renaming of the former B2 GC 'Sam Fay' 4-6-0s as class B19 in their few remaining years. 2871 retained its LNER 4,200 gallon tender as built in B17/4 form, and 2816 was similarly converted later in the year, but as it had been a B17/1 with short GE tender, that was replaced by a NE larger tender from a withdrawn C7 Atlantic. Six more followed in

The first Thompson rebuild of a B17, B2 2871 *Manchester City* in Works Grey, January 1946. Colling Turner/ MLS Collection

2871 a year later, repainted in LNER lined apple green and renamed *Royal Sovereign* for royal train duties and renumbered 1671 at King's Cross, 1947. C.R. Gordon-Stuart/ MLS Collection

1946, 2814, 2815, 2839 and the by then renumbered 1603, 1617 and 1632. 1607 was rebuilt in 1947 and the last, 61644, after nationalisation in March 1949. The final ten authorised were not rebuilt. The equipping of most of the B17s with 100A boilers raised their power and was cheaper than a complete rebuilding and by this time the B1s were proving themselves well able to cover the former B17 work on both the GE and GC lines. The rebuilt B2s showed little superiority over the B17/6s and were equally bad, if not worse riders, as mileage between overhauls rose.

All the remaining B2s were equipped with larger tenders to replace their former GE versions, most with former NER C7 varieties. 1615 and 1632 however inherited the former P1 2-8-2 freight engines' 7 ton capacity flush-sided tenders, although modifications were made caused by the need to remove the extensions to carry the P1s' booster equipment. All except 61644 appeared after rebuilding in plain black, the first three with just NE on the tender, the next three renumbered and LNER lettering. 2871 reappeared in February 1946 in LNER lined apple-green livery as, based at Cambridge, it was allocated royal train duties to and from Sandringham. It was renamed *Royal Sovereign* in April 1946. It retained its lined LNER green livery after nationalisation as 61671 and BRITISH RAILWAYS on the tender. After March 1952 it was in the standard Brunswick green with the BR 'lion & wheel' emblem on the tender, though still kept spotless for royal train duties. Other B2s were also painted LNER green during 1949 and 1950 before getting the BR dark green livery.

1607 *Blickling* equipped with an ex NE C7 tender, at Stratford, April 1948. Photomatic/MLS Collection

61617 *Ford* *Castle* at Stratford ex-works, the detail of the ex-NE tender visible in this photograph, 15 March 1953. H.C. Casserley/ MLS Collection

61615 ***Culford*** *Hall* with the former P1 large tender, at Stratford, 29 March 1953.
MLS Collection

61614 ***Castle*** *Hedingham* at Colchester, its home depot, just before the B2s from that depot were all concentrated at Cambridge in 1956.
MLS Collection

61639 *Norwich City* at Cambridge, 4 May 1958.
N. Fields/MLS

Like the B17s, the B2s lost their work with the early dieselisation of the Anglia services, and withdrawals took place in 1958 and 1959, 61617 being the first to go in August 1958, followed by 61603 and 61671 the next month. 61632 *Belvoir Castle* was renamed *Royal Sovereign* to take over the royal duties of the withdrawn 61671, but its reign was short-lived, itself being condemned in February 1959 as a result of cracks in the frame. 61607 was the last survivor of the class, withdrawn in December 1959, outlived by both B17/4s and B17/6s.

A very rundown 61616 *Fallodon* at March in 1959 with a row of early diesel shunters.
MLS Collection

The last B2 rebuild, 61644 *Earlham Hall* with an ex NE tender but flush coal rails, 1959. MLS Collection

61632 ***Belvoir*** *Castle* before renaming *Royal Sovereign* after the withdrawal of 61671, seen here at Colchester in the company of a J39 and K3, in 1955. 61632 had the other ex-P1 tender. G.A. Coltas/ MLS Collection

61632 lasted just five months after being named *Royal Sovereign* and was withdrawn in February 1959 after a defect was found that was uneconomic to repair. Here it is stored at Stratford after withdrawal, the nameplate and smokebox numberplate already removed, 25 February 1959. David Maidment

Operations

They were run in at Darlington Bank Top shed after rebuilding at the Works and were all allocated to the GE section, 61617 joining 61671 at Cambridge and covering for royal duties when necessary, including King George VI's funeral train from Sandringham to King's Lynn (70000 hauled the train from there to London). These two B2s worked to both Liverpool Street and King's Cross, while the other B2s went to Colchester for the Clacton-London services. In 1956 all the B2s were concentrated at Cambridge and remained there until withdrawn. They were prone to frame fractures and the royal 61671 was a particular culprit.

I had a run behind 61639 *Norwich City* on a Clacton train in 1952 returning from a stay with relatives in Chelmsford. I was determined to ride behind a 'namer', preferably a Britannia, but after I'd let go a succession of B1s, I accepted the B2 with some relief. Then six years later, during my twice weekly evening sessions at Liverpool Street in between college commitments, I had several relatively short runs behind B2s, all on the Cambridge line. 61614 was only experienced on a stopper to Cambridge as far as its first stop at Tottenham, but I had 61616 *Fallodon* twice on the 4.36pm Liverpool Street-King's Lynn *Fenman* as far as its first stop, Bishop's Stortford. I was not timing trains in those days but my memory is that it

1671 *Royal* *Sovereign* departs from Liverpool Street with a Cambridge train while sister B2 1617 *Ford Castle* awaits in the engine sidings for its next working, 9 August 1947. MLS Collection

1671 *Royal* *Sovereign* with a King's Cross-Cambridge buffet express on the GN main line, c1947. C.R. Gordon-Stuart/ MLS Collection

61671 *Royal* *Sovereign* at Potters Bar with a down Cambridge buffet express, 18 September 1954. MLS Collection

The other Cambridge based B2, 61617 *Ford Castle,* comes off the engine siding at Liverpool Street to move across to head a King's Lynn train, c1953. MLS Collection

61615 ***Culworth*** *Castle,* with the ex-P1 tender, transferred from Colchester to Cambridge in 1956, heading a King's Cross-Cambridge train out of Wood Green tunnel, c1957.
MLS Collection

61616 ***Fallodon*** with a two-coach special train organised by the Cambridge University Railway Club, 3 September 1959.
MLS Collection

61603 *Framlingham* ex-works at Stratford on the occasion of the visit of the Charterhouse School Railway Society visit, 1956. David Maidment

was more vigorous than the B17s I travelled behind on the same train. However, that might just have been the impression from hearing the harsher two-cylinder exhaust. My last B2 trip was in late 1958 with 61607 *Blickling* on a Cambridge semi-fast train as far as Broxbourne and I remember this as being one of the better runs (not a huge compliment). My last experience should have been in December 1958 with the renamed 61632, which I saw spotless at the head of a train for Colchester and Ipswich. I hurried to get a ticket to Shenfield, but by the time I returned, found it had failed and had been replaced by one of the few remaining B17s still with the original boiler, 61660, which proceeded to give me an excellent run, making up time from the late start.

They did the job, though they were eclipsed on the GE by the Britannias (and B1s) and ran turn and turn about with the B17s. They suffered frame fractures probably as a result of stress of the two cylinders on the lightweight frames and had the reputation of being very rough-riding in their final years.

61616 *Fallodon* waiting to depart from Liverpool Street with the 4.36pm *Fenman* to King's Lynn which the author took as far as Bishop's Stortford, March 1959. David Maidment

Colour Section

***Above*: The *City of Manchester* nameplate and works plate from 425 (5425/1491) mounted in the main club room of the Manchester Locomotive Society at Stockport station, from whose extensive archive the majority of photographs in this book are reproduced. David Maidment

B3/2 6166 *Earl Haig* leaving Aylesbury with a Manchester-Marylebone express, December 1938. MLS Collection

A colour postcard of the Paris Exhibition 'gold winner', 2006, in NER lined green livery, 1900. MLS Collection

A colour postcard of the Great Eastern 1500 of 1911. MLS Collection

A colour postcard of the North Eastern Railway B15 with Stumpf Uniflow cylinders, No.825.
MLS Collection

B16/3 61438 departing from Rotherham with a Sheffield - Skegness holiday express, 1959.
MLS Collection

B16/1 61423 near Great Ponton with an up freight, 1961. MLS Collection

B16/3 61435 heads an RCTS railtour to the Hawes branch and makes a photographic stop, 25 April 1964. MLS Collection

B16/3 61444 ex-works at Doncaster alongside Robinson O4 2-8-0 63618, 29 October 1961. N. Fields/MLS Collection

B12/3 61572, the only class survivor into the 1960s, at the head of the 3.55pm van train from Lowestoft to Norwich between Brundall and Whitlingham,24 September 1961. Roy Hobbs/Transport OnLine Archive

61572 two years after withdrawal and now privately owned heads the Wandering 1500 railtour depicted here on the Hitchin-Bedford branch, 5 October 1963. Roy Hobbs/Transport OnLine Archive

61572 on Norwich shed in steam a few months before withdrawal, 1961. Roy Hobbs/Transport OnLine Archive

61572 on Norwich shed a month after withdrawal, October 1961. Roy Hobbs/Transport OnLine Archive

B17/6 61610 *Honingham Hall* at March depot, May 1959. MLS Collection

B17/6 61657 *Doncaster Rovers*, c1958.
MLS Collection

B17/6 61658 *The Essex Regiment* departing from Colchester with a Clacton train, 1958. MLS Collection

B17/6 61620 *Clumber* passing Chaloners Whin Junction with a York-Harwich express, c1957.
K. Pirt/MLS Collection

61620 ***Clumber*** nears York with the Harwich-York express, c1957.
MLS Collection

B2 61639 *Norwich City,* 1958. MLS Collection

B1 61283 leaving Liverpool Street station with a down express, shortly before total dieselisation of the GE section, September 1962.
Roy Hobbs/Transport OnLine Archive

61179 with an up fast perishable freight on the GN main line, c1961. J. Davenport/MLS Collection

61008 *Kudu* arriving at Manchester Victoria with a with a train from York, 1962. MLS Collection

Three B1s, 61156, 61149 and 61375, line up to celebrate the last day of operation of Stratford depot, 8 September 1962. Roy Hobbs/Transport Online Archive

61324 at Cockburnspath with the *Scottish Rambler* railtour, 14 April 1963. Roy Hobbs/Transport Online Archive

61324 with a further shot of the 1963 *Scottish Rambler* railtour. Roy Hobbs/Transport OnLine Archive

61116 passes Alloa shed with an unfitted goods train. Two J38 0-6-0s are in the shed, including 65934, 17 April 1965. Roy Hobbs/Transport Online Archive

61132 on a pick-up goods at Anstruther, 16 June 1966. Roy Hobbs/Transport Online Archive

61345 on St Margarets shed, Edinburgh, alongside a V2, 18 April 1965. Roy Hobbs/Transport Online Archive

61396 passing an English Electric 2000hp D2XX and St Margarets shed with an empty stock train, 19 April 1965. Roy Hobbs/Transport Online Archive

61406 prepared for an LCGB railtour from Boston, with an Ivatt 4MT mogul 43108 off the M&GN section alongside, 24 April 1965. J.D. Darby/MLS Collection

Preserved B1 61306, restored to operation and in the 1947 LNER apple green livery, at the North Yorkshire Moors 40th Anniversary Gala in 2013, seen at Grosmont. Dr Phil Brown

Preserved 61264, running in LNER 1946 black livery as 1264, with the *Whitby Flyer* railtour in the Esk Valley between Castleton and Danby, 7 April 2018. Dr Phil Brown

***Below Left*: Preserved 61264** at Whitby station during a stint of working on the North Yorkshire Moors Railway, 2016. Dr Phil Brown

***Below right*: 61264 masquerading** as withdrawn sister engine 61002 *Impala* at the NYMR 40th Anniversary Gala event at Grosmont in 2013. Dr Phil Brown

The author's Hornby model (R3432) of 61580 purchased new in 1980 for £145, including 20 per cent discount – compare this with the earlier Hornby model of 61535 (R866) which the author purchased for £12 new in 1980 and painted himself in BR lined black. All model photos were taken on the author's home layout on Christmas Eve 2019. David Maidment

The author's repainted model of 61625 *Raby Castle*, a Hornby B17/4 chassis (R053) with Crownline body and tender parts, new in 1988 (estimated cost £46). David Maidment

The author's 2013 Hornby model (R2921) of B17/1 61637 *Thorpe Hall*, new in 2013. David Maidment

The author's Hornby model of B17/6 'Football' 61650 *Grimsby Town* (R2922) also new in 2013. David Maidment

The author's half completed modification of a Hornby B17/4 (R053) as B2 61607 *Blickling* using Crownline body and tender kit purchased in 1986 (estimated cost £47) but still awaiting the author to get round to painting it! David Maidment

A Replica/Dapol model (ref:11011) of B1 61026 *Ourebi* purchased new in 1988 for £40.
David Maidment

A Nu-Cast kit, assembled by Constructeon and painted by the author in 1984 at a cost of £80, before good production ones were on the market. The author also bought a Crownline kit for a B1 conversion of a Hornby B17 and had half completed the model when the Replica/Dapol model became available and since then the Hornby R3000 in 2011.
David Maidment

The Methodist Church in Nantwich has a 7¼in gauge steam railway (powered by a 'Joffra' 0-6-0 one-third scale of the trench engines in the First World War) running each Saturday morning for a children's club and children of all ages for donations to children's charities. The end of the short line is graced by this painting by local artist Susan Fishburne, which includes Nantwich station, the church's former minister and dog and a steam locomotive which – although red – looks uncannily like a named B1. Perhaps the painter thought it was a Crewe engine… David Maidment

APPENDIX

Great Central Class 8C (LNER B1/B18)

Dimensions

Cylinders	5195: 21in x 26in, 5196: 19in x 26in
Stephenson's valve gear	5195: 10in piston valves, 5196: slide valves
Boiler pressure	180psi
Heating surface	1,951sqft
Grate area	26.24sqft
Axleload	18tons 10 cwt
Weight – Engine	5195: 72tons 18 cwt, 5196: 71 tons
– Tender	48 tons 6 cwt
– Total	5195: 121 tons 4 cwt, 5196: 119 tons 6 cwt
Water capacity	4,000 gallons
Coal capacity	6 tons
Tractive effort	5195: 21,658lbs, 5196: 17,729lbs

Weight Diagram

C4 4-4-2 (similar to C18 4-6-0)

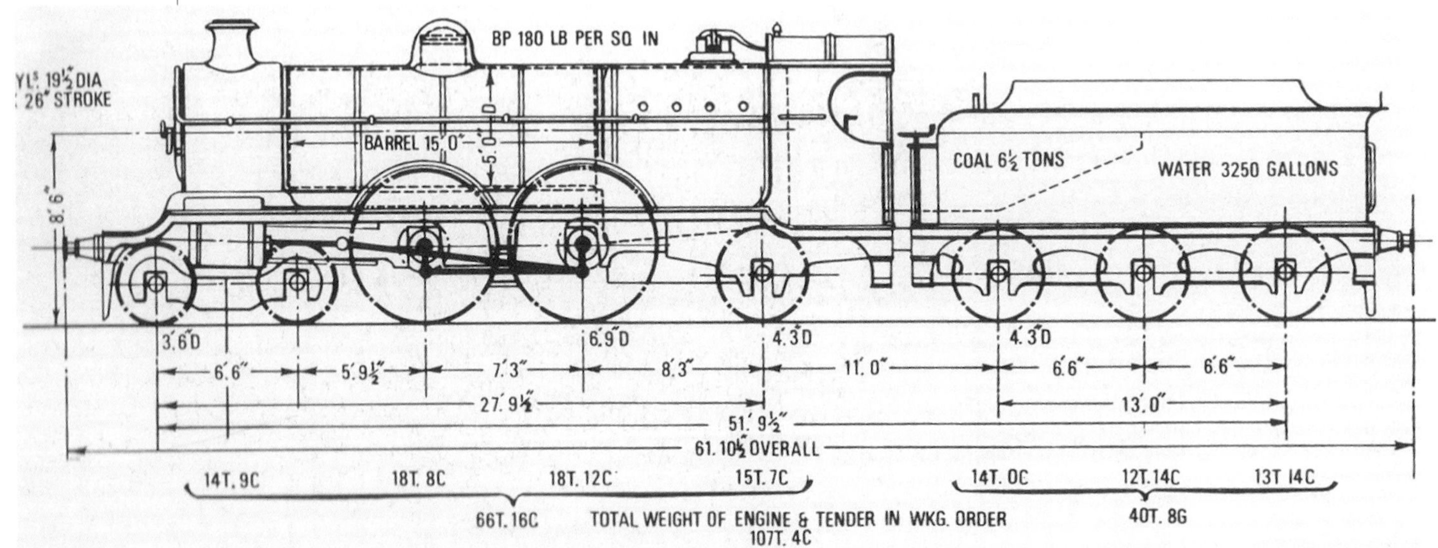

Statistics

No.	Built	1st LNER No.	2nd LNER No.	Superheated	1st depot	Last depot	Withdrawn
195	12/03	5195	1479	8/12*, 3/26	Gorton	Annesley	12/47
196	1/04	5196	1480	4/27	Gorton	Annesley	12/47

Great Central Class 1 (LNER B2/B19)

Dimensions

Cylinders (2 inside)	21½in x 26in (B2/2: 20in x 26in after 1922)
Coupled wheel diameter	6ft 9in
Bogie wheel diameter	3ft 6in
Stephenson's valve gear	10in piston valves
Boiler pressure	180psi
Heating surface	2,477sqft (B2/2: 2,387sqft)
Grate area	26sqft
Axleload	19 tons 10 cwt
Weight – Engine	75 tons 4 cwt
– Tender	48 tons 6 cwt
– Total	123 tons 10 cwt
Water capacity	4,000 gallons
Coal capacity	6 tons
Tractive effort	22,700lbs (B2/2: 19,644lbs)

Weight Diagram

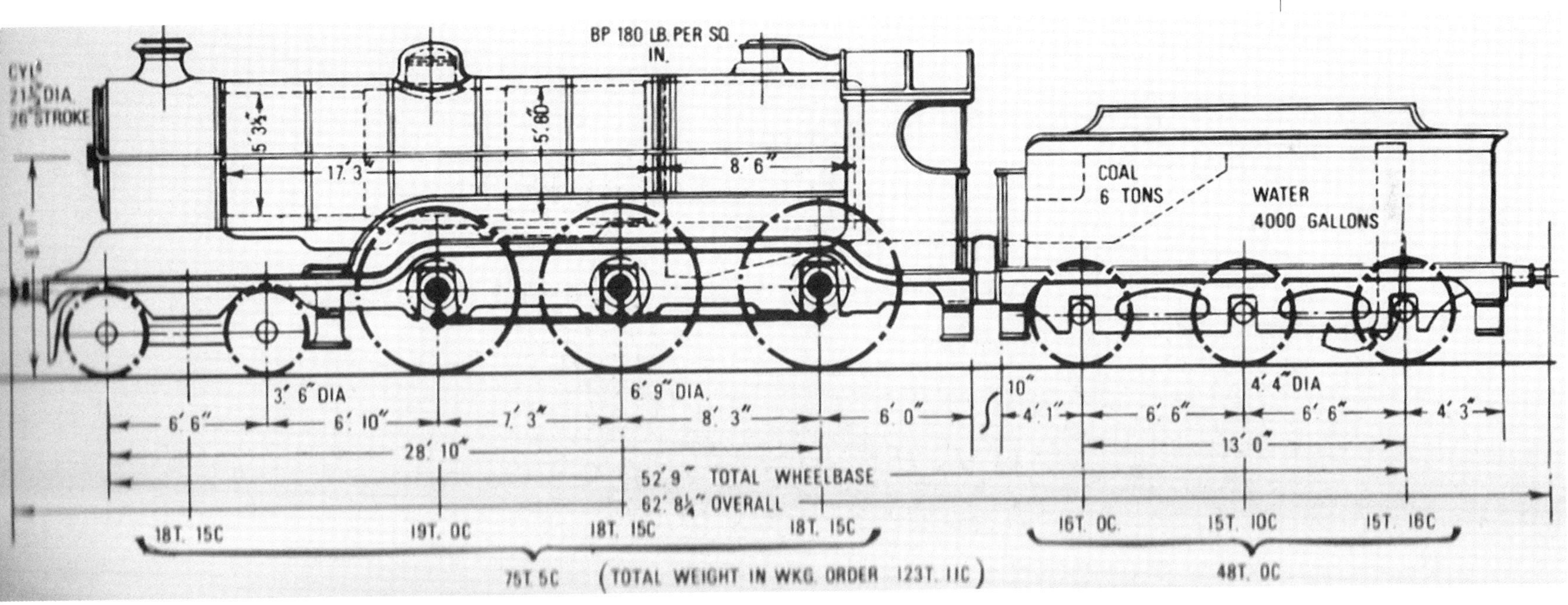

Statistics

No.	Built	Renumbered	Rebuilt	1st depot	Last depot	Withdrawn
423	12/12	5423, 1472, 1490	10/22	Gorton	Immingham	4/47
424	1/13	5424	5/22	Gorton	Immingham	11/45
425	2/13	5425, 1474, 1491		Gorton	Immingham	7/47
426	3/13	5426	8/38	Gorton	Immingham	12/44
427	3/13	5427, 1476, 1492	4/21	Gorton	Immingham	11/47
428	12/13	5428, 1477, 1493		Gorton	Immingham	4/47

Names:
423 *Sir Sam Fay*
424 *City of Lincoln*
425 *City of Manchester*
426 *City of Chester*
427 *City of London* (removed in 9/37 when B17 2870 named)
428 *City of Liverpool*

Great Central Class 9P (LNER B3)

Dimensions B3/1

Cylinders (4)	16 in x 26in
Coupled wheel diameter	6ft 9in
Bogie wheel diameter	3ft 6in
Stephenson's valve gear	8in piston valves (B3/2: Caprotti valve gear)
Boiler pressure	180psi
Heating surface	2,387sqft (incl 343sqft superheater)
Grate area	26sqft
Axleload	20 tons
Weight – Engine	79 tons 2 cwt
– Tender	48 tons 6 cwt
– Total	127 tons 8 cwt
Water capacity	4,000 gallons
Coal capacity	6 tons
Tractive effort	25,145lbs

Dimensions B3/3 (Thompson 1943)

As above except:

Cylinders (2 outside)	20in x 26in
Walchaerts valve gear	10in piston valves
Boiler pressure	225psi
Heating surface	2,020sqft
Grate area	27.9sqft
Axleload	18 tons 3 cwt
Weight – Engine	71 tons 7 cwt
– Total	119 tons 13 cwt
Tractive effort	24,555lbs

Weight Diagram

B3

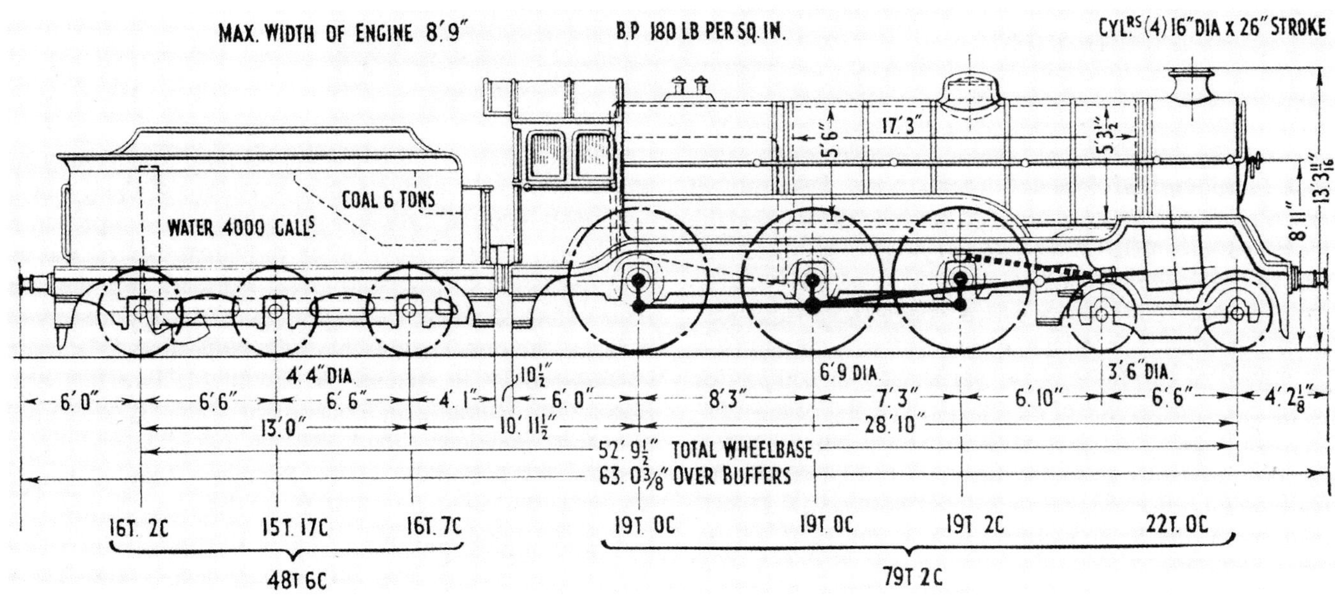

B3/2 Caprotti

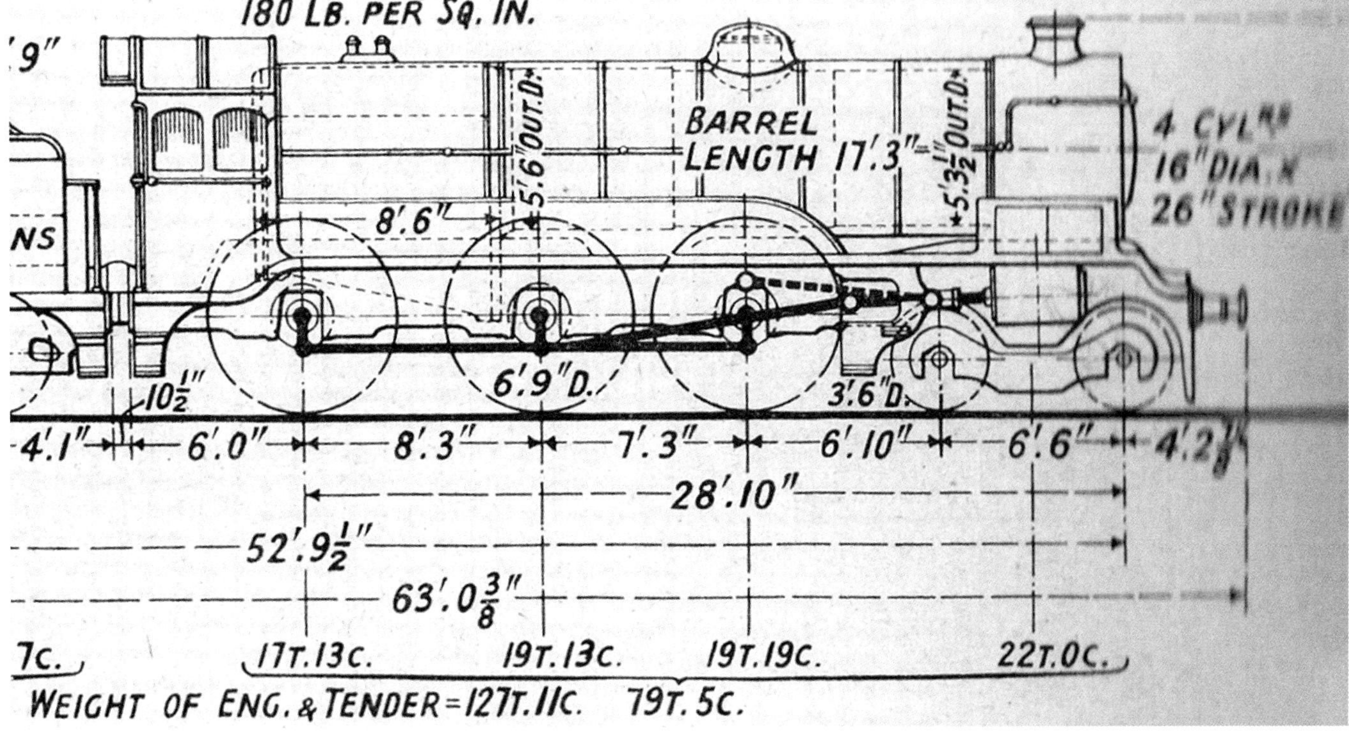

B3/3

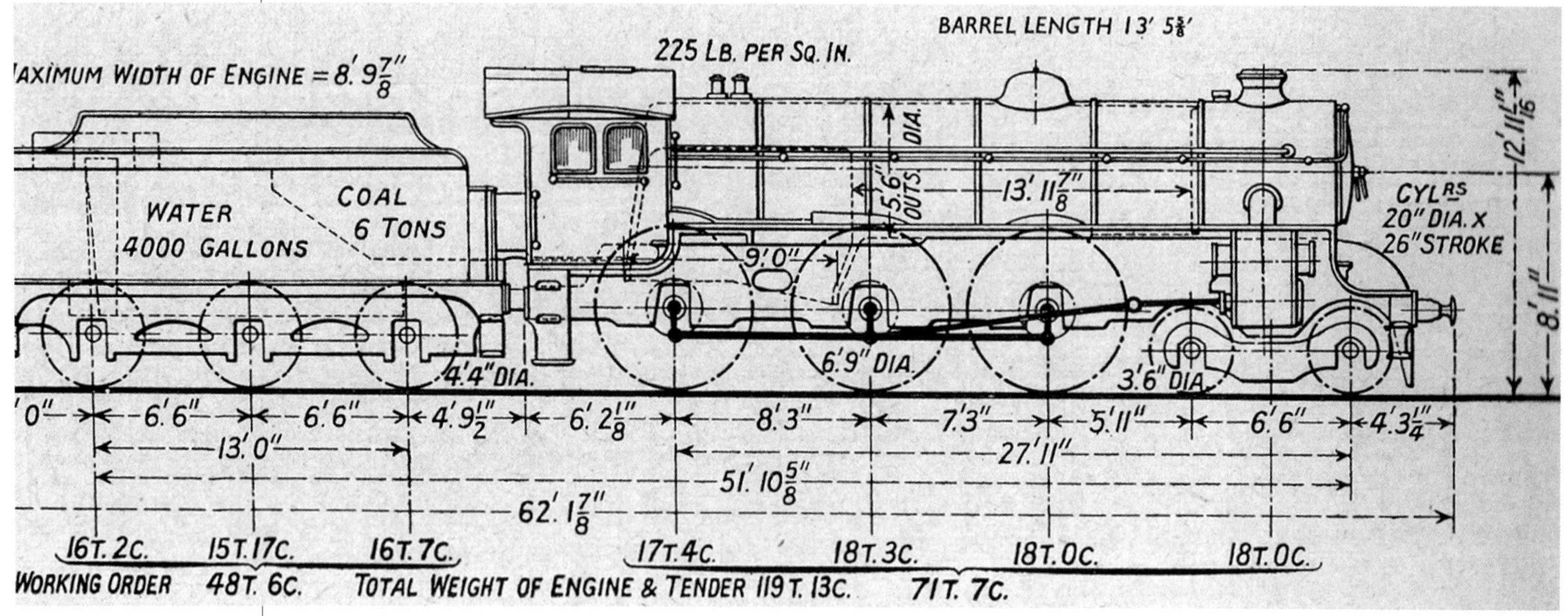

Statistics

No.	Built	Renumbered	Rebuilt	1st depot	Last depot	Withdrawn
1164	6/20	6164, 1481, 1495	6/39	Immingham	Immingham	9/47
1165	7/20	6165, 1482, 1496		Gorton	Lincoln	12/47
1166	8/20	6166, 1483, 1497, 61497	12/29, 10/43*	Gorton	Immingham	4/49
1167	9/20	6167, 1484, 1498	6/38	Gorton	Immingham	12/47
1168	10/20	6168, 1485	9/29	Immingham	Immingham	9/46
1169	11/17	6169, 1480, 1494		Gorton	Lincoln	12/47

* Rebuilt as B3/3

Names:
1164 *Earl Beatty*
1165 *Valour*
1166 *Earl Haig* (removed 10/43)
1167 *Lloyd George* (removed 8/23)
1168 *Lord Stuart of Wortley*
1169 *Lord Faringdon*

Great Central Class 8F (LNER B4)

Dimensions

Cylinders (2 outside)	19 in x 26in (six rebuilt as B4/2 with 21in x 26in)
Coupled wheel diameter	6ft 7in
Bogie wheel diameter	3ft 6in
Stephenson's valve gear	slide valves (B4/2 with 10in piston valves)

Boiler pressure	180psi
Heating surface	1,951sqft (1,975sqft after superheating)
Grate area	26.24sqft
Axleload	18 tons 8 cwt
Weight – Engine	70 tons 14 cwt (B4/2t: 71 tons 15 cwt)
– Tender	48 tons 6 cwt
– Total	119 tons (B4/2: 120 tons 1 cwt)
Water capacity	4,000 gallons
Coal capacity	6 tons
Tractive effort	18,178lbs (B4/2: 22,206lbs)

Weight Diagram

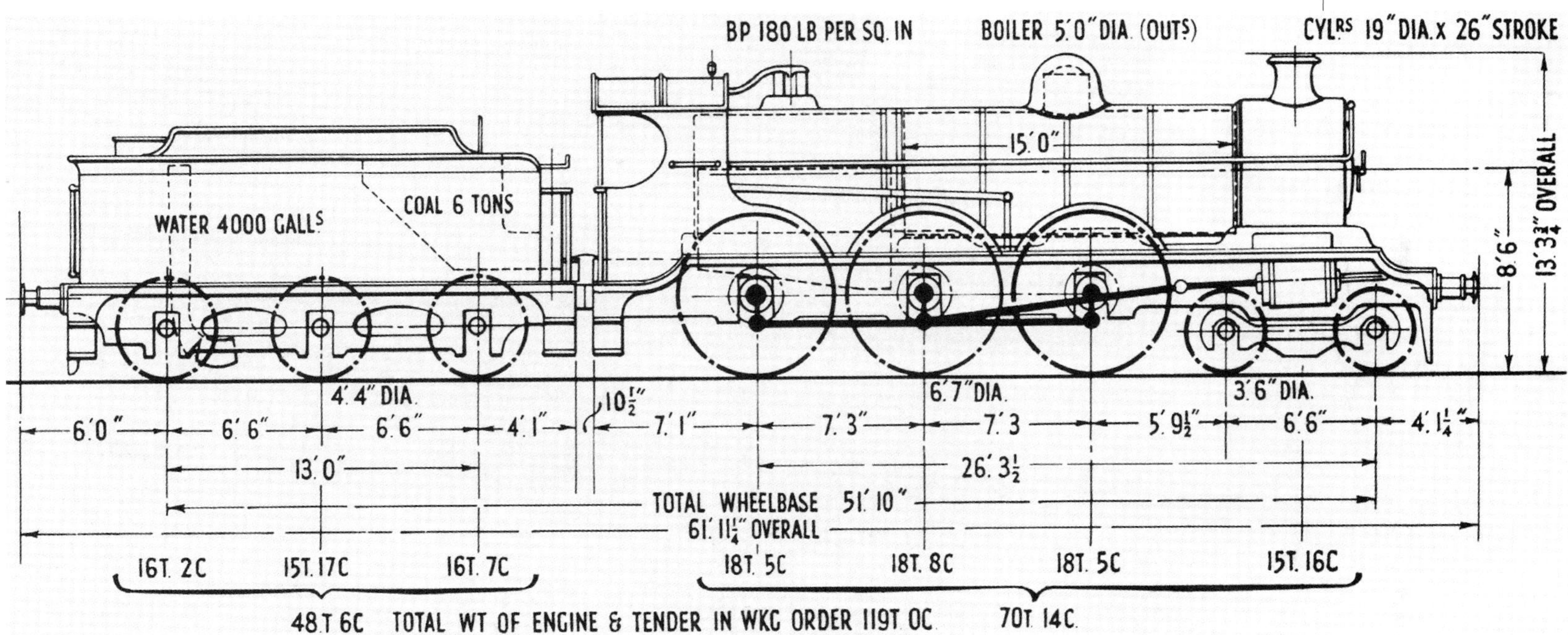

Statistics

No.	**Built**	**Renumbered**	**S'heated**	**Rebuilt**	**1st depot**	**Last depot**	**Withdrawn**	
1095	6/06	6095	10/27	10/27	Neasden	Lincoln	2/44	
1096	6/06	6096, 1481	11/27		Gorton	Lincoln	7/47	
1097	6/06	6097, 1482, 61482	5/26		Grimsby	Lincoln	11/50	Named *Immingham*
1098	6/06	6098, 1483, 61483	10/28	8/34	Neasden	Copley Hill	9/49	
1099	6/06	6099, 1484	12/26		Neasden	Ardsley	11/47	
1100	6/06	6100, 1485, 61485	1/26	5/32 *		Ardsley	6/49	
1101	6/06	6101, 1486	4/25	6/27 *		Ardsley	10/47	
1102	6/06	6102, 1487	9/27*			Ardsley	12/47	
1103	7/06	6103, 1488, 61488	5/27	5/27 *		Copley Hill	10/48	
1104	7/06	6104, 1489	3/27	3/27	Neasden	Lincoln	7/47	

* First allocation either Gorton or Grimsby

Great Central Class 8 (LNER B5)

Dimensions

Cylinders (2 outside)	19 in x 26in (B5/3: 21in x 26in)
Coupled wheel diameter	6ft 1in
Bogie wheel diameter	3ft 6in
Stephenson's valve gear	slide valves
Boiler pressure	180psi
Heating surface	1,795sqft (superheated: 1,568sqft)
Grate area	23.5sqft
Axleload	18 tons
Weight – Engine	65 tons 2 cwt (superheated: 64 tons 3 cwt)
– Tender	44 tons 3 cwt, (4,000 gallon: 48 tons 6 cwt)
– Total	109 tons 5 cwt (4000 gallon: 113 tons 8 cwt)
Water capacity	Initially 3,250 gallons, 4,000 from 1905/6
Coal capacity	6 tons
Tractive effort	19,672lbs

Weight Diagram

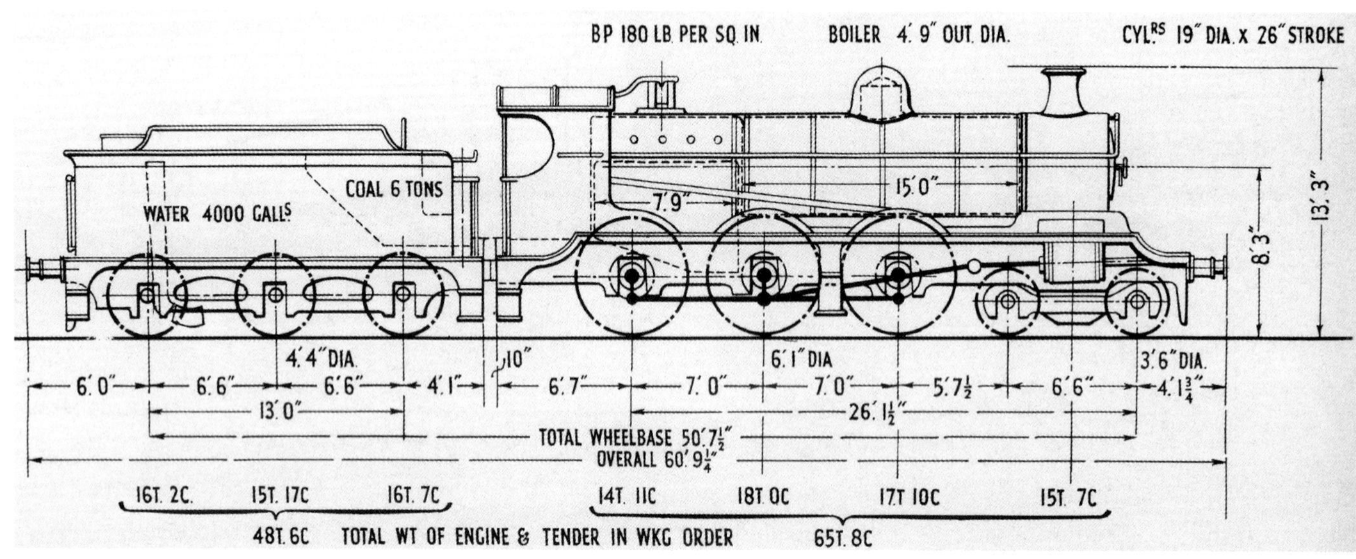

Statistics

No.	Built	Renumbered	S'heated	Rebuilt	1st depot	Last depot	Withdrawn
180	1/04	5180, 1683	2/31	8/38	Gorton	Mexborough	12/47
181	1/04	5181, 1684	12/32		**	Mexborough	5/47
182	1/04	5182, 1685, 61685	4/33		**	Mexborough	3/48
183	2/04	5183, 1686, 61686	7/35	6/36	**	Mexborough	6/50
184	2/04	5184, 1687	6/23	8/24*	**	Lincoln	7/47
185	2/04	5185, 1688, 61688	5/28	5/28	**	Mexborough	11/49
186	2/04	5186, 1689, 61689	1/28		**	Mexborough	10/49
187	3/04	5187, 1690, 61690	7/30	3/37	**	Mexborough	4/48

No.	Built	Renumbered	S'heated	Rebuilt	1st depot	Last depot	Withdrawn
1067	11/02	6067, 1678	9/28	8/30	Grimsby	Mexborough	11/47
1068	12/02	6068, 1679	1/26		#	Mexborough	12/47
1069	12/02	6069, 1680, 61680	1/33		#	Mexborough	11/48
1070	12/02	6070	5/36		#	Immingham	3/39
1071	12/02	6071, 1681, 61681	3/28		#	Mexborough	6/48
1072	12/02	6072, 1690, 61690	5/30	7/35	#	Mexborough	4/48

* Fitted with O4 boiler, heating surface, 1,745sqft, grate area 26.24sqft, engine weight 67 tons 18 cwt
** Gorton, Grimsby or Neasden
# Grimsby or Neasden

Great Central Class 8N (LNER B6)

Dimensions

Cylinders (2 outside)	21 in x 26in
Coupled wheel diameter	5ft 8in
Bogie wheel diameter	3ft 6in
Stephenson's valve gear	slide valves
Boiler pressure	180psi
Heating surface	2,123sqft (incl 308sqft superheating)
Grate area	26.24sqft
Axleload	18 tons 4 cwt
Weight – Engine	72 tons 18 cwt
– Tender	48 tons 6 cwt
– Total	121 tons 4 cwt
Water capacity	4,000 gallons
Coal capacity	6 tons
Tractive effort	25,798lbs

Weight Diagram

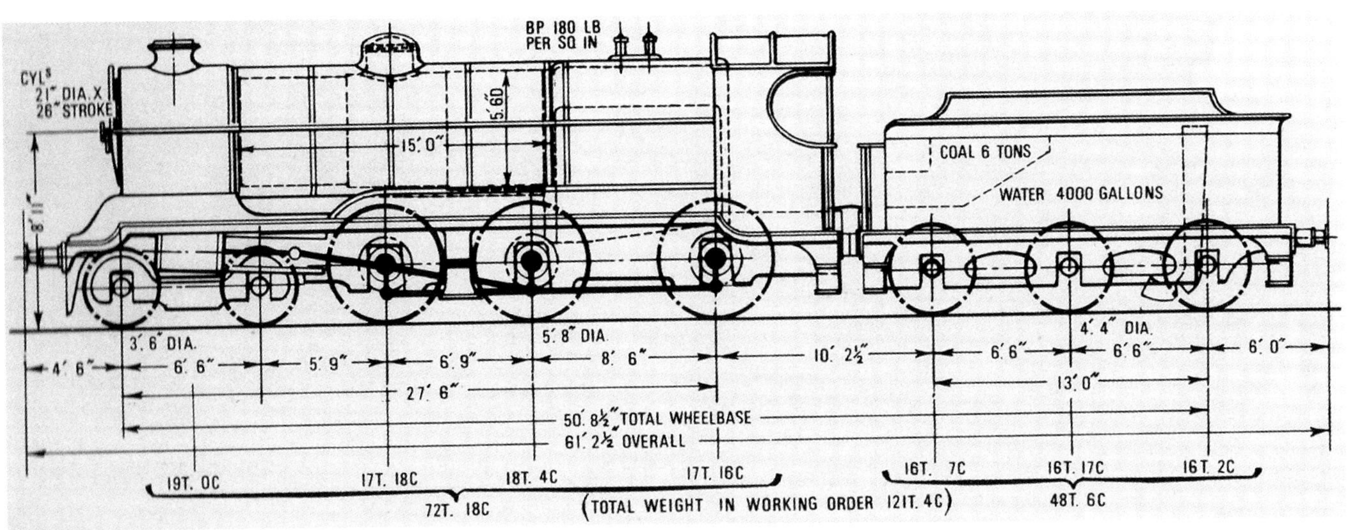

Statistics

No.	Built	Renumbered	1st depot	Last depot	Withdrawn
416	7/18	5416, 1346	Gorton	Ardsley	11/47
52	3/21	5052, 1347	Woodford	Ardsley	12/47
53	4/21	5053, 1348	Woodford	Ardsley	12/47

Great Central Class 9Q (LNER B7)

Dimensions

Cylinders (4)	16in x 26in
Coupled wheel diameter	5ft 8in
Bogie wheel diameter	3ft 6in
Stephenson's valve gear	8in piston valves
Boiler pressure	180psi
Heating surface	2,387sqft (incl 343sqft superheating)
Grate area	26sqft
Axleload	19 tons 10 cwt
Weight – Engine	79 tons 10 cwt
– Tender	48 tons 6 cwt
– Total	127 tons 16cwt
Water capacity	4,000 gallons
Coal capacity	6 tons
Tractive effort	29,952lbs

Weight Diagram

B7

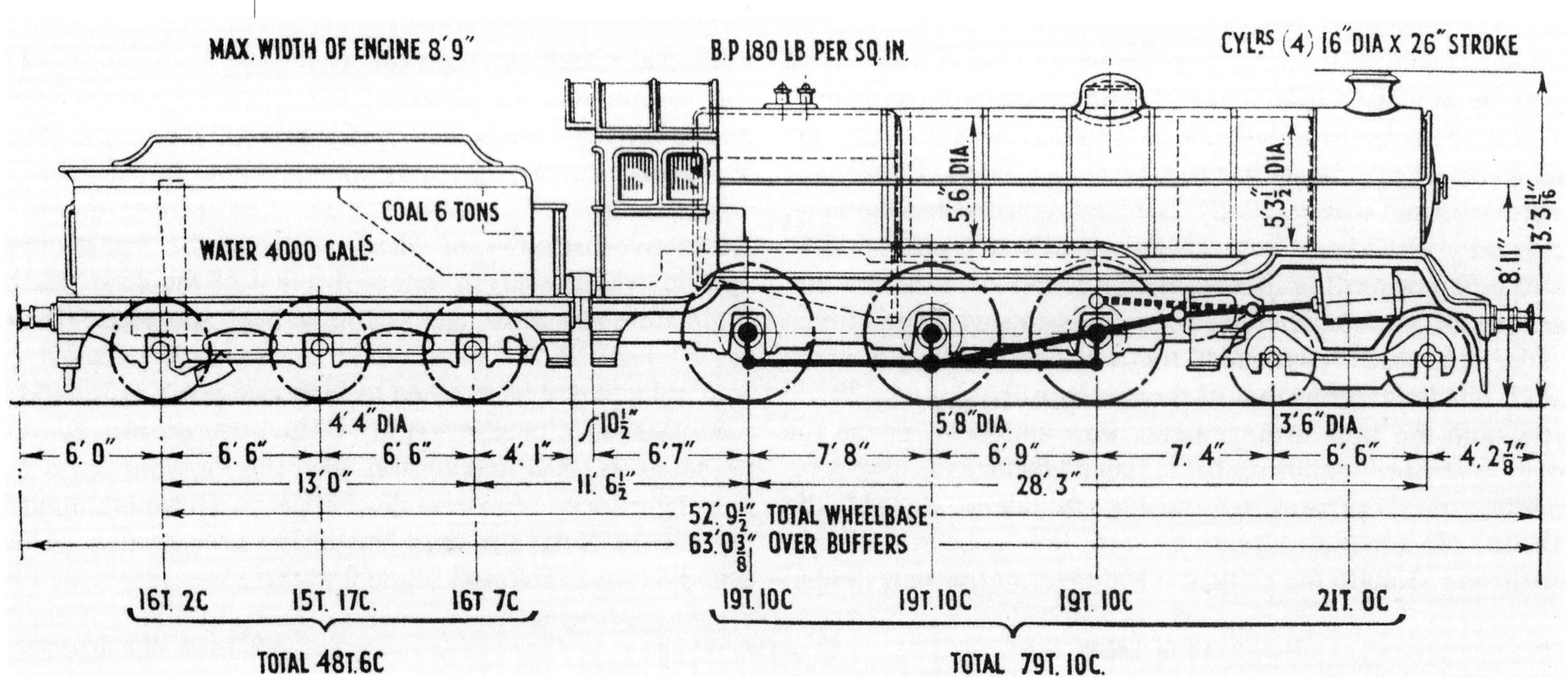

B7 proposed rebuild

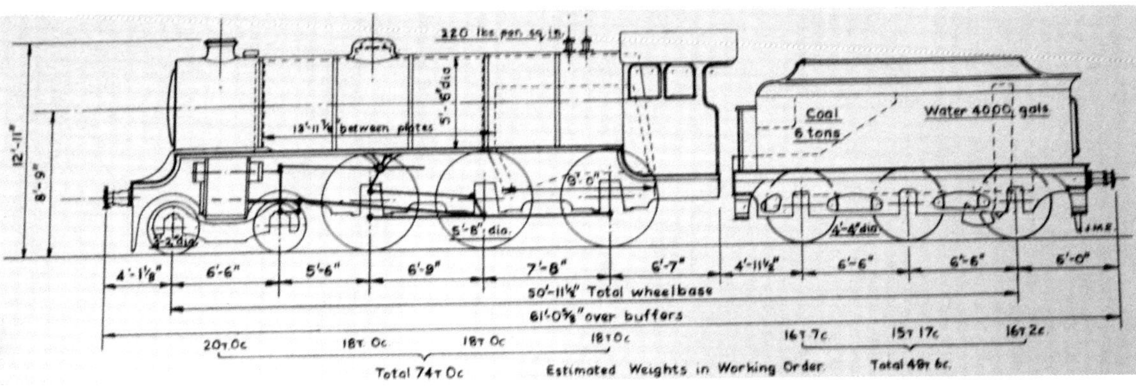

Statistics

No.	Built	Renumbered	1st depot	Last depot	Withdrawn	
72	5/21	5072, 1360, 61360	Gorton	Darnall	9/48	
73	6/21	5073, 1361, 61361	Gorton	Darnall	3/49	
78	7/21	5078, 1362, 61362	Gorton	Darnall	4/49	
36	9/21	5036, 1363, 61363	Neasden	Darnall	6/48	Alt cyls 5/40
37	10/21	5037, 1364, 61364	Neasden	Gorton	6/48	
38	10/21	5038, 1365, 61365, 61702	Neasden	Darnall	6/49	Alt cyls 12/40
458	10/21	5458, 1366, 61366	Neasden	Darnall	12/48	
459	10/21	5459, 1367, 61367, 61703	Neasden	Gorton	9/49	
460	10/21	5460, 1368, 61368	Neasden	Gorton	10/48	
461	11/21	5461, 1369, 61369	Neasden	Gorton	8/48	Alt cyls 9/46
462	11/21	5462, 1370, 61370	Neasden	Gorton	11/48	Alt cyls 3/37
463	11/21	5463, 1371, 61371	Neasden	Gorton	1/49	
464	11/21	5464, 1372, 61372	Neasden	Darnall	9/48	Alt cyls 1/43
465	8/21	5465, 1373, 61373	Sheffield	Gorton	8/48	Alt culs 9/45
466	10/21	5466, 1374, 61374	Sheffield	Gorton	9/48	Alt cyls 11/41
467	2/22	5467, 1375, 61375, 61704	Woodford	Gorton	6/49	Alt cyls 12/47
468	3/22	5468, 1376, 61376	Woodford	Gorton	12/48	Alt cyls 3/36
469	4/22	5469, 1377, 61377, 61705	Woodford	Darnall	2/50	Alt cyls 1/41
470	5/22	5470, 1378, 61378	Gorton	Darnall	8/48	
471	6/22	5471, 1379, 61379	Gorton	Darnall	2/49	Alt cyls 11/43
472	6/22	5472, 1380, 61380	Gorton	Gorton	8/48	Alt cyls 6/41
473	7/22	5473, 1381, 61381, 61706	Gorton	Gorton	12/49	
474	8/22	5474, 1382, 61382, 61707	Gorton	Gorton	6/49	
31	7/22	5031, 1383, 61383	Leicester	Darnall	5/48	
32	7/22	5032, 1384, 61384	Leicester	Darnall	8/48	
33	8/22	5033, 1385, 61385	Leicester	Gorton	1/49	Alt cyls 9/37
34	8/22	5034, 1386, 61386, 61708	Gorton	Darnall	6/49	
35	8/22	5035, 1387, 61387, 61709	Gorton	Darnall	1/50	
475	8/23	5475, 1388, 61388, 61710	Neasden	Gorton	2/50	
476	8/23	5476, 1389, 61389	Neasden	Gorton	2/49	
477	9/23	5477, 1390, 61390	Gorton	Gorton	11/48	
478	10/23	5478, 1391, 61391, 61711	Gorton	Gorton	7/50	

No.	Built	Renumbered	1st depot	Last depot	Withdrawn	
479	11/23	5479, 1392, 61392, 61712	Gorton	Gorton	6/49	
480	11/23	5480, 1393, 61393	Gorton	Gorton	8/48	Alt cyls as built
481	12/23	5481, 1394, 61394	Gorton	Gorton	4/48	
482	12/23	5482, 1395, 61395	Gorton	Gorton	11/48	Alt cyls as built
5483	2/24	1396, 61396, 61713	Gorton	Gorton	9/49	Alt cyls as built
5484	3/24	1397, 61397	Gorton	Darnall	6/48	Alt cyls as built

Great Central Class 1A (LNER B8)

Dimensions

Cylinders (2 inside)	21½in x 26in
Coupled wheel diameter	5ft 7in
Bogie wheel diameter	3ft 6in
Stephenson's valve gear	10in piston valves
Boiler pressure	180psi
Heating surface	2,387sqft (incl 343sqft superheating; 2,477sqft from 1923)
Grate area	26sqft
Axleload	19 tons 10 cwt
Weight – Engine	74 tons 7 cwt
– Tender	48 tons 6 cwt
– Total	122 tons 13cwt
Water capacity	4,000 gallons
Coal capacity	6 tons
Tractive effort	27,445lbs

Weight Diagram

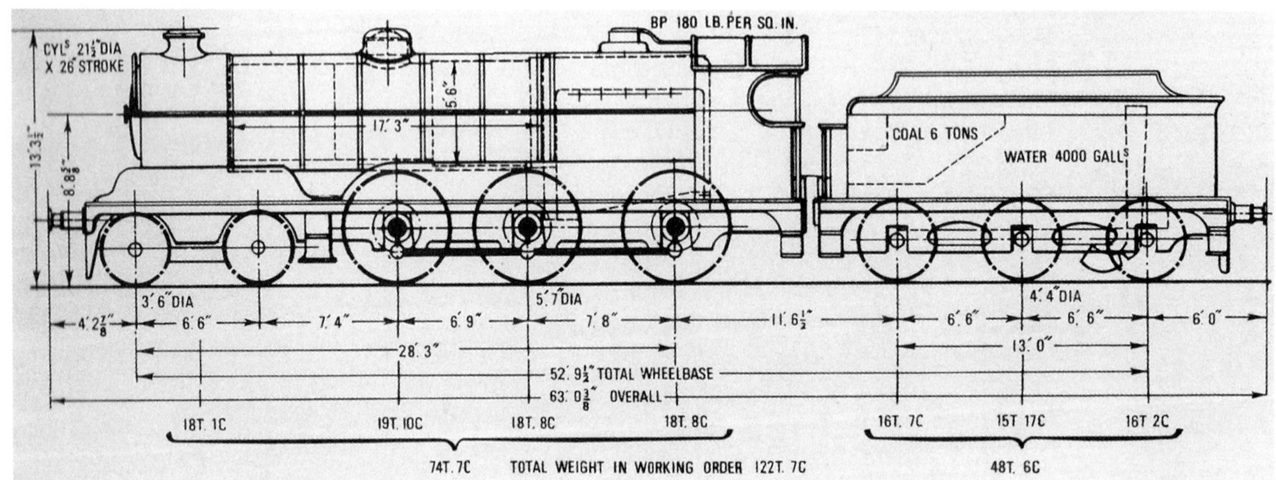

Statistics

No.	Built	Renumbered	1st depot	Last depot	Withdrawn
4*	6/13	5004, 1349	Gorton	Sheffield Darnall	11/47
439*	7/14	5439, 1350	**	Sheffield Darnall	8/47
440	8/14	5440, 1351	**	Sheffield Darnall	10/47
441	9/14	5441, 1352	**	Annesley	5/47

No.	Built	Renumbered	1st depot	Last depot	Withdrawn
442	9/14	5442, 1353, 61353	**	Sheffield Darnall	3/49
443	10/14	5443, 1354, 61354	**	Sheffield Darnall	3/48
444	10/14	5444, 1355, 61355	**	Sheffield Darnall	9/48
445	11/14	5445, 1356,	**	Sheffield Darnall	8/47
446*	11/14	5446, 1357, 61357	**	Sheffield Darnall	4/49
279*	12/14	5279, 1358, 61358	**	Sheffield Darnall	8/48
280	1/15	5280, 1359	**	Annesley	3/47

* 4 named *Glenalmond*
* 439 named *Sutton Nelthorpe*
* 446 named *Earl Roberts of Kandahar*
* 279 named *Earl Kitchener of Khartoum*
** Allocated between Gorton, Neasden & Immingham

Great Central Class 8G (LNER B9)

Dimensions

Cylinders (2 outside)	19in x 26in
Coupled wheel diameter	5ft 4in
Bogie wheel diameter	3ft 6in
Stephenson's valve gear	slide valves
Boiler pressure	180psi
Heating surface	1,951sqft (1,568sqft incl 230sqft superheating from 1924)
Grate area	23.75sqft
Axleload	18 tons
Weight – Engine	67 tons 6 cwt
– Tender	48 tons 6 cwt
– Total	115 tons 12cwt
Water capacity	4,000 gallons
Coal capacity	6 tons
Tractive effort	22,438lbs

Weight Diagram

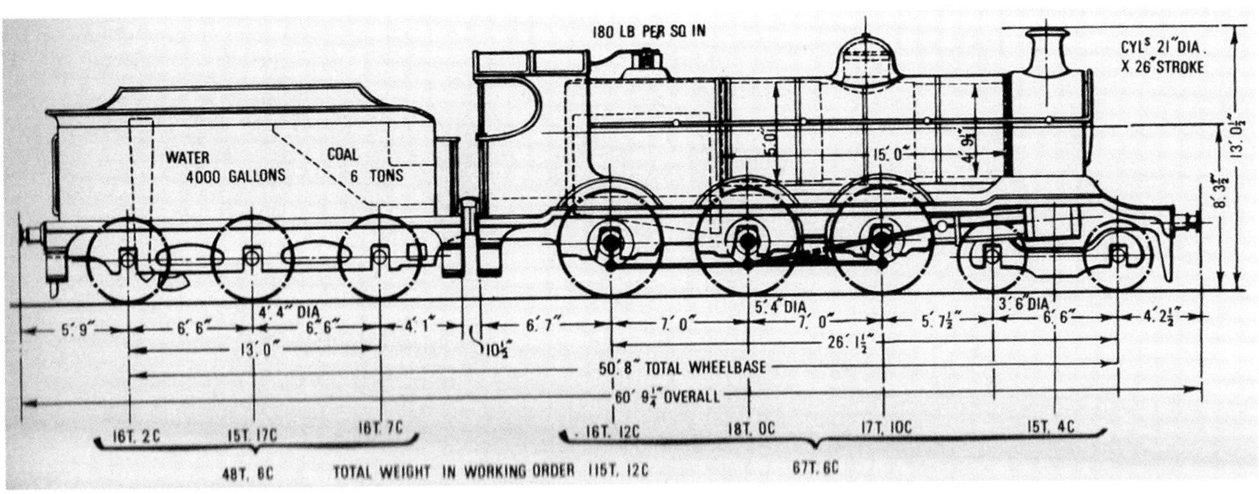

Statistics

No.	Built	Renumbered	S'heated	1st depot	Last depot	Withdrawn
1105	9/06	6105, 1469, 61469	8/27	Gorton	CLC depots**	4/49
1106	9/06	6106, 1470, 61470	1/26	Lincoln	CLC	11/48
1107	9/06	6107, 1471	1/29	Lincoln	CLC	11/47
1108	9/06	6108, 1472	6/28	Lincoln	CLC	6/47
1109	9/06	6109, 1473	11/24*	Gorton	CLC	12/47
1110	9/06	6110, 1474	8/26	Gorton	CLC	10/47
1111	10/06	6111, 1475, 61475	10/24	Lincoln	CLC	5/49
1112	10/06	6112, 1476, 61476	12/24	Lincoln	CLC	8/48
1113	10/06	6113, 1477	12/25	Gorton	CLC	8/47
1114	10/06	6114, 1478	4/29	Gorton	CLC	12/47

* 1109 fitted with 21in x 26in cylinders & piston valves in 11/14.
** Cheshire Lines Committee (CLC) depots: Stockport, Trafford Park & Liverpool

Great Eastern Class 1500 (LNER B12)

Dimensions

Cylinders (2 inside)	20in x 28in
Coupled wheel diameter	6ft 6in
Bogie wheel diameter	3ft 3in
Stephenson's valve gear	10in piston valves
Boiler pressure	180psi
Heating surface	1,834.2sqft (incl 201.6sqft superheating)
Grate area	26.5sqft
Axleload	15 tons 13 cwt
Weight – Engine	63 tons
– Tender	38 tons 6 cwt
– Total	101 tons 6 cwt
Water capacity	3,700 gallons
Coal capacity	4 tons
Tractive effort	21,969lbs

Weight Diagram

B12/1

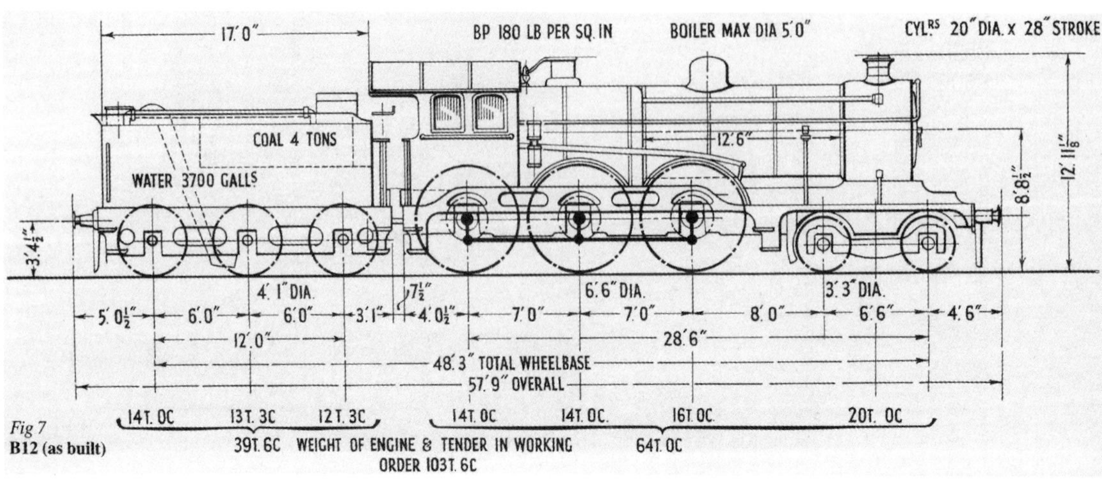

Fig 7
B12 (as built)

B12/3

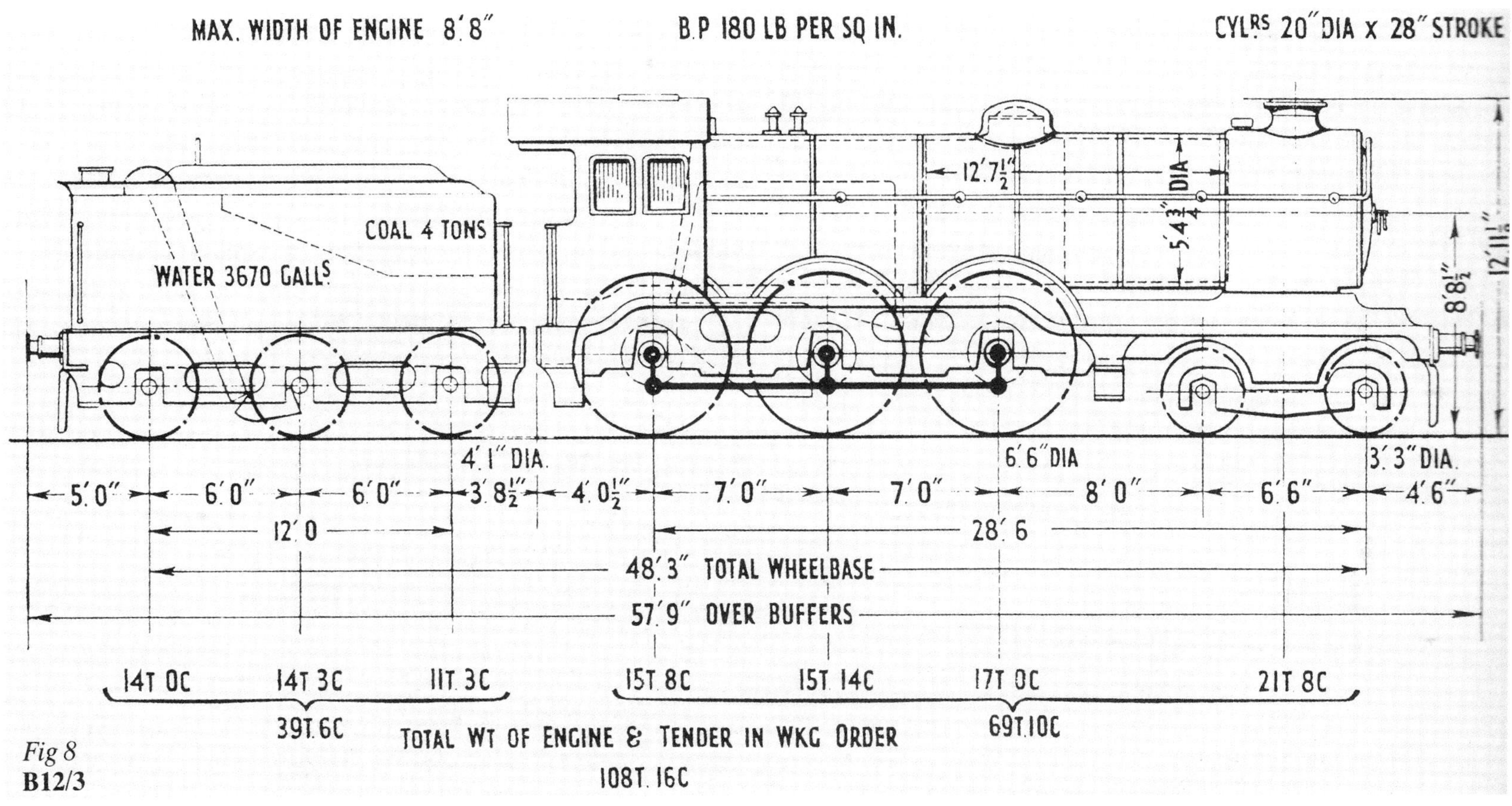

Fig 8
B12/3

Statistics

No.	Built	Renumbered	ACF1	B12/3	1st depot	Last depot	Withdrawn
1500	12/11	8500, 1500	12/31-12/40	*	Stratford	Keith	6/48
1501	2/12	8501, 1501, 61501	7/31-2/41		Stratford	Keith	5/53
1502	2/12	8502, 1502, 61502			Stratford	Keith	4/54
1503	3/12	8503, 1503, 61503	4/31-11/37		Stratford	Keith	5/51
1504	5/12	8504, 1504, 61504	4/31-5/42	*	Stratford	K'brewster	6/50
1505	2/13	8505, 1505, 61505	12/27-12/39	*	Stratford	K'brewster	3/52
1506	2/13						7/13 Accident
1507	3/13	8507, 1507, 61507	6/32-8/41	*	Stratford	Keith	2/53
1508	3/13	8508, 1508, 61508	10/31-8/41	*	Parkeston	Keith	4/53
1509	4/13	8509, 1509	2/32-4/35	4/35	Norwich	Ipswich	10/48
1510	4/13	8510, 1510	6/31-12/37	12/37	Norwich	Yarmouth	6/49
1511	5/13	8511, 1511, 61511	11/31-6/41	*	Parkeston	K'brewster	5/52
1512	6/13	8512, 7426, 1512, 61512	12/32-10/37	10/37	Cambridge	Stratford	1/57
1513	6/13	8513, 1513, 61513	10/31-9/41		Norwich	K'brewster	2/53
1514	6/13	8514, 1514, 61514	11/32-2/38	2/38	Cambridge	Norwich	10/59
1515	11/13	8515, 1515, 61515	5/32-7/38	7/38	Ipswich	Colchester	11/51
1516	11/13	8516, 1516, 61516		11/32	Norwich	Cambridge	7/58 B12/2: 12/26
1517	11/13	8517, 1517	12/27-2/34	2/34	Norwich	Stratford	10/48

No.	Built	Renumbered	ACF1	B12/3	1st depot	Last depot	Withdrawn
1518`	12/13	8518, 1518	1/32-2/35	2/35	Ipswich	Stratford	12/47
1519	12/13	8519, 1519, 61519	6/32-5/35	5/35	Ipswich	Norwich	12/57
1520	4/14	8520, 1520, 61520	4/32-1/40	1/40	Cambridge	Norwich	6/57
1521	4/14	8521, 1521, 61521	12/31-2/41		Cambridge	K'brewster	7/52
1522	4/14	8522, 1522	3/33-2/37	2/37	Cambridge	Stratford	8/47
1523	5/14	8523, 7437, 1523, 61523	12/27-9/35	9/35	Ipswich	Stratford	3/55
1524	5/14	8524, 1524, 61524	6/31-6/41	*	Cambridge	Keith	11/53
1525	6/14	8525, 1525, 61525		1/34	Stratford	Stratford	8/51 B12/2: 9/28
1526	6/14	8526, 1526, 61526	2/32-11/42	*	Cambridge	K'brewster	10/51
1527	8/14	8527, 1527	1/32-1/35	1/35	Cambridge	Stratford	9/47
1528	8/14	8528, 1528, 61528	4/33-3/39		Cambridge	K'brewster	7/53
1529	9/14	8529, 1529, 61529	11/31--/40		Ipswich	K'brewster	2/50
1530	11/14	8530, 1530, 61530	4/32-5/38	5/38	Cambridge	Cambridge	11/59
1531	11/14	8531, 1531	5/31-2/42		Stratford	K'brewster	11/47
1532	12/14	8532, 1532	5/32-8/41	*	Parkeston	Keith	7/53 B12/2: 4/30
1533	12/14	8533, 1533, 61533		10/37	Stratford	Cambridge	11/59 B12/2: 9/29
1534	2/15	8534		8/32-7/41	Stratford	Yarmouth	6/45
1535	3/15	8535, 7449, 1535, 61535	5/32-10/35	10/35	Ipswich	Norwich	12/59
1536	5/15	8536, 1536, 61536	6/31-?		Parkeston	K'brewster	12/49
1537	7/15	8537, 1537, 61537	9/32-4/39	4/39	Ipswich	Ipswich	4/57
1538	7/15	8538, 1538, 61538	12/32-6/37	6/37	Ipswich	Peterborough	1/57
1539	6/17	8539, 1539, 61539	3/32-11/40		Ipswich	Keith	11/54
1540	7/17	8540, 1540, 61540	6/32-10/34	10/34	Ipswich	Yarmouth B'ch	10/57
1541	6/20	8541, 1541, 61541		5/36	Stratford	Grantham	1/57
1542	7/20	8542, 1542, 61542	2/32-2/35	2/35	Stratford	Norwich	7/58
1543	7/20	8543, 1543, 61543	7/32-12/41		Stratford	K'brewster	6/53
1544	7/20	8544, 1544	7/32-2/35	2/35	Stratford	Stratford	9/47
1545	8/20	8545, 1545, 61545		11/36	Stratford	Yarmouth B'ch	1/57
1546	9/20	8546, 1546, 61546	2/32-2/38	2/38	Stratford	Cambridge	5/59
1547	9/20	8547, 1547, 61547		7/37	Stratford	Norwich	10/58
1548	5/21	8548, 1548	10/31-?		Stratford	K'brewster	12/46
1549	6/21	8549, 1549, 61549	7/32-7/41	1/44	Stratford	Cambridge	1/59
1550	10/20	8550, 1550, 61550		5/56	Stratford	Stratford	1/57
1551	10/20	8551, 1551	3/34-?		Stratford	K'brewster	1/47
1552	12/20	8552, 1552, 61552	4/34-?	7/39	Ipswich	K'brewster	7/52
1553	12/20	8553, 7467, 1553, 61553	6/32-5/37	5/37	Stratford	Cambridge	8/58
1554	1/21	8554, 1554, 61554	8/32-11/35	11/35	Stratford	Cambridge	9/58
1555	1/21	8555, 1555, 61555		10/35	Stratford	Cambridge	10/57
1556	2/21	8556, 7470, 1556, 61556	1/32-5/35	5/35	Stratford	Norwich	12/57
1557	2/21	8557, 1557, 61557		12/34	Stratford	Colchester	1/57
1558	2/21	8558, 7472, 1558, 61558		11/35	Stratford	Cambridge	4/59
1559	2/21	8559, 1559, 61559		5/36	Stratford	Colchester	9/51
1560	4/21	8560, 1560, 61560	11/32-3/41		Stratford	K'brewster	5/52

No.	Built	Renumbered	ACF1	B12/3	1st depot	Last depot	Withdrawn
1561	3/20	8561, 1561, 61561		4/37	Ipswich	Ipswich	9/58
1562	4/20	8562, 7476, 1562, 61562		4/38	Ipswich	Ipswich	8/55
1563	4/20	8563, 1563, 61563	9/32-12/40		Ipswich	K'brewster	4/53
1564	4/20	8564, 1564, 61564	11/32-7/35	7/35	Ipswich	Ipswich	11/58
1565	5/20	8565, 7479, 1565, 61565		2/37	Ipswich	Peterborough	1/57
1566	5/20	8566, 1566, 61566		5/36	Ipswich	Norwich	1/59
1567	5/20	8567, 1567, 61567	4/32-4/35	4/35	Norwich	Bury St Edm'ds	11/58
1568	6/20	8568, 7482, 1568, 61568	10/31-4/41	4/41	Norwich	Norwich	8/59
1569	6/20	8569, 1569, 61569	5/32-12/33	12/33	Norwich	Ipswich	1/57
1570	6/20	8570, 1570, 61570	5/32-6/41	11/43	Norwich	Ipswich	3/58
8571	8/28	1571, 61571		7/33	Stratford	Norwich	12/59 Built as B12/2
8572	8/28	1572, 61572		12/33	Stratford	Norwich	9/61 Built as B12/2 Preserved
8573	8/28	1573, 61573		7/33	Stratford	Cambridge	1/59 Built as B12/2
8574	8/28	7488, 1574, 61574		7/33	Stratford	Grantham	1/57 Built as B12/2
8575	9/28	1575, 61575		11/33	Stratford	Cambridge	4/59 Built as B12/2
8576	9/28	1576, 61576		8/32	Stratford	Cambridge	1/59 Built as B12/2
8577	9/28	7491, 1577, 61577	11/31-1/34	1/34	Stratford	Cambridge	9/59 Built as B12/2
8578	9/28	1578, 61578		10/32	Stratford	Stratford	1/57 Built as B12/2
8579	9/28	1579, 61579		5/32	Stratford	Stratford	1/57 Built as B12/2
8580	10/28	1580, 61580		9/32	Stratford	Cambridge	3/59 Built as B12/2

Notes: B12/2 rebuilt with Lentz poppet valve gear
* B12/1 rebuilt to B12/4 with J20 round topped boiler replacing Belpaire firebox between 1943 and 1948

North Eastern Class S (LNER B13)

Dimensions

Cylinders (2 outside)	20in x 26in
Coupled wheel diameter	6ft 1 ¼ in
Bogie wheel diameter	3ft 7 ¼ in
Stephenson's valve gear	8¾ in piston valves (2001-3 built with slide valves)
Boiler pressure	160psi (2001-3 built with 200psi)
Heating surface	1,769sqft (later 1,659sqft incl 276sqft superheating)
Grate area	23sqft
Axleload	19 tons 14 cwt
Weight – Engine	64 tons 6 cwt
– Tender	43 tons 10 cwt
– Total	107 tons 16 cwt
Water capacity	3,940 gallons
Coal capacity	5 tons
Tractive effort	19,309lbs (2001-3: 24,136lbs as built)

Weight Diagram

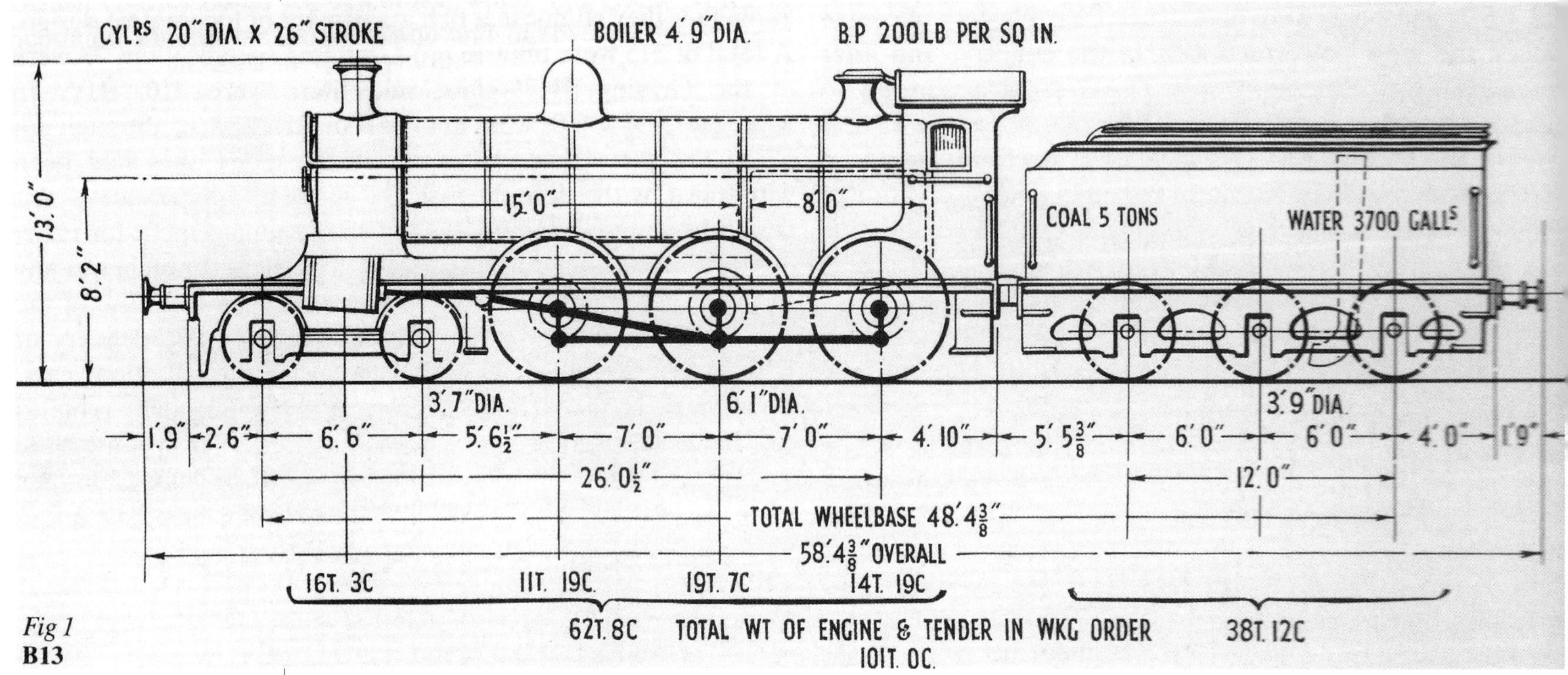

Fig 1
B13

Statistics

No.	Built	Superheated	1st depot	Last depot	Withdrawn
2001	6/99	2/16	Gateshead	Dairycoates	6/31
2002	6/99	7/24	Gateshead	Blaydon	7/31
2003	9/99	5/20	Gateshead	Dairycoates	7/31
2004	12/99	4/21	Gateshead	Dairycoates	8/28
2005	12/99	11/16	Gateshead	York	11/28
2006	12/99	4/18	Gateshead	Neville Hill	6/31
2007	3/00	6/16	Gateshead	Blaydon	10/28
2008	5/00	4/17	Gateshead	Neville Hill	12/29
2009	6/00	7/15	Gateshead	Dairycoates	7/31
2010	6/00	4/16	Gateshead	Dairycoates	7/31
726	4/06	11/15	Dairycoates	Dairycoates	12/36
740	4/06	7/14	Dairycoates	Dairycoates	9/32
757	4/06	3/18	Heaton	Dairycoates	5/32
760	5/06	4/15	Dairycoates	Dairycoates	3/31
761	6/06	11/24	Heaton	Service stock	5/51 Renumbered 1699 10/46
763	6/06	1/16	Dairycoates	Dairycoates	4/29
766	6/06	12/16	Blaydon	Darlington	10/31
768	6/06	8/18	Dairycoates	Dairycoates	5/29
775	8/06	12/20	Blaydon	York	8/36

No.	Built	Superheated	1st depot	Last depot	Withdrawn
1077	8/06	6/18	Heaton	York	11/31
738	6/08	8/16	Tweedmouth	Dairycoates	7/38
739	6/08	2/25	Tweedmouth	Neville Hill	7/32
741	6/08	5/17	Tweedmouth	Tweedmouth	1/30
743	7/08	10/17	Neville Hill	Neville Hill	5/32
744	7/08	11/15	Dairycoates	Dairycoates	12/31
745	8/08	12/21	Tweedmouth	Tweedmouth	12/31
746	8/08	3/18	Dairycoates	Colwick	11/31
747	9/08	10/20	Tweedmouth	Dairycoates	8/32
748	9/08	3/15	Dairycoates	Dairycoates	10/38
749	10/08	11/15	Dairycoates	Dairycoates	4/30
750	11/08	1/15	Neville Hill	Neville Hill	11/32
751	11/08	11/13	Dairycoates	Dairycoates	5/36
752	11/08	3/20	Heaton	Tweedmouth	6/34
753	12/08	11/16	Neville Hill	Dairycoates	10/38
754	1/09	7/22	Tweedmouth	Dairycoates	12/36
755	1/09	8/17	Dairycoates	Dairycoates	2/34
756	1/09	11/19	Blaydon	Dairycoates	9/34
758	2/09	11/15	Dairycoates	Dairycoates	5/30
759	3/09	9/23	Heaton	Dairycoates	10/38
762	3/09	6/17	Neville Hill	Neville Hill	5/37

North Eastern Class S1 (LNER B14)

Dimensions

Cylinders (2 outside)	20in x 26in
Coupled wheel diameter	6ft 8¼ in
Bogie wheel diameter	3ft 7¼ in
Stephenson's valve gear	8¾ in piston valves
Boiler pressure	200psi (175psi when superheated))
Heating surface	1,769sqft (later 1857.8sqft incl 390.1sqft superheating)
Grate area	23sqft
Axleload	19 tons 10 cwt
Weight – Engine	67 tons 2 cwt
– Tender	41 tons 2 cwt
– Total	108 tons 4 cwt
Water capacity	3,940 gallons
Coal capacity	5 tons
Tractive effort	22,069lbs (later 19,310lbs when superheated)

Statistics

No.	Built	Superheated	1st depot	Last depot	Withdrawn
2111	12/00	10/13	Gateshead	Dairycoates	7/29
2112	6/01	4/16	Gateshead	Dairycoates	4/31
2113	6/01	6/15	Gateshead	Dairycoates	10/30
2114	6/01	5/15	Gateshead	Dairycoates	10/30
2115	8/01	4/17	Gateshead	Dairycoates	6/29

North Eastern Class S2 (LNER B15)

Dimensions

Cylinders (2 outside)	20in x 26in
Coupled wheel diameter	6ft 1¼ in
Bogie wheel diameter	3ft 7¼ in
Stephenson's valve gear	8¾in piston valves
Boiler pressure	180psi (175psi when superheated))
Heating surface	2,297sqft (later 2,366sqft incl 545sqft superheating)
Grate area	23sqft
Axleload	19 tons 4 cwt
Weight – Engine	68 tons 17 cwt (70 tons 14 cwt superheated)
– Tender	41 tons 2 cwt
– Total	109 tons 19 cwt (111 tons 16 cwt superheated)
Water capacity	3,940 gallons
Coal capacity	5 tons
Tractive effort	21,723lbs (later 21,555lbs when superheated)

825 with Stumpf Uniflow cylinders

As above superheated locomotives except:

Walschaerts valve gear	Piston valves with Uniflow
Axleload	19 tons 9 cwt
Weight – Engine	71 tons 14 cwt
– Total	112 tons 16 cwt

Statistics

No.	Built	Renumbered	Superheated	1st depot	Last depot	Withdrawn
782	12/11	1313, 1691	2/26	Heaton	Dairycoates	12/46
786	12/11		12/28	Heaton	Dairycoates	9/37
787	2/12	1314, 1692	6/20	Heaton	Dairycoates	12/46
788	2/12		2/19	Heaton	Dairycoates	9/37
791	2/12		7/27	Heaton	Starbeck	10/37
795	3/12	1315	5/28	Heaton	Dairycoates	12/45
796	3/12	1316	8/22	Heaton	Dairycoates	12/45
797	5/12		As built	Heaton	Selby	11/37
798	6/12	1317	As built	Heaton	Dairycoates	10/45
799	6/12		As built	Heaton	York	11/37
813	9/12	1318	As built	Scarborough	Dairycoates	3/44
815	9/12	1319, 1693	As built	Doncaster	Dairycoates	5/47
817	10/12	1320, 1694	As built	York	Dairycoates	4/46
819	10/12	1321, 1695	As built	Neville Hill	Dairycoates	12/46
820	11/12	1322, 1696	As built	York	Dairycoates	12/47
821	11/12	1323, 1697	As built	York	Dairycoates	11/46
822	11/12	1324	As built	York	Dairycoates	2/44
823	12/12	1325	As built	York	Dairycoates	10/44
824	12/12	1326, 1698	As built	Darlington	Dairycoates	4/46
825*	3/13	1327	As built	Heaton	Dairycoates	2/44

* Stumpf Uniflow cylinders rebuilt with conventional cylinders, 3/24

North Eastern Class S3 (LNER B16)

Dimensions

Cylinders (3)	18½in x 26in
Coupled wheel diameter	5ft 8in
Bogie wheel diameter	3ft 1in
Stephenson's valve gear	8¾in piston valves
Boiler pressure	180psi (175psi when superheated))
Heating surface	1,958sqft (incl 392sqft superheating)
Grate area	27sqft
Axleload	20 tons
Weight – Engine	77 tons 14 cwt
– Tender	46 tons 12 cwt
– Total	124 tons 6 cwt
Water capacity	4,125 gallons
Coal capacity	5 tons10 cwt
Tractive effort	30,031lbs

B16/2

As above except:

Walchaerts/Gresley conjugated gear, 9in piston valves

Axleload	20 tons 3 cwt
Weight – Engine	79 tons 4 cwt
– Total	125 tons 16 cwt

B16/3

As B16/2 except:

Walchaerts valve gear	3 independent sets
Axleload	20 tons
Weight – Engine	78 tons 19 cwt
– Total	125 tons 11 cwt

Weight Diagram

B16/1

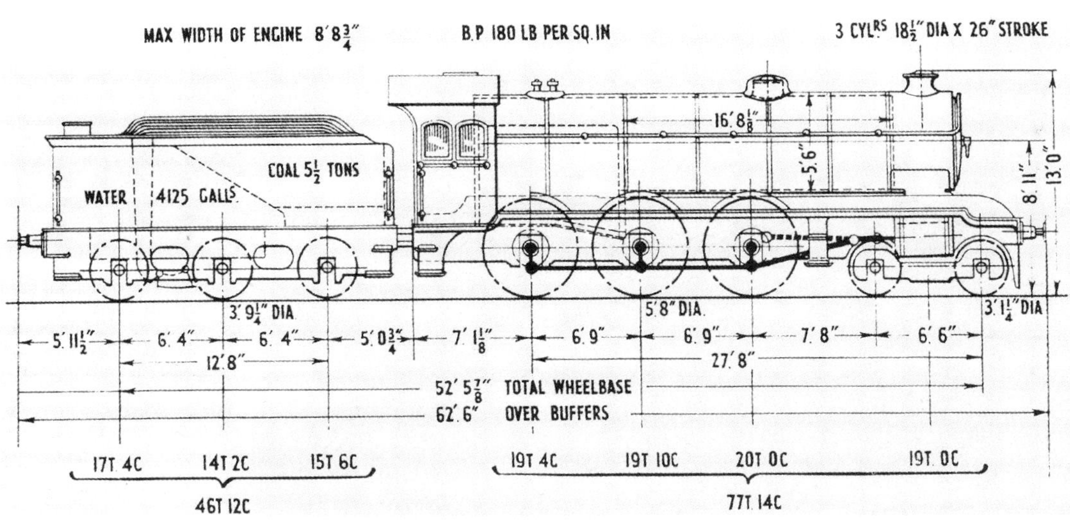

B16/3

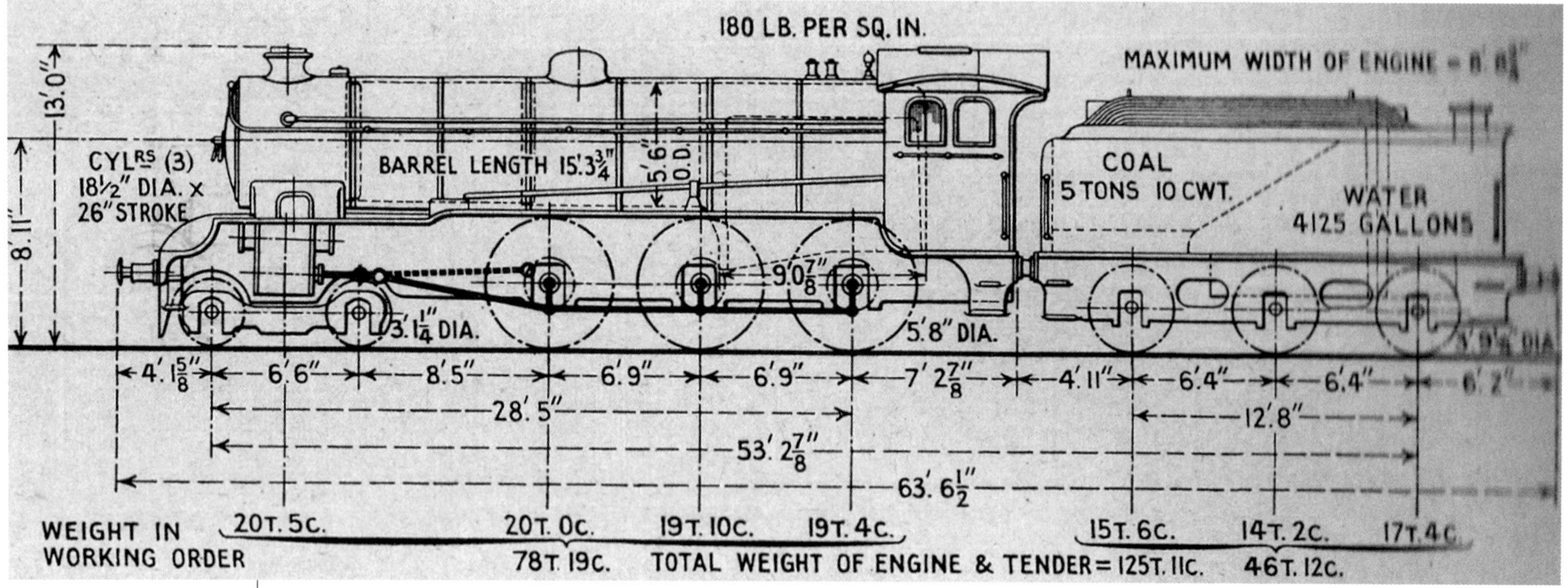

Statistics

No.	Built	Renumbered	B16/2	B16/3	1st depot	Last depot	Withdrawn
840	12/19	1400, 61400, 61469			Heaton	York	10/60
841	12/219	1401, 61401, 61470			Heaton	Neville Hill	11/59
842	12/19	1402, 61402, 61471			Heaton	Neville Hill	9/60
843	12/19	1403, 61472		9/45	Heaton	Dairycoates	4/64
844	12/19	1404, 61404, 61473			York	York	9/61
845	4/20	1405, 61405, 61474			York	Selby	1/58
846	3/20	1406, 61406, 61475	1/40		Heaton	Dairycoates	4/63
847	3/20	1407, 61407, 61476		6/45	York	Mirfield	9/63
848	4/20	1408, 61477			York	York	2/60
849	4/20	1409, 61478			York	York	12/60
906	6/20	1410, 61410			Heaton	York	10/60
908	8/20	1411, 61411			York	Mirfield	9/61
909	8/20	1412, 61412			Tweedmouth	Mirfield	9/61
911	8/20	1413, 61413			York	Mirfield	9/61
914	9/20	1414, 61414			Heaton	Mirfield	9/61
915	9/20	1415, 61415			York	Neville Hill	9/61
920	9/20	1416, 61416			Gateshead	Mirfield	5/61
921	10/20	1417, 61417		12/45	York	York	9/62
922	11/20	1418, 61418		4/44	Heaton	Dairycoates	6/64
923	11/20	1419, 61419			York	York	9/61
924	12/20	1420, 61420		10/45	Tweedmouth	Dairycoates	9/63
925	12/20				York	York	6/42
926	12/20	1421, 61421	3/40		Tweedmouth	York	6/64

No.	Built	Renumbered	B16/2	B16/3	1st depot	Last depot	Withdrawn
927	12/20	1422, 61422			York	York	9/61
928	1/21	1423, 61423			Tweedmouth	York	9/61
929	2/21	1424, 61424			Neville Hill	York	10/60
930	2/21	1425, 61425			Heaton	York	9/61
931	3/21	1426, 61426			Neville Hill	York	9/59
932	3/21	1427, 61427			Heaton	Neville Hill	3/60
933	3/21	1428, 61428			York	Neville Hill	10/60
934	4/21	1429, 61429			Heaton	Neville Hill	9/61
936	4/21	1430, 61430			York	York	10/59
937	5/21	1431, 61431			Heaton	York	9/61
942	6/21	1432, 61432			York	Neville Hill	7/61
943	6/21	1433, 61433			Heaton	York	11/59
2363	11/22	1434, 61434		4/49	Gateshead	York	6/64
2364	11/22	1435, 61435	6/37		York	Dairycoates	7/64
2365	12/22	1436, 61436			Gateshead	York	9/61
2366	1/23	1437, 61437	2/40		York	Dairycoates	6/64
2367	1/23	1438, 61438	11/39		Gateshead	Dairycoates	6/64
2368	2/23	1439, 61439		8/45	York	York	8/62
2369	3/23	1440, 61440			Gateshead	York	8/60
2370	3/23	1441, 61441			York	York	10/59
2371	4/23	1442, 61442			Gateshead	Neville Hill	2/60
2372	4/23	1443, 61443			York	York	9/61
2373	5/23	1444, 61444		5/45	York	Dairycoates	6/64
2374	5/23	1445, 61445			York	Scarborough	7/61
2375	5/23	1446, 61446			Gateshead	Neville Hill	1/61
2376	6/23	1447, 61447			York	Mirfield	9/61
2377	5/23	1448, 61448		7/44	Gateshead	York	6/64
2378	7/23	1449, 61449		9/44	York	Mirfield	7/63
2379	6/23	1450, 61450			Gateshead	York	9/61
2380	7/23	1451, 61451			York	York	9/61
2381	8/23	1452, 61452			Gateshead	York	9/61
2382	8/23	1453, 61453		9/47	York	Dairycoates	6/63
1371	10/23	1454, 61454		12/44	York	York	6/64
1372	10/23	1455, 61455	11/39		Heaton	York	9/63
1373	10/23	1456, 61456			Heaton	York	8/60
1374	10/23	1457, 61457	10/39		York	York	6/64
1375	10/23	1458, 61458			Tweedmouth	York	11/59
1376	11/23	1459, 61459			Tweedmouth	York	9/61
1377	11/23	1460, 61460			York	York	9/61
1378	11/23	1461, 61461		8/48	Tweedmouth	Mrfield	9/63
1379	11/23	1462, 61462			Heaton	York	5/61
1380	12/23	1463, 61463		11/47	Neville Hill	Dairycoates	6/64
1381	12/23	1464, 61464		4/45	Darlington	Mirfield	9/63
1382	12/23	1465, 61465			Darlington	York	1/60
1383	12/23	1466, 61466			Heaton	York	7/61
1384	1/24	1467, 61467		10/44	Tweedmouth	Dairycoates	6/64
1385	1/24	1468, 61468		5/47	Heaton	Mirfield	9/63

LNER Class B17

Dimensions

B17/1

Cylinders (3)	17½in x 26in
Coupled wheel diameter	6ft 8in
Bogie wheel diameter	3ft 2in
Walchaerts/Gresley conjugated gear with 8in piston valves	
Boiler pressure	200psi
Heating surface	2,020sqft (incl 344sqft superheating)
Grate area	27.5sqft
Axleload	18 tons
Weight – Engine	76 tons 13 cwt
– Tender	39 tons 8 cwt
– Total	116 tons 1 cwt
Water capacity	3,700 gallons
Coal capacity	4 tons
Tractive effort	25,380lbs

B17/4

As B17/1 with large LNER tender:

Axleload	18 tons 7 cwt
Weight – Engine	77 tons 5 cwt
– Tender	52 tons
– Total	129 tons 5 cwt
Water capacity	4,200 gallons
Coal capacity	7 tons 10 cwt

B17/5

B17/4 streamlined in 1937

As B17/4 above except:

Axleload	19 tons 16 cwt
Weight – Engine	80 tons 10 cwt
– Tender	52 tons 13 cwt
– Total	133 tons 3 cwt

B17/6

B17/1 &/4 with B1 100A boiler

As B17/1 & 4 except:

Boiler pressure	225psi
Heating surface	2,005sqft (incl 344sqft superheating)
Grate area	27.9sqft
Axleload	18 tons 3 cwt
Weight – Engine	77 tons 3 cwt
– Total	116 tons 11 cwt (129 tons 3 cwt ex B17/4)
Tractive effort	28,553lbs

Weight Diagram

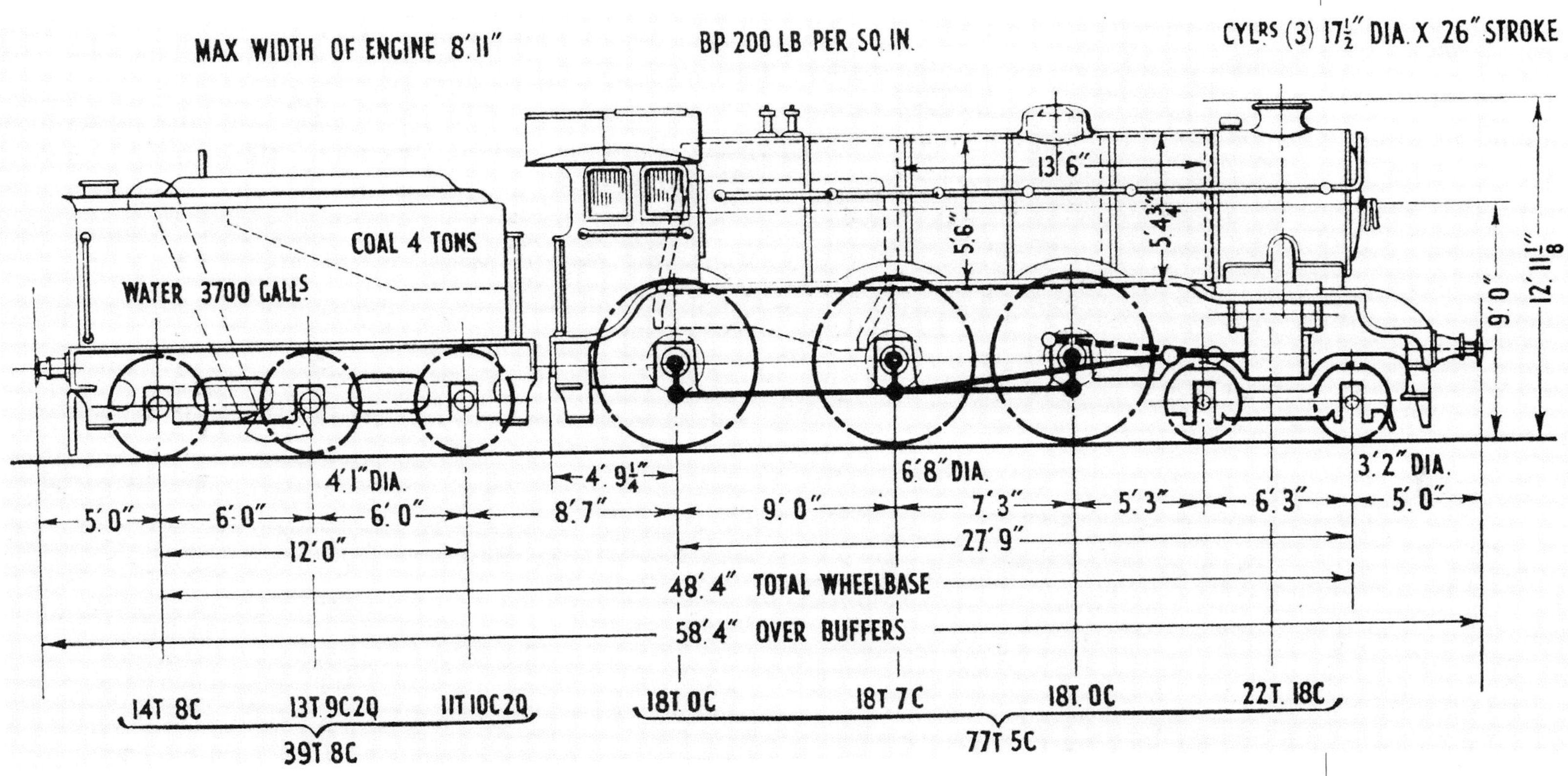

Statistics

No.	Built	Renumbered	B17/6	1st depot	Last depot	Withdrawn
B17/1						
2800	12/28	1600, 61600	6/50	Stratford	Stratford	7/58
2801	12/28	1601, 61610		Stratford	Stratford	1/58
2802	11/28	1602, 61602	10/51	Gorton	Yarmouth	1/58
2803	12/28			Stratford	Ipswich	Rebuilt as B2, 10/46
2804	12/28	1604, 61604	11/51	Stratford	Stratford	8/53
2805	12/28	1605, 61605	1/48	Stratford	Stratford	5/58
2806	12/28	1606, 61606	3/50	Stratford	Colchester	9/58
2807	12/28	1607		Ipswich	Stratford	Rebuilt as B2, 5/47
2808	12/28	1608, 61608	10/50	Stratford	Cambridge	3/60
2809	12/28	1609, 61609	1/52	Gorton	Ipswich	6/58
2810	8/30	1610, 61610	10/53	Stratford	Cambridge	1/60
2811	8/30	1611, 61611	2/56	Stratford	Norwich	10/59
2812	10/30	1612, 61612	3/50	Stratford	Ipswich	9/59
2813	10/30	1613, 61613	12/51	Stratford	Cambridge	12/59
2814	10/30			Stratford	Cambridge	Rebuilt as B2, 11/46
2815	10/30			Stratford	Stratford	Rebuilt as B2, 4/46

No.	Built	Renumbered	B17/6	1st depot	Last depot	Withdrawn
2816	10/30			Gorton	Cambridge	Rebuilt as B2, 11/45
2817	11/30	1617		Cambridge	Cambridge	Rebuilt as B2, 12/46
2818	11/30	1618, 61618	4/58	Cambridge	Cambridge	1/60
2819	11/30	1619, 61619	1/53	Cambridge	March	9/58
2820	11/30	1620, 61620	12/51	Ipswich	King's Lynn	1/60
2821	11/30	1621, 61621	1/55	Ipswich	March	11/58
2822	1/31	1622, 61622	10/43	Colchester	Yarmouth	9/58
2823	2/31	1623, 61623	4/48	Colchester	Cambridge	7/59
2824	2/31	1624, 61624		Colchester	March	3/53
2825	2/31	1625, 61625		Ipswich	Cambridge	12/59
2826	3/31	1626, 61626	4/55	Ipswich	Cambridge	1/60
2827	3/31	1627, 61627	11/48	Stratford	March	7/59
2828	3/31	1628, 61628	12/48	Stratford	Cambridge	9/52
2829	4/31	1629, 61629		Stratford	Ipswich	9/59
2830	4/31	1630, 61630	12/48	Stratford	March	8/58
2831	5/31	1631, 61631	10/57	Stratford	Ipswich	4/59
2832	5/31			Doncaster	Norwich	Rebuilt as B2, 7/46
2833	5/31	1633, 61633	8/48	Doncaster	March	9/59
2834	6/31	1634, 61634	1/57	Gorton	March	8/58
2835	7/31	1635, 61635	1/49	Doncaster	March	1/59
2836	7/31	1636, 61636	5/50	Ipswich	Norwich	10/59
2837	3/33	1637, 61637	11/57	Norwich	Ipswich	9/59
2838	3/33	1638, 61638	12/48	Norwich	March	3/58
2839	5/33			Norwich	Norwich	Rebuilt as B2, 1/46
2840	5/33	1640, 61640	5/55	Gorton	Cambridge	11/58
2841	5/33	1641, 61641	2/49	Gorton	March	1/60
2842	5/33	1642, 61642	1/49	Gorton	Cambridge	9/58
2843	5/35	1643, 61643	10/54	Norwich	March	7/58
2844	5/35	1644		Norwich	Norwich	Rebuilt as B2, 3/49
2845	6/35	1645, 61645	12/52	Ipswich	March	2/59
2846	8/35	1646, 61646	2/51	March	March	1/59
2847	9/35	1647, 61647	2/58	March	Cambridge	11/59
B17/4						
2848	3/36	1648, 61648	10/57	Leicester	Stratford	12/58
2849	3/36	1649, 61649	3/54	Leicester	Ipswich	2/59
2850	3/36	1650, 61650	2/55	Leicester	Colchester	9/58
2851	3/36	1651, 61651	6/53	Leicester	Colchester	8/59
2852	4/36	1652, 61652	3/48	Leicester	Cambridge	9/59
2853	4/36	1653, 61653	5/54	Leicester	March	1/60
2854	4/36	1654, 61654	4/48	Leicester	Norwich	11/59
2855	4/36	1655, 61655	7/50	Leicester	Cambridge	4/59
2856	5/36	1656, 61656	11/53	Neasden	March	1/60
2857	5/36	1657, 61657	10/50	Neasden	March	6/60
2858	5/36	1658, 61658	9/50	Neasden	Stratford	12/59
2859	6/36	1659, 61659	7/49	Gorton	Lowestoft	3/60 Streamlined B17/5 1937

No.	Built	Renumbered	B17/6	1st depot	Last depot	Withdrawn
2860	6/36	1660, 61660		Gorton	March	6/60
2861	6/36	1661, 61661	8/55	Gorton	Cambridge	7/59
2862	1/37	1662, 61662	3/55	Gorton	Stratford	12/59
2863	2/37	1663, 61663	11/51	Sheffield	Stratford	2/60
2864	1/37	1664, 61664	10/43	Sheffield	March	6/60
2865	1/37	1665, 61665	8/49	Sheffield	Yarmouth	4/59
2866	2/37	1666, 61666	12/47	Woodford	Stratford	3/60
2867	4/37	1667, 61667		Woodford	Cambridge	6/58
2868	4/37	1668, 61668	6/49	Leicester	Stratford	8/60
2869	5/37	1669, 61669	9/49	Gorton	Ipswich	9/58
2870	5/37	1670, 61670	4/51	Leicester	Lowestoft	4/60 Streamlined B17/5 1937
2871	6/37			Gorton	Stratford	Rebuilt as B2 8/45
2872	7/37	1672, 61672	9/50	Gorton	Lowestoft	3/60

Names & Renaming

Sandringham Class

		Nearby Location
2800	*Sandringham*	King's Lynn
2801	*Holkham*	Wells-next-the-Sea
2802	*Walsingham*	Fakenham
2803	*Framlingham*	Saxmundham
2804	*Elveden*	Thetford
2805	*Burnham Thorpe* (renamed *Lincolnshire Regiment*, 4/38)	Hunstanton
2806	*Audley End*	Saffron Walden
2807	*Blickling*	Aylsham
2808	*Gunton*	Cromer
2809	*Quidenham*	Thetford
2810	*Honingham Hall*	Norwich/Dereham
2811	*Raynham Hall*	Fakenham
2812	*Houghton Hall*	King's Lynn/Fakenham
2813	*Woodbastwick Hall*	Norwich/Cromer
2814	*Castle Hedingham*	Halstead
2815	*Culford Hall*	Bury St Edmunds
2816	*Fallodon*	Alnwick
2817	*Ford Castle*	Coldstream
2818	*Wynyard Park*	Stockton/Sedgefield
2819	*Welbeck Abbey*	Worksop
2820	*Clumber*	Worksop
2821	*Hatfield House*	Hatfield (Herts)
2822	*Alnwick Castle*	Alnwick
2823	*Lambton Castle*	Chester-le-Street
2824	*Lumley Castle*	Chester-le-Street
2825	*Raby Castle*	Staindrop
2826	*Brancepeth Castle*	Bishop Auckland/Durham
2827	*Aske Hall*	Richmond (Yorks)
2828	*Harewood House*	Leeds/Harrogate
2829	*Naworth Castle*	Brampton (Cumberland)

	Names & Renaming	**Nearby Location**
2830	*Thoresby Park* (renamed *Tottenham Hotspur* 1/38)	Worksop
2831	*Serlby Hall*	Retford
2832	*Belvoir Castle*	Grantham
2833	*Kimbolton Castle*	Huntingdon
2834	*Hinchingbrooke*	Huntingdon
2835	*Milton*	Peterborough
2836	*Harlaxton Manor*	Grantham
2837	*Thorpe Hall*	Thorpe-le-Soken
2838	*Melton Hall*	Melton Constable
2839	*Rendlesham Hall* (renamed *Norwich City*, 1/38)	Wickham Market
2840	*Somerleyton Hall*	Lowestoft
2841	*Gayton Hall*	King's Lynn
2842	*Kilverstone Hall*	Thetford
2843	*Champion Lodge*	Maldon
2844	*Earlham Hall*	Norwich
2845	*The Suffolk Regiment*	
2846	*Gilwell Park*	Chingford
2847	*Helmingham Hall*	Ipswich/Yarmouth

	Football Class	**Nameplate Panel Colours**
2848	*Arsenal*	Red
2849	*Sheffield United*	Red & white
2850	*Grimsby Town*	Black & white
2851	*Derby County*	White
2852	*Darlington*	Black & white
2853	*Huddersfield Town*	Blue & white
2854	*Sunderland*	Red & white
2855	*Middlesbrough*	Red
2856	*Leeds United*	Blue & gold (later white)
2857	*Doncaster Rovers*	Red & white
2858	*Newcastle United* (renamed *The Essex Regiment*, 6/36)	Black & white
2859	*Norwich City* (renamed *East Anglian*, 9/37)	Green & yellow
2860	*Hull City*	Blue (later Yellow & black)
2861	*Sheffield Wednesday*	Blue & white
2862	*Manchester United*	Red
2863	*Everton*	Blue
2864	*Liverpool*	Red
2865	*Leicester City*	Blue
2866	*Nottingham Forest*	Red
2867	*Bradford*	Black, yellow & red
2868	*Bradford City*	Claret & amber
2869	*Barnsley*	Red
2870	*Manchester City* (renamed *Tottenham Hotspur*, 5/37 & renamed *City of London*, 9/37) (Tottenham, White with cockerel badges)	
2871	*Manchester City* (renamed *Royal Sovereign*, 8/45)	Blue
2872	*West Ham United*	Claret & blue (later red)

LNER Class B1

Dimensions

Cylinders (2 outside)	20in x 26in
Coupled wheel diameter	6ft 2in
Bogie wheel diameter	3ft 2in
Walchaerts valve gear with 10in piston valves	
Boiler pressure	225psi
Heating surface	2,005sqft (incl 344sqft superheating)
Grate area	27.9sqft
Axleload	17 tons 15 cwt
Weight – Engine	71 tons 3 cwt
– Tender	52 tons 10 cwt
– Total	123 tons 13 cwt
Water capacity	4,200 gallons
Coal capacity	7 tons 10 cwt
Tractive effort	26,878lbs

Weight Diagram

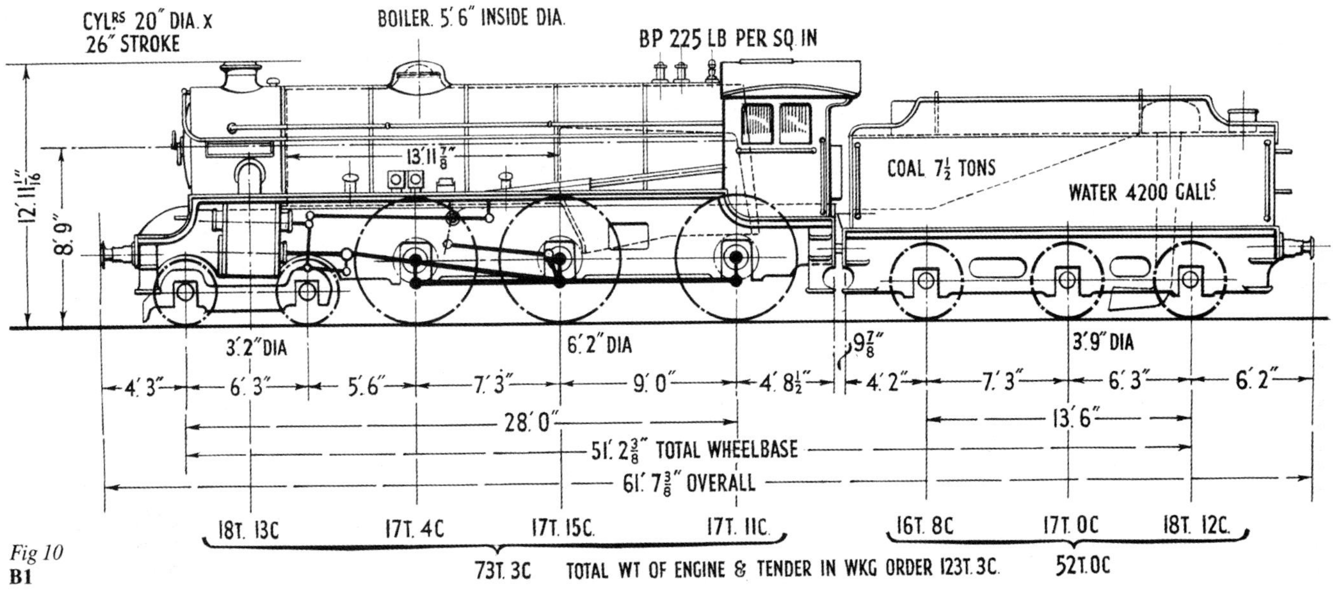

Fig 10
B1

Statistics

No.	Built	Renumbered	Name	1st depot	Last depot	Withdrawn
8301	12/42	1000, 61000	*Springbok*	Gorton	Colwick	3/62
8302	6/43	1001, 61001	*Eland*	Stratford	Doncaster	9/63
8303	9/43	1002, 61002	*Impala*	Haymarket	Dairycoates	6/67
8304	11/43	1003, 61003	*Gazelle*	Norwich	Colwick	12/65
8305	12/43	1004, 61004	*Oryx*	Stratford	Canklow	12/63
8306	2/44	1005, 61005	*Bongo*	Stratford	March	9/62

No.	Built	Renumbered	Name	1st depot	Last depot	Withdrawn
8307	3/44	1006, 61006	*Blackbuck*	Gorton	Lincoln	9/63
8308	4/44	1007, 61007	*Klipspringer*	Haymarket	Ayr	2/64
8309	5/44	1008, 61008	*Kudu*	Gateshead	Carstairs	12/66
8310	6/44	1009, 61009	*Hartebeeste*	Neville Hill	Lincoln	9/62
1010	11/46	61010	*Wildebeeste*	Botanic Gdns	Dairycoates	11/65
1011	11/46	61011	*Waterbuck*	Ardsley	Gorton	11/62
1012	11/46	61012	*Puku*	Dairycoates	York	6/67
1013	12/46	61013	*Topi*	Ardsley	Wakefield	12/66
1014	12/46	61014	*Oribi*	Tweedmouth	North Blyth	12/66
1015	1/47	61015	*Duiker*	York	Wakefield	11/62
1016	1/47	61016	*Inyala*	York	Low Moor	10/65
1017	1/47	61017	*Bushbuck*	York	York	11/66
1018	2/47	61018	*Gnu*	York	York	11/65
1019	2/47	61019	*Nilghai*	Heaton	York	3/67
1020	2/47	61020	*Gemsbok*	Heaton	York	11/62
1021	3/47	61021	*Reitbok*	Heaton	York	6/67
1022	3/47	61022	*Sassaby*	Heaton	Wakefield	11/66
1023	4/47	61023	*Hirola*	Heaton	Low Moor	10/65
1024	4/47	61024	*Addax*	Tweedmouth	Wakefield	5/66
1025	4/47	61025	*Pallah*	Tweedmouth	Alnmouth	12/62
1026	4/47	61026	*Ourebi*	Doncaster	Immingham	2/66
1027	5/47	61027	*Madoqua*	New England	Sheffield	9/62
1028	5/47	61028	*Umseke*	Neasden	Woodford	10/62
1029	6/47	61029	*Chamois*	King's Cross	Dundee	12/66
1030	6/47	61030	*Nyala*	Stockton	Low Moor	9/67
1031	7/47	61031	*Reedbuck*	Copley Hill	Ardsley	11/64
1032	8/47	61032	*Stembok*	Stockton	Dairycoates	11/66
1033	8/47	61033	*Dibatag*	Bradford	Canklow	3/63
1034	10/47	61034	*Chiru*	York	Wakefield	12/64
1035	10/47	61035	*Pronghorn*	York	York	12/66
1036	11/47	61036	*Ralph Assheton*	Gorton	Doncaster	9/62
1037	11/47	61037	*Jairou*	Darlington	Darlington	5/64
1038	12/47	61038	*Blacktail*	Darlington	Gateshead	6/64
1039	12/47	61039	*Steinbok*	Darlington	Doncaster	6/65
1040	4/46	61040	*Roedeer*	Stratford	Wakefield	7/66
1041	4/46	61041		Stratford	New England	4/64
1042	5/46	61042		Cambridge	Doncaster	4/66
1043	5/46	61043		Norwich	March	7/62
1044	5/46	61044		Norwich	Canklow	3/64
1045	5/46	61045		Norwich	Stratford	9/62
1046	5/46	61046		Norwich	Cambridge	4/62
1047	6/46	61047		Norwich	Sheffield	9/62
1048	6/46	61048		Norwich	Stratford	9/62
1049	6/46	61049		Norwich	York	11/65
1050	6/46	61050	Dept 30	Norwich	Langwith	4/68
1051	6/46	61051	Dept 31	Norwich	Langwith	3/66
1052	6/46	61052		Ipswich	March	9/62

No.	Built	Renumbered	Name	1st depot	Last depot	Withdrawn
1053	6/46	61053		Ipswich	York	2/63
1054	6/46	61054		Ipswich	March	9/62
1055	7/46	61055		Ipswich	Doncaster	2/66
1056	7/47	61056		Ipswich	Immingham	4/64
1057	7/46	61057		Ipswich	Ipswich	4/50 Accident
1058	7/46	61058		Ipswich	Immingham	2/66
1059	7/46	61059	Dept 17	Ipswich	March	4/66
1060	8/46	61060		Neville Hill	Lincoln	9/62
1061	8/46	61061		Perth	Ardsley	9/65
1062	8/46	61062		Neville Hill	York	8/64
1063	8/46	61063		Sheffield	Woodford	3/62
1064	8/46	61064		K'brewster	Carlisle Canal	10/62
1065	8/46	61065		Neville Hill	Dairycoates	9/64
1066	8/46	61066		Sheffield	March	9/62
1067	8/46	61067		K'brewster	Parkhead	12/62
1068	8/46	61068		Neville Hill	Ardsley	6/63
1069	8/46	61069		Neville Hill	York	8/63
1070	8/46	61070		Eastfield	Colwick	8/65
1071	8/46	61071		Eastfield	York	2/63
1072	9/46	61072		Eastfield	Dundee	5/67
1073	9/46	61073		Eastyfield	New England	9/63
1074	9/46	61074		Botanic Gdns	New England	9/63
1075	9/46	61075		Gorton	Mexborough	9/63
1076	9/46	61076		Haymarket	St Margarets	9/65
1077	9/46	61077		Gorton	Gorton	5/62
1078	9/46	61078		Gorton	Woodhead	10/62
1079	9/46	61079		Gorton	Immingham	6/62
1080	9/46	61080		Botanic Gdns	Dairycoates	3/64
1081	10/46	61081		Haymarket	Dundee	6/64
1082	10/46	61082		Gorton	Immingham	12/62
1083	10/46	61083		Gorton	Canklow	9/63
1084	10/46	61084		Botanic Gdns	York	6/64
1085	10/46	61085		Gorton	Leicester	11/61
1086	10/46	61086		Gorton	York	12/62
1087	10/46	61087		Sheffield	Doncaster	12/65
1088	10/46	61088		Sheffield	Colwick	9/63
1089	10/46	61089		Sheffield	LMR	4/66
1090	10/46	61090		Sheffield	Mexborough	9/63
1091	10/46	61091		Sheffield	New England	9/62
1092	10/46	61092		Sheffield	LMR	2/66
1093	11/46	61093		Doncaster	Langwith	7/65
1094	11/46	61094		Doncaster	Colwick	6/65
1095	11/46	61095		Doncaster	Lincoln	12/63
1096	11/46	61096		Hitchin	March	9/62
1097	11/46	61097		Hitchin	New England	1/65
1098	11/46	61098		Hitchin	Immingham	7/65
1099	11/46	61099		Hitchin	Thornton Jcn	9/66

No.	Built	Renumbered	Name	1st depot	Last depot	Withdrawn
1100	11/46	61100		Gateshead	Copley Hill	11/62
1101	11/46	61101		Dundee	Dunfermline	12/66
1102	12/46	61102		Dundee	Dundee	4/67
1103	12/46	61103		Thornton Jn	Thornton Jn	7/66
1104	12/46	61104		Stratford	Canklow	4/64
1105	12/46	61105	Dept 27	Hitchin	New England	5/66
1106	12/46	61106		Hitchin	Woodford	11/62
1107	12/46	61107		Hitchin	Doncaster	8/65
1108	12/46	61108		Sheffield	St Margarets	12/62
1109	12/46	61109		Sheffield	New England	7/64
1110	12/46	61110		Sheffield	Ardsley	10/65
1111	12/46	61111		Sheffield	Sheffield	9/62
1112	12/46	61112		King's Cross	Mexborough	12/62
1113	12/46	61113		King's Cross	Lincoln	9/63
1114	1/47	61114		King's Cross	Immingham	9/62
1115	1/47	61115		York	Wakefield	5/67
1116	1/47	61116		Eastfield	Carstairs	7/66
1117	1/47	61117		Eastfield	St Margarets	2/64
1118	1/47	61118		Thornton Jn	Thornton Jn	7/64
1119	1/47	61119		Stratford	March	11/63
1120	1/47	61120		Doncaster	Retford	1/65
1121	1/47	61121		King's Cross	Doncaster	4/66
1122	1/47	61122		Sheffield	New England	11/63
1123	1/47	61123		Sheffield	York	5/67
1124	2/47	61124		Doncaster	Doncaster	9/62
1125	2/47	61125		Doncaster	Doncaster	12/63
1126	2/47	61126		Doncaster	Retford	9/63
1127	2/47	61127		Doncaster	Frodingham	8/65
1128	2/47	61128		Sheffield	Doncaster	12/62
1129	2/47	61129		King's Cross	Wakefield	9/65
1130	2/47	61130		Gorton	Immingham	9/62
1131	2/47	61131		Gorton	Wakefield	12/66
1132	2/47	61132		K'brewster	Thornton Jn	9/66
1133	2/47	61133		K'brewster	Thornton Jn	9/66
1134	3/47	61134		K'brewster	Dalry Road	10/65
1135	3/47	61135		Stratford	Doncaster	9/63
1136	3/47	61136		Gorton	Woodford	10/62
1137	3/47	61137		Gorton	Gorton	5/62
1138	3/47	61138	Dept 26	Gorton	New England	10/67
1139	4/47	61139		Sheffield	Sheffield	9/62
1140	4/47	61140		Gorton	Motherwell	12/66
1141	4/47	61141		Gorton	Colwick	7/65
1142	4/47	61142		Gorton	Colwick	9/63
1143	4/47	61143		Gorton	Immingham	2/64
1144	4/47	61144		Gorton	Immingham	4/64
1145	4/47	61145		Gorton	Colwick	1/66
1146	4/47	61146		K'brewster	Thornton Jn	3/64

No.	Built	Renumbered	Name	1st depot	Last depot	Withdrawn
1147	4/47	61147		K'brewster	Dundee	12/65
1148	4/47	61148		K'brewster	Thornton Jn	9/66
1149	4/47	61149		Stratford	March	9/62
1150	4/47	61150		Sheffield	Sheffield	9/62
1151	4/47	61151		Sheffield	Sheffield	9/62
1152	5/47	61152		Sheffield	Immingham	4/64
1153	5/47	61153		Sheffield	Canklow	1/65
1154	5/47	61154		Sheffield	Sheffield	9/62
1155	5/47	61155		Gorton	Mexborough	3/64
1156	5/47	61156		Gorton	March	11/63
1157	5/47	61157		Gorton	Doncaster	8/65
1158	5/47	61158		Gorton	Doncaster	4/66
1159	5/47	61159		Gorton	Immingham	9/63
1160	5/47	61160		Gorton	Doncaster	9/63
1161	5/47	61161		Gorton	Wakefield	12/66
1162	5/47	61162		Gorton	New England	12/64
1163	5/47	61163		Neasden	Colwick	9/62
1164	5/47	61164		Neasden	Sheffield	9/62
1165	5/47	61165		Mexborough	Canklow	11/64
1166	5/47	61166		Mexborough	Sheffield	9/62
1167	5/47	61167		Mexborough	Canklow	12/64
1168	6/47	61168		Mexborough	Immingham	10/65
1169	6/47	61169		Neasden	Mexborough	12/63
1170	6/47	61170		Doncaster	Doncaster	7/62
1171	6/47	61171		Grantham	March	9/62
1172	6/47	61172		Eastfield	Dundee	12/65
1173	6/47	61173		Darlington	York	1/67
1174	6/47	61174		Doncaster	New England	12/63
1175	6/47	61175		Grantham	Colwick	12/63
1176	6/47	61176		Darlington	York	11/65
1177	6/47	61177		Grantham	Colwick	9/63
1178	6/47	61178		Haymarket	St Margarets	2/64
1179	6/47	61179		Sheffield	Immingham	1/65
1180	6/47	61180		Eastfield	Dundee	5/67
1181	7/47	61181	Dept 18	Sheffield	March	12/65
1182	7/47	61182		Gorton	March	9/62
1183	7/47	61183		Sheffield	Sheffield	7/62
1184	7/47	61184		Gorton	St Margarets	12/62
1185	7/47	61185		Leicester	Immingham	10/64
1186	7/47	61186		Leicester	Woodford	11/62
1187	7/47	61187		Leicester	Woodford	9/62
1188	7/47	61188		Leicester	Colwick	11/65
1189	8/47	61189	*Sir William Gray*	Stockton	York	5/67
1190	5/47	61190		Doncaster	Colwick	6/65
1191	5/47	61191		Doncaster	St Margarets	8/65
1192	5/47	61192		Leicester	Woodford	10/62
1193	5/47	61193		Doncaster	Doncaster	9/62

No.	Built	Renumbered	Name	1st depot	Last depot	Withdrawn
1194	5/47	61194	Dept 28	Doncaster	Colwick	6/66
1195	5/47	61195		Immingham	Frodingham	11/65
1196	5/47	61196		Doncaster	Doncaster	9/65
1197	5/47	61197		Eastfield	Ayr	6/64
1198	6/47	61198		Tweedmouth	York	4/65
1199	6/47	61199		Tweedmouth	York	1/67
1200	6/47	61200		King's Cross	King's Cross	12/62
1201	6/47	61201		Doncaster	Agecroft	1/62
1202	6/47	61202		Immingham	Lincoln	9/62
1203	6/47	61203		King's Cross	March	7/62
1204	6/47	61204	Dept 19	Immingham	March	2/66
1205	6/47	61205	Dept 20	Grantham	March	1/65
1206	7/47	61206		New England	Woodford	9/62
1207	6/47	61207		New England	New England	12/63
1208	7/47	61208		Retford	Doncaster	9/65
1209	7/47	61209		New England	Colwick	9/62
1210	7/47	61210		New England	Doncaster	2/66
1211	7/47	61211		Retford	Retford	11/62
1212	7/47	61212		Retford	Retford	11/64
1213	7/47	61213		Retford	Retford	4/64
1214	7/47	61214		Stockton	Low Moor	5/65
1215	7/47	61215	*William Henton Carver*	Botanic Gdns	Ardsley	3/65
1216	7/47	61216		York	York	1/67
1217	8/47	61217		Carlisle Canal	Carlisle Canal	3/62
1218	8/47	61218		Neville Hill	Ardsley	7/65
1219	8/47	61219		Carlisle Canal	St Margarets	6/64
1220	8/47	61220		Stockton	West Hartlepool	10/65
1221	8/47	61221	*Sir Alexander Erskine-Hill*	Carlisle Canal	Dundee	3/65
1222	8/47	61222		Carlisle Canal	Carlisle Canal	1/62
1223	8/47	61223		Leicester	Immingham	1/66
1224	8/47	61224		Heaton	Wakefield	7/66
1225	8/47	61225		Leicester	Doncaster	6/65
1226	8/47	61226		Stratford	Stratford	9/62
1227	8/47	61227		Leicester	Colwick	9/63
1228	8/47	61228		Leicester	Sheffield	9/62
1229	9/47	61229		Ardsley	Bradford	6/64
1230	9/47	61230		Ardsley	Bradford	11/62
1231	9/47	61231		Doncaster	Retford	7/62
1232	9/47	61232		Stratford	Parkeston	2/66
1233	9/47	61233	Dept 21	Stratford	March	4/66
1234	9/47	61234		Stratford	Sheffield	8/62
1235	9/47	61235		Stratford	Immingham	9/62
1236	9/47	61236		Stratford	March	9/62
1237	9/47	61237	*Geoffrey H Kitson*	Neville Hill	Wakefield	12/66
1238	9/47	61238	*Leslie Runciman*	Gateshead	York	2/67
1239	10/47	61239		York	Gorton	8/62
1240	10/47	61240	*Harry Hinchcliffe*	York	Wakefield	12/66

No.	Built	Renumbered	Name	1st depot	Last depot	Withdrawn
1241	10/47	61241	*Viscount Ridley*	Heaton	Heaton	12/62
1242	10/47	61242	*Alexander Reith Gray*	K'brewster	Dalry Road	7/64
1243	10/47	61243	*Sir Harold Mitchell*	Eastfield	Ayr	5/64
1244	10/47	61244	*Strang Steel*	Haymarket	St Margarets	10/65
1245	10/45	61245	*Murray of Elibank*	Haymarket	Dalry Road	7/65
1246	10/47	61246	*Lord Balfour of Burleigh*	Doncaster	St Margarets	12/62
1247	10/47	61247	*Lord Burghley*	Doncaster	Colwick	6/62
1248	10/47	61248	*Geoffrey Gibbs*	Doncaster	Colwick	11/65
1249	10/47	61249	*Fitzherbert Wright*	Doncaster	Canklow	6/64
1250	10/47	61250	*A. Harold Bibby*	Doncaster	Doncaster	4/66
1251	11/47	61251	*Oliver Bury*	King's Cross	Immingham	4/64
1252	11/47	61252	Dept 22	Ipswich	March	5/64
1253	11/47	61253		Stratford	Stratford	9/62
1254	11/47	61254		Stratford	March	9/62
1255	11/47	61255		Heaton	Dairycoates	6/67
1256	11/47	61256		Neville Hill	York	11/65
1257	11/47	61257		Neville Hill	West Hartlepool	10/65
1258	11/47	61258		Neville Hill	Lincoln	1/64
1259	11/47	61259		Neville Hill	Ardsley	8/65
1260	11/47	61260		Eastfield	St Margarets	12/62
1261	11/47	61261		Eastfield	Thornton Junction	9/66
1262	12/47	61262		Thornton Jcn	Dunfermline	4/67
1263	12/47	61263		Dundee	Dundee	12/66
1264	12/47	61264	Dept 29	Stratford	Colwick	7/67 Preserved
1265	12/47	61265		Doncaster	Leicester	2/62
1266	12/47	61266		King's Cross	Sheffield	9/62
1267	12/47	61267		Ardsley	West Hartlepool	12/62
1268	12/47	61268		Ardsley	Ardsley	12/64
1269	12/47	61269		Lincoln	Gorton	12/63
1270	12/47	61270		Norwich	Doncaster	9/63
1271	12/47	61271		Norwich	Woodford	7/62
1272	12/47	61272	Dept 25	Norwich	New England	11/65
1273	12/47	61273		Darlington	York	5/63
1274	1/48	61274		Darlington	Wakefield	11/64
1275	1/48	61275		Darlington	York	10/65
1276	1/48	61276		Darlington	York	6/65
1277	1/48	61277		K'brewster	Dundee	6/64
1278	1/48	61278		Dundee	Dundee	4/67
1279	1/48	61279		Lincoln	Doncaster	9/63
1280	1/48	61280		Lincoln	March	9/62
1281	1/48	61281		Lincoln	LMR	2/66
1282	1/48	61282		Colwick	New England	9/62
1283	2/48	61283		Colwick	Stratford	9/62
1284	2/48	61284		Immingham	Lincoln	9/62
1285	2/48	61285		Cambridge	Colwick	12/65
1286	2/48	61286		Cambridge	March	9/62
1287	2/48	61287		Cambridge	March	9/62

No.	Built	Renumbered	Name	1st depot	Last depot	Withdrawn
E1288	2/48	61288		Darlington	York	1/64
E1289	2/48	61289		Darlington	Dairycoates	6/67
E1290	2/48	61290		Darlington	Carlisle Canal	3/62
E1291	2/48	61291		Darlington	Ardsley	5/65
E1292	2/48	61292		Thornton Jcn	Dundee	9/65
E1293	2/48	61293		Dundee	Dundee	8/66
E1294	3/48	61294		Bradford	St Margarets	11/64
E1295	3/48	61295		Ardsley	Ardsley	11/62
E1296	3/48	61296		Ardsley	Wakefield	11/62
E1297	3/48	61297		Ardsley	Ardsley	11/62
E1298	3/48	61298		Leicester	Gorton	6/62
E1299	3/48	61299		Leicester	Colwick	7/65
E1300	3/48	61300	Dept 23	March	March	11/65
E1301	3/48	61301		Cambridge	Stratford	9/62
E1302	3/48	61302		Cambridge	LMR	4/66
E1303	3/48	61303		Darlington	York	11/66
61304	3/38			Dairycoates	Ardsley	10/65
61305	4/48			Dairycoates	Dairycoates	10/63
61306	4/48			Dairycoates	Low Moor	9/67 Preserved
61307	4/48			K'brewster	St Margarets	11/66
61308	4/48			K'brewster	Thornton Jcn	11/66
61309	4/48			Ardsley	Wakefield	1/67
61310	4/48			Ardsley	Ardsley	4/65
61311	4/48			Sheffield	Stratford	9/62
61312	4/48			Sheffield	Mexborough	3/64
61313	4/48			Gorton	Langwith	11/65
61314	4/48			Gorton	New England	12/63
61315	4/48		Dept 32	Gorton	Langwith	4/68
61316	5/48			Gorton	Canklow	12/62
61317	5/48			Gorton	Immingham	9/62
61318	5/48			Immingham	Immingham	9/63
61319	5/48			Borough Gdns	York	12/66
61320	5/48			Borough Gdns	Wakefield	8/65
61321	5/48			Borough Gds	Ardsley	8/64
61322	5/48			Borough Gdns	Dairycoates	2/66
61323	5/48			K'brewster	March	11/63
61324	6/48			K'brewster	St Margarets	10/65
61325	6/48			Immingham	Immingham	9/63
61326	6/48			Gorton	Doncaster	3/66
61327	6/48			Gorton	Canklow	2/65
61328	6/48			Immingham	Immingham	9/63
61329	6/48			New England	Doncaster	4/66
61330	6/48			New England	Thornton Jcn	11/66
61331	6/48			New England	New England	9/63
61332	6/48			Cambridge	Thornton Jcn	12/62
61333	7/48			Cambridge	Parkhead	12/62
61334	7/48			Norwich	Gorton	12/63

No.	Built	Renumbered	Name	1st depot	Last depot	Withdrawn
61335	7/48			Stratford	Stratford	9/62
61336	8/48			Stratford	Colwick	9/63
61337	8/48			Neville Hill	Low Moor	9/67
61338	8/48			Neville Hill	Wakefield	1/65
61339	9/48			Neville Hill	Copley Hill	11/62
61340	11/48			Eastfield	Dundee	4/67
61341	12/48			Eastfield	St Margarets	12/63
61342	1/49			Eastfield	Motherwell	12/66
61343	2/49			Aberdeen	Thornton Jcn	3/66
61344	3/49			Eastfield	Thornton Jcn	9/66
61345	4/49			Aberdeen	St Margarets	7/66
61346	4/49			K'brewster	Thornton Jcn	6/64
61347	5/49			K'brewster	Thornton Jcn	4/67
61348	6/49			K'brewster	Colwick	12/65
61349	7/49			K'brewster	Thornton Jcn	8/66
61350	7/49			K'brewster	Dunfermline	11/66
61351	8/49			K'brestwer	Dalry Road	7/64
61352	8/49			K'brewster	Gorton	10/62
61353	9/49			K'brewster	Wakefield	8/65
61354	9/49			St Margarets	Dundee	4/67
61355	9/49			St Margarets	Ayr	6/64
61356	9/49			St Margarets	St Margarets	7/64
61357	10/49			St Margarets	St Margarets	6/65
61358	10/49			St Margarets	Thornton Jcn	12/63
61359	10/49			St Margarets	St Margarets	12/63
61360	3/50			Stratford	Doncaster	4/66
61361	3/50			Stratford	Colwick	12/65
61362	3/50			Stratford	Stratford	9/62
61363	4/50			Stratford	March	9/62
61364	4/50			Lincoln	New England	9/62
61365	4/50			Immingham	Immingham	7/65
61366	4/50			Immingham	Immingham	12/62
61367	4/50			Colwick	Doncaster	8/65
61368	4/50			Colwick	Woodford	1/62
61369	5/50			Colwick	Gorton	12/63
61370	10/50			Lincoln	Frodingham	7/65
61371	10/50			Lincoln	March	9/62
61372	12/50			Immingham	Langwith	6/65
61373	12/50			Immingham	Sheffield	9/62
61374	2/51			Immingham	Immingham	9/63
61375	2/51		Dept 24	Immingham	March	4/66
61376	4/51			Colwick	Leicester	2/62
61377	5/51			Colwick	Langwith	9/63
61378	5/51			Colwick	March	11/63
61379	6/51		*Mayflower*	Colwick	Immingham	8/62
61380	8/51			Colwick	Woodford	3/62
61381	9/51			Colwick	Gorton	11/62

No.	Built	Renumbered	Name	1st depot	Last depot	Withdrawn
61382	9/51			Ardsley	Ardsley	12/64
61383	10/51			Ardsley	Low Moor	1/63
61384	10/51			Ardsley	Immingham	1/66
61385	10/51			Ardsley	Ardsley	10/65
61386	10/51			Ardsley	North Blyth	12/66
61387	11/51			Ardsley	Wakefield	10/65
61388	11/51			Ardsley	Wakefield	6/67
61389	11/51			New England	Frodingham	11/65
61390	12/51			New England	LMR	2/66
61391	12/51			New England	New England	9/62
61392	12/51			New England	Colwick	6/65
61393	1/52			Doncaster	Mexborough	9/63
61394	1/52			Doncaster	Langwith	11/65
61395	2/52			Carlisle	Gorton	10/62
61396	2/52			Eastfield	St Margarets	9/65
61397	3/52			St Margarets	St Margarets	6/65
61398	3/52			St Margarets	Dundee	11/64
61399	4/52			Doncaster	Canklow	9/63
61400	3/50			K'brewster	Thornton Jcn	12/64
61401	4/50			K'brewster	Thornton Jcn	4/64
61402	4/50			K'brewster	Dundee	6/64
61403	4/50			K'brewster	Dundee	7/66
61404	5/50			K'brewster	St Margarets	11/65
61405	5/50			Lincoln	Lincoln	9/62
61406	5/50			Lincoln	Doncaster	4/66
61407	6/50			Immingham	Thornton Jcn	6/67
61408	6/50			Immingham	Immingham	12/62
61409	6/50			Immingham	Lincoln	9/63

LNER Class B2

Dimensions

Cylinders (2 outside)	20inx 26in
Coupled wheel diameter	6ft 8in
Bogie wheel diameter	3ft 2in
Walchaerts valve gear with 10in piston valves	
Boiler pressure	225psi
Heating surface	2,005sqft (incl 344sqft superheating)
Grate area	27.9sqft
Axleload	18 tons 12 cwt
Weight – Engine	73 tons 10 cwt
– Tender	52 tons 10 cwt (LNER)
	44 tons 2 cwt (NER)
	51 tons 8 cwt (ex P1)
– Total	126 tons (with LNER tender)
Water capacity	4,200 gallons (LNER)
	4,125 gallons (NER)
	4,700 gallons (ex P1)

Coal capacity	7 tons 10 cwt (LNER) 5 tons 10 cwt (NER) 7 tons (ex P1)
Tractive effort	24,863lbs

Weight Diagram

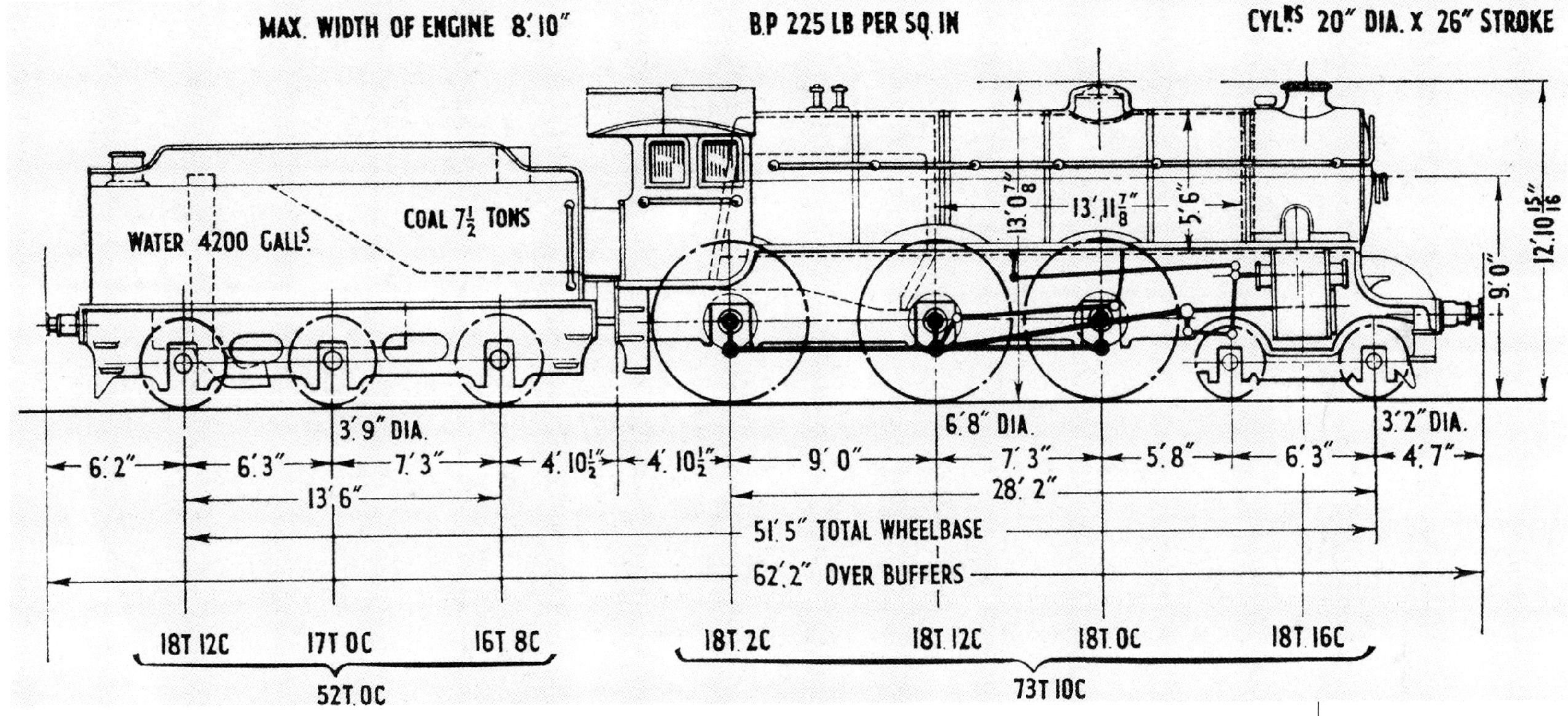

Statistics

No.	Rebuilt	Renumbered	Name	1st depot	Last depot	Withdrawn
1603	10/46	61603	*Framlingham*	Ipswich	Cambridge	9/58 *NER
1607	5/47	61607	*Blickling*	Colchester	Cambridge	12/59 *NER
2814	11/46	1614, 61614	*Castle Hedingham*	Cambridge	Cambridge	6/59 *NER
2815	4/46	1615, 61615	*Culford Hall*	Parkeston	Cambridge	2/59 * ex P1
2816	8/46	1616, 61616	*Fallodon*	Parkeston	Cambridge	9/59 *NER
1617	12/46	61617	*Ford Castle*	Cambridge	Cambridge	8/58 *NER
1632	7/46	61632	*Belvoir Castle* ***	Parkeston	Cambridge	2/59 * ex P1
2839	1/46	1639, 61639	*Norwich City*	Norwich	Cambridge	5/59 *NER
61644	3/49		*Earlham Hall*	Colchester	Cambridge	11/59 * NER
2871	2/46	1671, 61671	*Manchester City* **	Cambridge	Cambridge	9/58 * LNER

* Tender type
** renamed *Royal Sovereign*, 4/46
*** renamed *Royal Sovereign*, 10/58

BIBLIOGRAPHY

Allen, Cecil J., *Trains Illustrated, Speed in East Suffolk,* Ian Allan, November 1956.

Bradley, R.P., *LNER 4-6-0s,* David & Charles, 1988

Hardy, R.H.N., Bird, Chris, & Butcher, David, *B12s Remembered,* The Midland & Great Northern Joint Railway Society, 2011

Haresnape, Brian & Rowledge, Peter, *Robinson Locomotives,* Ian Allan 1982

Hughes, Geoffrey, *LNER 4-6-0s at Work,* Ian Allan 1988

Railway Correspondence & Travel Society, *Locomotives of the L.N.E.R. Part 2B, Tender Engines, Classes B1-B19,* RCTS 1975.

Stewart,I.R., *Steam to Southend Victoria,* Railway World February 1982.

Tuplin, W.A.,*Trains Illustrated, The Holden 4-6-0s of the G.E.R.* Ian Allan, February 1955

Tuplin, W.A., *Great Central Steam,* George Allen & Unwin Ltd., 1967

Yeadon's Register, *LNER Locomotives Volume 5 Gresley B17 and Thompson B2 Classes*, Book Law Publications, 2001

Yeadon's Register, *LNER Locomotives Volume 6 Thompson B1 Class,* Book Law Publications, 2001

Yeadon's Register, *LNER Locomotives Volume 17 Class B13 to B16,* Book Law Publications, 2000

Yeadon's Register, *LNER Locomotives Volume 22 Class B1 (B18) to B9,* Book Law Publications, 2001

INDEX

Photographs (Black & White)

Photographs (Colour)

Locations

Photographs (Black & White)

Locomotives (Great Central)

Locomotives (Great Eastern)

Photographs (Colour)